A
SONG
IN MY
HEART

366 Devotions from Our Best-Loved Hymns

ROBERT J. MORGAN

a division of Baker Publishing Group
Grand Rapids, Michigan

© 2010 by Robert J. Morgan

Published by Revell
a division of Baker Publishing Group
PO Box 6287, Grand Rapids, MI 49516-6287
www.revellbooks.com

Repackaged edition published 2021
ISBN 978-0-8007-4048-1
ISBN 978-0-8007-4132-7 (casebound)

Previously published in 2010 under the title *Near to the Heart of God: Meditations on 366 Best-Loved Hymns*

Printed in the United States of America

The Library of Congress has cataloged the original edition as follows:
Morgan, Robert J., 1952–
    Near to the heart of God : meditations on 366 best-loved hymns / Robert J. Morgan.
        p.   cm.
    Includes index.
    ISBN 978-0-8007-3395-7 (pbk.)
    1. Devotional calendars. 2. Hymns—Devotional use. 3. Hymns—History and criticism. I. Title.
    BV340.M67 2010
    264'.23—dc22   2010017872

Published in association with Yates & Yates, www.yates2.com.

Permissions for lyrics on page 375.

21 22 23 24 25 26 27   7 6 5 4 3 2 1

To
Audrey Claire

Fill Thou my life, O Lord my God,
In every part with praise.

—Horatius Bonar

Introduction

Call it therapeutic theology. Hymns are distillations of the richest truths of God, versified, emotionalized, set to music, and released in the mind and from the mouth. They're miniature Bible studies that lead us effortlessly to worship, testimony, exhortation, prayer, and praise. They're bursts of devotional richness with rhyme and rhythm. They clear our minds, soothe our nerves, verbalize our worship, summarize our faith, and sing our great Redeemer's praise.

From our first recorded hymn—the song of Moses in Exodus 15—to today's more recent choruses, we join the choir of the ages when, filled with the Spirit, we sing to ourselves in psalms, hymns, and spiritual songs, singing and making melody in our hearts to the Lord. We tune our hearts to the frequency of heaven and join in a song of sweet accord and thus surround the throne.

When the Bible tells us to sing "a new song" to the Lord, it's telling us that every generation needs to write its own music. If a time ever comes when the younger generation isn't writing praises to the Lord, Christianity is dead. Jesus said wise people bring out of their storehouses treasures both old and new. My church, the Donelson Fellowship in Nashville, sings songs both ancient and modern every Sunday. I love the newer music.

But pray don't lose the old hymns.

The rediscovery of the hymnal can be soul-bolstering. It's a spiritual journey into biblical truth, Christian history, and timeless worship. In olden times, many of the hymns were written by pastors and theologians, often to summarize and conclude their sermons. I'm alarmed at the rapidity with which many of our great old hymns are losing their voice in today's churches.

But they don't have to be lost to you or me.

Every morning when I walk out the front door on my way to work, I quietly sing a hymn aloud, whichever one happens to be on my mind. I have a short commute (around the side of the house and in my office door), but that hymn sets the tone for my day.

Preparing this devotional book of daily hymns has likewise set the tone for my year, because in addition to reviewing some of the most beloved hymns of all time, I've excavated the vault of history and found some forgotten treasures, such as Joseph Conder's great hymn "Day by Day the Manna Fell," with lines of rare poignancy like these:

"Day by day" the promise reads,
Daily strength for daily needs. . . .

And . . .

Oh, to live exempt from care,
By the energy of prayer. . . .

Admittedly, not all hymns have retained their richness. Time and language change, and I can't imagine any church today singing the Isaac Watts hymn "Blest Is the Man Whose Bowels Move." Yes, that really is the name and first line of the hymn ("Blest is the man whose bowels move and melt with pity to the poor"), but the meaning of the word *bowels* was much different in 1719.

Some hymns, however, will never be truly out-of-date. Here are 366 examples that have stood the test of time. Some are well-known, and the rest should be. If you'd like to hear the music to any or all of these, there are several hymn-centered websites that provide the opportunity of listening to the tunes. If you'd like to find my other books, including several on the history of our hymns, or if you'd like to contact me, please visit www.robertjmorgan.com.

In addition to thanking Isaac Watts, Charles Wesley, Fanny Crosby, and the rest of our hymn-writing friends, I want to express special thanks to three ministry partners and fellow hymn lovers who have made this book possible:

My editor, Andrea Doering, who helped conceive this project and who has been an uplifting voice, enthusiastic supporter, and skillful guide.

My agent, Chris Ferebee, whose wise counsel and calming effect are always much appreciated.

And my dear wife, Katrina, who is my partner in writing and ministry, as well as in life and marriage.

So shall each fear, each fret, each care
Be turned into a song,
And every winding of the way
The echo shall prolong;
So shall no part of day or night
From sacredness be free;
But all my life, in every step
Be fellowship with Thee.

Amazing Grace

Perhaps you'll be surprised to learn that "Amazing Grace" is a New Year's hymn. On Friday morning, **January 1, 1773**, John Newton, former slave trader and infidel, preached a New Year's message from 1 Chronicles 17:16–17 in his church at Olney, England. Newton opened his sermon, saying, "The Lord bestows many blessings upon His people, but unless He likewise gives them a thankful heart, they lose much of the comfort they might have." He told his church to look back at God's goodness, look around at God's promises, and look forward to future usefulness. In concluding, Newton introduced a poem he'd written for the occasion, the hymn "Amazing Grace."

> Amazing grace, how sweet the sound
> That sav'd a wretch like me!
> I once was lost, but now am found,
> Was blind, but now I see.
>
> 'Twas grace that taught my heart to fear,
> And grace my fears reliev'd;
> How precious did that grace appear,
> The hour I first believ'd!
>
> Thro' many dangers, toils and snares,
> I have already come;
> 'Tis grace has brought me safe thus far,
> And grace will lead me home.
>
> The earth shall soon dissolve like snow,
> The sun forbear to shine;
> But God, who call'd me here below,
> Will be forever mine.

Who am I, O LORD . . . that You have brought me this far?

—1 Chronicles 17:16

Praise Ye the Triune God

Elizabeth Rundle Charles was born **January 2, 1828**, into a prominent family in the Devon area of England. She began writing poetry in childhood, and her early works were commended by Alfred Lord Tennyson. Elizabeth was a bundle of talent—a linguist, painter, musician, poet, church historian, and author who wrote over fifty books. In her trinitarian hymn "Praise Ye the Triune God," she used unrhymed but splendid verse to praise our God, Three in One. Last year when I preached a series of sermons on the subject of the Trinity, we taught this old hymn to our young congregation who thought it "quaint," especially the part about "young men and maidens."

> Praise ye the Father for His lovingkindness;
> Tenderly cares He for His erring children;
> Praise Him, ye angels, praise Him in the heavens,
> Praise ye Jehovah!
>
> Praise ye the Savior—great is His compassion;
> Graciously cares He for His chosen people;
> Young men and maidens, older folks and children,
> Praise ye the Savior!
>
> Praise ye the Spirit, Comforter of Israel,
> Sent of the Father and the Son to bless us;
> Praise ye the Father, Son and Holy Spirit,
> Praise ye the Triune God!

The grace of the Lord Jesus Christ, and the love of God, and the communion of the Holy Spirit be with you all. Amen.

—2 Corinthians 13:14

We Rest on Thee

On Tuesday, **January 3, 1956**, a handful of missionaries gathered at their base in the Ecuadorian jungle and sang "We Rest on Thee," one of their favorite hymns. Then Jim Elliot, Nate Saint, Ed McCully, Roger Yoderian, and Peter Fleming began flying supplies to a jungle outpost where they set up camp, hoping to reach a Stone Age tribe with the gospel. It ended tragically when the five men were attacked and slain. Their story and the subsequent evangelization of the Aucas were captured in a book by Elizabeth Elliot, Jim's widow, which drew its name from the final stanza of this hymn sung the morning the five heroes left for Auca territory—*Through Gates of Splendor*. (This hymn can be sung to the same tune as "Be Still My Soul.")

> We rest on Thee, our Shield and our Defender!
> We go not forth alone against the foe;
> Strong in Thy strength, safe in Thy keeping tender,
> We rest on Thee, and in Thy Name we go.
> Strong in Thy strength, safe in Thy keeping tender,
> We rest on Thee, and in Thy Name we go.
>
> We go in faith, our own great weakness feeling,
> And needing more each day Thy grace to know:
> Yet from our hearts a song of triumph pealing,
> "We rest on Thee, and in Thy Name we go."
> Yet from our hearts a song of triumph pealing,
> "We rest on Thee, and in Thy Name we go."
>
> We rest on Thee, our Shield and our Defender!
> Thine is the battle, Thine shall be the praise;
> When passing through the gates of pearly splendor,
> Victors, we rest with Thee, through endless days.
> When passing through the gates of pearly splendor,
> Victors, we rest with Thee, through endless days.

Open to me the gates of righteousness; I will go through them.

—Psalm 118:19

My Times of Sorrow and of Joy

Benjamin Beddome, among the earliest of the British hymnists, was born in 1717 and grew up to become a doctor. Following his conversion in 1737, he entered the ministry and served fifty-two years as pastor of the Baptist church in the English town of Burton-on-the-Water. Every Sunday he wrote an original hymn to be sung following his sermon. On **January 4, 1778**, Beddome's sermon was from Psalm 31:15: "My times are in Your hand," and his hymn, "My Times of Sorrow and of Joy," is given below. As Beddome preached that day, he was unaware that his beloved son, who had just finished his medical studies, had died in Edinburgh following a sudden illness. In the coming hours, Beddome was greatly comforted by his own hymn, which has ever since been a comfort to multitudes of others.

My times of sorrow and of joy,
Great God, are in Thy hand.
My choicest comforts come from Thee,
And go at Thy command.

If Thou shouldst take them all away,
Yet would I not repine;
Before they were possessed by me,
They were entirely Thine.

Nor would I drop a murmuring word,
Though the whole world were gone,
But seek enduring happiness
In Thee, and Thee alone.

Here perfect bliss can ne'er be found,
The honey's mixed with gall;
Midst changing scenes and dying friends,
Be Thou my all in all.

My times are in Your hand.

—Psalm 31:15

A Shelter in the Time of Storm

Rev. V. J. Charlesworth was a prolific Christian worker during the Victorian era and a close associate of the great Charles Haddon Spurgeon. He was born in 1839 in Essex and became pastor of London's Surrey Chapel in 1864. Five years later, Spurgeon recruited him for the leadership team at the Metropolitan Tabernacle and to oversee Stockwell Orphanage, one of Spurgeon's many ministries. Charlesworth wrote a number of hymns, including this one, "A Shelter in the Time of Storm." He died **January 5, 1915**.

The Lord's our Rock, in Him we hide,
A Shelter in the time of storm;
Secure whatever ill betide,
A Shelter in the time of storm.

A shade by day, defense by night,
A Shelter in the time of storm;
No fears alarm, no foes afright,
A Shelter in the time of storm.

O Rock divine, O Refuge dear,
A Shelter in the time of storm;
Be Thou our Helper ever near,
A Shelter in the time of storm.

Oh, Jesus is a Rock in a weary land,
A weary land, a weary land;
Oh, Jesus is a Rock in a weary land,
A Shelter in the time of storm.

For You have been a strength to the poor, a strength to the needy in his distress, a refuge from the storm, a shade from the heat.

—Isaiah 25:4

Of the Father's Love Begotten

Epiphany comes from a Greek word meaning "manifestation," and it's an important date on the Christian calendar. It speaks of God's manifestation of Christ to the world, either at His presentation to the Magi or at His baptism. As early as the third century, **January 6** was celebrated in the Eastern church to commemorate Christ's baptism. In the fourth century, the Western church began celebrating Epiphany to commemorate the day of the Magi's visit. In the fifth century, Aurelius Prudentius gave the world this Latin hymn, "Of the Father's Love Begotten," which is often used on Epiphany. Sung to the medieval tune "Divinum Mysterium," it's one of Christianity's most hauntingly beautiful hymns of wonder.

Of the Father's love begotten, ere the worlds began to be,
He is Alpha and Omega, He the source, the ending He,
Of the things that are, that have been, and that future years shall
see,
Evermore and evermore!

O ye heights of heaven adore Him; angel hosts, His praises sing;
Powers, Dominions, bow before Him, and extol our God and
King;
Let no tongue on earth be silent, every voice in concert ring,
Evermore and evermore!

Christ, to Thee with God the Father, and, O Holy Ghost, to
Thee,
Hymn and chant and high thanksgiving, and unwearied praises
be:
Honor, glory, and dominion, and eternal victory,
Evermore and evermore!

This is My commandment, that you love
one another, as I have loved you.

—John 15:12

In the Garden

January 7, 1868, is the birthday of Charles Austin Miles, a pharmacologist and photographer who made his greatest mark as a hymnist and writer of gospel songs, including "There's a New Name Written Down in Glory," "Dwelling in Beulah Land," and "If Jesus Goes with Me." In March of 1912, as Miles was in his darkroom waiting for some film to develop, he read the story from John 20 of Jesus Christ's resurrection. He imagined himself in the garden of the empty tomb and visualized the wonder of seeing the risen Christ. Out of this experience, he wrote this beloved hymn.

> I come to the garden alone,
> While the dew is still on the roses;
> And the voice I hear, falling on my ear,
> The Son of God discloses.
>
> He speaks, and the sound of His voice
> Is so sweet, The birds hush their singing,
> And the melody that He gave to me,
> Within my heart is ringing.
>
> I'd stay in the garden with Him,
> Though the night around me be falling,
> But He bids me go; Through the voice of woe,
> His voice to me is calling.
>
> *And He walks with me, And He talks with me,*
> *And He tells me I am His own;*
> *And the joy we share as we tarry there,*
> *None other has ever known.*

Then the disciples were glad when they saw the Lord.

—John 20:20

When I Survey the Wondrous Cross

Lowell Mason is among the giants of American hymnody. He was born **January 8, 1792**, in Medfield, Massachusetts, but he grew up in the Deep South. Though at first he went into banking, eventually he became the first music teacher in the American public school system. He also served as music director for various churches and as a music publisher and compiler of hymnals. We know him for composing the melodies for "Joy to the World," "O for a Thousand Tongues to Sing," "Nearer, My God, to Thee," "There Is a Fountain," and this great hymn by Isaac Watts, "When I Survey the Wondrous Cross." Lowell Mason is rightly called the Father of American Church Music.

When I survey the wondrous cross
On which the Prince of glory died,
My richest gain I count but loss,
And pour contempt on all my pride.

Forbid it, Lord, that I should boast,
Save in the death of Christ my God!
All the vain things that charm me most,
I sacrifice them to His blood.

See from His head, His hands, His feet,
Sorrow and love flow mingled down!
Did e'er such love and sorrow meet,
Or thorns compose so rich a crown?

Were the whole realm of nature mine,
That were a present far too small;
Love so amazing, so divine,
Demands my soul, my life, my all.

*But what things were gain to me, these
I have counted loss for Christ.*

—Philippians 3:7

Trusting Jesus

Simple, daily faith saves us from chronic worry. When we abide in Christ and rest in His promises, no alarm can overwhelm us for long, and no anxiety can sustain its attack. That's the theme of this beloved song written by Edgar P. Stites, a Civil War veteran and riverboat captain. Stites was converted in the revival of 1857 and became a Methodist preacher. He wrote "Trusting Jesus" in 1876. Evangelist D. L. Moody saw the words in a newspaper and handed the clipping to his music director, Ira Sankey, who wrote the melody and popularized it in the Moody-Sankey campaigns. Edgar Stites passed away on **January 9, 1921.**

Simply trusting every day,
Trusting through a stormy way;
Even when my faith is small,
Trusting Jesus, that is all.

Singing if my way is clear,
Praying if the path be drear;
If in danger for Him call;
Trusting Jesus, that is all.

Trusting Him while life shall last,
Trusting Him till earth be past;
Till within the jasper wall,
Trusting Jesus, that is all.

Trusting as the moments fly,
Trusting as the days go by;
Trusting Him whate'er befall,
Trusting Jesus, that is all.

My heart trusted in Him, and I am helped.
—Psalm 28:7

Anywhere with Jesus

In the early 1800s, John Cadbury, a Quaker and teetotaler, opened a coffee and tea shop in the center of Birmingham, England. He soon became known for his cocoa, giving rise to the Cadbury Chocolate Company. John's granddaughter, Helen, who was born on **January 10, 1877**, became an heir of the Cadbury fortune. A dedicated Christian, Helen married the famous song leader Charles M. Alexander, and the two traveled the world for Christ and founded the Pocket Testament League. Charles died of a heart attack in 1920 at age fifty-three. Helen labored for Christ until her death in 1969 at age ninety-two. She isn't primarily known as a hymnist, but she did contribute the last two stanzas to this great old hymn by Jessie Pounds.

Anywhere with Jesus I can safely go,
Anywhere He leads me in this world below;
Anywhere without Him dearest joys would fade;
Anywhere with Jesus I am not afraid.

Anywhere with Jesus, over land and sea,
Telling souls in darkness of salvation free;
Ready as He summons me to go or stay,
Anywhere with Jesus when He points the way.

Anywhere with Jesus I can go to sleep,
When the darkening shadows round about me creep,
Knowing I shall waken nevermore to roam;
Anywhere with Jesus will be home, sweet home.

Anywhere, anywhere! Fear I cannot know;
Anywhere with Jesus I can safely go.

Wherever you send us we will go.

—Joshua 1:16

Rock of Ages

Daniel Draper, an English Methodist, spent thirty years planting churches and schools in Australia, then took a year's furlough in England. When the time came to return to Australia, he boarded the steamship *London*. A gale hit the ship in the Bay of Biscay, and Draper spent his last hours evangelizing the 250 passengers. In the end, only three passengers were rescued, and one of them reported Draper's last words: "Those of you who are not converted, now is the time; not a minute to be lost." As the ship slipped beneath the sea on **January 11, 1866**, the passengers were singing Augustus Toplady's famous hymn "Rock of Ages" in their final moments.

Rock of Ages, cleft for me,
Let me hide myself in Thee;
Let the water and the blood,
From Thy riven side which flowed,
Be of sin the double cure;
Save from wrath and make me pure.

Not the labor of my hands
Can fulfill Thy law's demands;
Could my zeal no respite know,
Could my tears for ever flow,
All for sin could not atone;
Thou must save, and Thou alone.

While I draw this fleeting breath,
When my eyelids close in death,
When I soar to worlds unknown,
See Thee on Thy judgment throne,
Rock of Ages, cleft for me,
Let me hide myself in Thee.

When my heart is overwhelmed, lead me
to the rock that is higher than I.

—Psalm 61:2

Whosoever Meaneth Me

Ed McConnell, born in Atlanta on **January 12, 1892**, was a pioneer of religious broadcasting and children's television. In 1922, he began broadcasting the radio show *Hymn Time* on the National Broadcasting Company. Between 1929 and 1953, he hosted the children's television classic *Smilin' Ed McConnell and His Buster Brown Gang*, assisted by his animal cohosts, Midnight the Cat and Squeaky the Mouse. Years before, McConnell had written "Whosoever Meaneth Me" while assisting his father in evangelistic meetings in Spirit Lake, Iowa. He was eighteen years old at the time.

> I am happy today, and the sun shines bright,
> The clouds have been rolled away;
> For the Savior said, whosoever will
> May come with Him to stay.
>
> All my hopes have been raised, O His Name be praised,
> His glory has filled my soul;
> I've been lifted up, and from sin set free,
> His blood has made me whole.
>
> O what wonderful love, O what grace divine,
> That Jesus should die for me;
> I was lost in sin, for the world I pined,
> But now I am set free.
>
> *"Whosoever" surely meaneth me,*
> *Surely meaneth me, O surely meaneth me;*
> *"Whosoever" surely meaneth me,*
> *"Whosoever" meaneth me.*

Whosoever believeth in him should not perish, but have eternal life.

—John 3:15 KJV

Jesus Christ, Our Blessèd Savior

During the Middle Ages, congregational singing largely disappeared from the church, replaced by professional choristers whose songs accompanied the Mass. The pre-Reformation hero John Hus began writing some of the first of what would become known as Protestant hymns. After Hus was martyred, Bishop Luke of Prague printed history's first hymnbook in a vernacular language. It was published on **January 13, 1501.** Luther's German hymnal appeared later, in 1519; and the first hymnbook with musical notes appeared in 1531. To this day, many Lutheran hymnals feature this great communion hymn by the Bohemian reformer John Hus:

> Jesus Christ, our blessèd Savior,
> Turned away God's wrath forever;
> By His bitter grief and woe
> He saved us from the evil Foe.
>
> As His pledge of love undying
> He, this precious food supplying,
> Gives His body with the bread
> And with the wine the blood He shed.
>
> Praise the Father, Who from heaven
> Unto us such food hath given
> And, to mend what we have done,
> Gave into death His only Son.
>
> If thy heart this truth professes,
> And thy mouth thy sin confesses,
> His dear guest thou here shalt be,
> And Christ Himself shall banquet thee.

Our Savior Jesus Christ . . . has abolished death and brought life and immortality to light through the gospel.

—2 Timothy 1:10

Jesus! What a Friend for Sinners

When I first heard this hymn during college chapel services, I loved it not just for its words by Wilbur Chapman but for its tune by Rowland Pritchard. The melody to "Jesus, What a Friend for Sinners" is called "Hyfrydol," the Welsh word for "cheerful." Remarkably, Prichard, who was born on **January 14, 1811**, composed this piece as a teenager and never became a professional musician. He spent most of his life as a loom tender's assistant in a flannel manufacturing plant in the north of Wales. But his greatest weaving was the tapestry of notes he composed before he was twenty. We also use "Hyfrydol" as the tune for the Christmas carol "Come, Thou Long Expected Jesus," and for several other hymns as well. It's one of Christianity's most cheerful melodies.

Jesus! what a Friend for sinners!
Jesus! Lover of my soul;
Friends may fail me, foes assail me,
He, my Savior, makes me whole.

Jesus! what a strength in weakness!
Let me hide myself in Him.
Tempted, tried, and sometimes failing,
He, my Strength, my victory wins.

Jesus! what a Guide and Keeper!
While the tempest still is high,
Storms about me, night o'ertakes me,
He, my Pilot, hears my cry.

Hallelujah! what a Savior!
Hallelujah! what a Friend!
Saving, helping, keeping, loving,
He is with me to the end.

Be of good cheer! It is I; do not be afraid.

—Matthew 14:27

Search Me, O God

January 15 was a special day to revivalist J. Edwin Orr. He was born **January 15, 1915**, and January 15 became a red-letter day for him. It was on subsequent anniversaries of his birth that he was converted, married, ordained, and appointed a chaplain in the US Air Force. In my library is a prized set of travelogue books he wrote when, as a young man, he hitchhiked the world in evangelistic work. I once mentioned these books to him, and he waved them off as "early attempts" at writing. But I treasure them and they still inspire me as much as his later, more scholarly works. His hymn "Search Me, O God" was written hurriedly in 1936 at a revival meeting in Ngaruawahia, New Zealand.

Search me, O God,
And know my heart today;
Try me, O Savior,
Know my thoughts, I pray.
See if there be
Some wicked way in me;
Cleanse me from every sin
And set me free.

I praise Thee, Lord,
For cleansing me from sin;
Fulfill Thy Word,
And make me pure within.
Fill me with fire
Where once I burned with shame;
Grant my desire
To magnify Thy Name.

Search me, O God, and know my heart; try me, and know my anxieties; and see if there is any wicked way in me, and lead me in the way everlasting.

—Psalm 139:23–24

God of the World!

This lesser-known hymn comes from the pen of a great American Christian educator, Sewall Sylvester Cutting, who wanted to show the power of God in nature, science, providence, and grace. Cutting was born in Windsor, Vermont, in 1813 and enjoyed a long and distinguished career as a pastor, an editor, an educator, and a denominational leader. On **January 16, 1882**, he was in his son's home in Brooklyn when he suffered a paralyzing seizure. He lingered for about three weeks before passing away. The words he penned vividly portray our Lord's great power as Creator.

God of the world! near and afar,
Thy glories shine in earth and star;
We see Thy love in opening flower,
In distant orb Thy wondrous power.

God of our lives! The throbbing heart
Doth at Thy beck its action start;
Throbs on, obedient to Thy will,
Or ceases at Thy fatal chill.

God of eternal life! Thy love
Doth every stain of sin remove;
The cross, the cross, its hallowed light
Shall drive from earth her cheerless night.

God of all goodness! To the skies
Our hearts in grateful anthems rise;
And to Thy service shall be given
The rest of life, the whole of heaven.

The heavens declare the glory of God; and the firmament shows His handiwork.

—Psalm 19:1

Wherever He Leads I'll Go

A three-day Sunday school convention concluded in Clanton, Alabama, on **January 17, 1936.** The Southern Baptist hymnist B. B. McKinney was attending the convention, and he dined with his friend, missionary R. S. Jones, who was speaking at the gathering. Over dinner, Jones confided to McKinney that health problems were preventing him from returning to his work in Brazil. McKinney, deeply concerned, asked what he was going to do. "I don't know," replied Jones, "but wherever He leads I'll go." Inspired by that answer, McKinney wrote the words and music to this tremendous hymn of commitment in his hotel room before the evening session.

"Take up thy cross and follow Me," I heard my Master say;
"I gave My life to ransom thee, Surrender your all today."
Wherever He leads I'll go, Wherever He leads I'll go,
I'll follow my Christ who loves me so, Wherever He leads I'll go.

He drew me closer to His side, I sought His will to know,
And in that will I now abide, Wherever He leads I'll go.
Wherever He leads I'll go, Wherever He leads I'll go,
I'll follow my Christ who loves me so, Wherever He leads I'll go.

It may be thru' the shadows dim, Or o'er the stormy sea,
I take my cross and follow Him, Wherever He leadeth me.
Wherever He leads I'll go, Wherever He leads I'll go,
I'll follow my Christ who loves me so, Wherever He leads I'll go.

My heart, my life, my all I bring To Christ who loves me so;
He is my Master, Lord, and King, Wherever He leads I'll go.
Wherever He leads I'll go, Wherever He leads I'll go,
I'll follow my Christ who loves me so, Wherever He leads I'll go.

These are the ones who follow the Lamb wherever He goes.

—Revelation 14:4

Footprints of Jesus

On many occasions, we sang this hymn in the mountain church where I was raised. Today is the birthday of its author, Mary Bridges Slade, born **January 18, 1826**. She was an educator by trade, a pastor's wife by marriage, and a hymnist by grace. "Footprints of Jesus," her best-known hymn, follows the footsteps of Christ through the three years of His ministry and on to heaven, reminding us that we're to follow in His steps.

Sweetly, Lord, have we heard Thee calling,
Come, follow Me!
And we see where Thy footprints falling
Lead us to Thee.

Though they lead o'er the cold, dark mountains,
Seeking His sheep;
Or along by Siloam's fountains,
Helping the weak.

If they lead through the temple holy,
Preaching the Word;
Or in homes of the poor and lowly,
Serving the Lord.

Then at last when on high He sees us,
Our journey done,
We will rest where the steps of Jesus
End at His throne.

Footprints of Jesus,
That make the pathway glow;
We will follow the steps of Jesus
Where'er they go.

He said to him, "Follow Me." So he arose and followed Him.

—Matthew 9:9

Deeper, Deeper

Standing among the graves at Evergreen Cemetery in Los Angeles, California, is a well-preserved marker reading: "Bishop Charles Price Jones, Founder of Church of Christ (Holiness), USA. December 9, 1865–**January 19, 1949**. Jesus Only." Rev. C. P. Jones was born to slave parents in Georgia at the end of the Civil War. He came to Christ in 1884 and was soon preaching the gospel and writing hymns, including "I Would Not Be Denied" and "Jesus Only." All his life, Jones faced racist violence, including death threats and church fires. Jones wrote many of his hymns to comfort himself in danger. After moving to California, he became a leader in the holiness movement, and his song "Deeper, Deeper," which I remember singing many times as a child in church, reflects his theme of growing in the grace of our Lord.

> Deeper, deeper in the love of Jesus
> Daily let me go;
> Higher, higher in the school of wisdom,
> More of grace to know.
>
> Deeper, deeper, blessèd Holy Spirit,
> Take me deeper still,
> Till my life is wholly lost in Jesus,
> And His perfect will.
>
> Deeper, deeper in the faith of Jesus,
> Holy faith and true;
> In His pow'r and soul exulting wisdom
> Let me peace pursue.
>
> *O deeper yet, I pray,*
> *And higher every day,*
> *And wiser, blessèd Lord,*
> *In Thy precious, holy Word.*

But grow in the grace and knowledge of
our Lord and Savior Jesus Christ.

—2 Peter 3:18

Teach Me to Pray

Albert Simpson Reitz, author of over one hundred hymns, was born **January 20, 1879**, into a Methodist minister's family. In 1903, he got a job as a YMCA worker in Topeka, Kansas, and five years later began traveling as the song director for evangelist Henry Ostrom. Next came studies at the Moody Bible Institute in Chicago, following which Reitz was ordained into the Baptist ministry. He served various churches until his retirement in Inglewood, California, in 1952. Rev. Reitz composed "Teach Me to Pray" in 1925, following a heartwarming Day of Prayer at the Rosehill Baptist Church in Los Angeles, where he served as a pastor.

Teach me to pray, Lord, teach me to pray;
This is my heart-cry, day unto day.
I long to know Thy will and Thy way;
Teach me to pray, Lord, teach me to pray.

Power in prayer, Lord, power in prayer!
Here 'mid earth's sin and sorrow and care,
Men lost and dying, souls in despair,
O give me power, power in prayer!

My weakened will, Lord, Thou canst renew;
My sinful nature Thou canst subdue.
Fill me just now with power anew,
Power to pray and power to do!

Living in Thee, Lord, and Thou in me,
Constant abiding, this is my plea;
Grant me Thy power, boundless and free,
Power with men and power with Thee.

It came to pass, as He was praying in a certain place, when He ceased, that one of His disciples said to Him, "Lord, teach us to pray."

—Luke 11:1

The Solid Rock

Edward Mote was born **January 21, 1797**, to parents who ran a public house on a downtrodden London street. He was apprenticed to a cabinetmaker but eventually became a Baptist preacher in the village of Horsham. One day, while going about his work, it came to his mind to write a hymn on the "Gracious Experience of the Christian." He started with the refrain, "On Christ the solid Rock I stand, / All other ground is sinking sand." Later in the day, he sang his hymn for a dying woman. It proved such a comfort that Mote went home and wrote more verses by the fireplace. After "The Solid Rock" was printed in a gospel magazine, it gained widespread popularity and was included in hymnals everywhere.

My hope is built on nothing less
Than Jesus' blood and righteousness.
I dare not trust the sweetest frame,
But wholly lean on Jesus' name.

His oath, His covenant, His blood,
Support me in the whelming flood.
When all around my soul gives way,
He then is all my hope and stay.

When He shall come with trumpet sound,
Oh may I then in Him be found.
Dressed in His righteousness alone,
Faultless to stand before the throne.

On Christ the solid Rock I stand,
All other ground is sinking sand;
All other ground is sinking sand.

The LORD lives! Blessed be my Rock! Let the
God of my salvation be exalted.

—Psalm 18:46

Face to Face

Carrie Breck, an Oregon homemaker, raised five daughters and wrote over two thousand poems, many of them composed as she rocked her babies. One day she sent this poem, "Face to Face," to a musician named Grant Tullar who, just the night before he received it, had written a tune that perfectly fit the words. The tune had actually come to Grant over a nearly empty jar of jelly, but that's another story. The text and tune were instantly married and have lived happily ever after.

Carrie Breck was born **January 22, 1855.**

Face to face with Christ, my Savior,
Face to face—what will it be,
When with rapture I behold Him,
Jesus Christ who died for me?

Only faintly now I see Him,
With the darkened veil between,
But a blessèd day is coming,
When His glory shall be seen.

Face to face—oh, blissful moment!
Face to face—to see and know;
Face to face with my Redeemer,
Jesus Christ who loves me so.

Face to face I shall behold Him,
Far beyond the starry sky;
Face to face in all His glory,
I shall see Him by and by!

Now we see in a mirror, dimly, but then face to face.

—1 Corinthians 13:12

Pour Out Thy Spirit from On High

James Montgomery was only five when his parents left him in boarding school and shipped off as missionaries to the West Indies, never to be seen again. Remarkably, James grew up to be a prominent publisher, hymnist, and avid supporter of overseas missions. He wrote four hundred hymns, the best-known being the Christmas carol "Angels from the Realms of Glory." Among his lesser-known hymns is this wonderful prayer for Christian workers. A copy in the author's handwriting says it was written on **January 23, 1833,** for "a meeting of the clergy." It's usually sung to the tune "Duke Street" ("Jesus Shall Reign Where'er the Sun"). Offer it today as a prayer for your pastor or church staff!

> Pour out Thy Spirit from on high;
> Lord, Thine assembled servants bless;
> Graces and gifts to each supply,
> And clothe Thy priests with righteousness.
>
> Within Thy temple when they stand,
> To teach the truth, as taught by Thee,
> Savior, like stars in Thy right hand
> May all Thy Church's pastors be.
>
> To watch and pray and never faint,
> By day and night, strict guard to keep,
> To warn the sinner, cheer the saint,
> Nourish Thy lambs, and feed Thy sheep.
>
> Then, when their work is finished here,
> May they in hope their charge resign;
> When the Chief Shepherd shall appear,
> O God, may they and we be Thine.

I will pour out My Spirit in those days.

—Acts 2:18

In the Sweet By and By

For many years, the African nation of Burundi was controlled by a series of Tutsi military dictators who persecuted Christians. On **January 24, 1964**, a pastor named Yona Kanamuzeyi was arrested and driven away in a jeep. At the military camp, after asking permission to write in his journal, he scribbled that he was going to heaven and asked that the journal be given to his wife. His hands were then tied and he walked to his execution singing, "There's a land that is fairer than day. . . ." Shots rang out, Kanamuzeyi fell to the ground, and his body was rolled into the stream. He was one of an estimated 45 million people martyred for Christ in the twentieth century.*

There's a land that is fairer than day,
And by faith we can see it afar;
For the Father waits over the way
To prepare us a dwelling place there.

We shall sing on that beautiful shore
The melodious songs of the blessed;
And our spirits shall sorrow no more,
Not a sigh for the blessing of rest.

To our bountiful Father above,
We will offer our tribute of praise
For the glorious gift of His love
And the blessings that hallow our days.

In the sweet by and by,
We shall meet on that beautiful shore;
In the sweet by and by,
We shall meet on that beautiful shore.

The city had no need of the sun or of the moon to
shine in it, for the glory of God illuminated it.

—Revelation 21:23

* The story of Pastor Yona Kanamuzeyi and the persecution of Christians in Rwanda is told by James and Marti Hefley in their book *By Their Blood: Christian Martyrs of the Twentieth Century* (Baker Books). The statistic of 45 million comes from media reports quoting Nina Shea in her book on Christian persecution titled *In the Lion's Den* (Broadman & Holman).

Peace, Perfect Peace

Happy birthday to Edward Bickersteth, who was born on **January 25, 1825**. Though he became a vicar and a bishop in the Church of England, he's best remembered for his hymns. "Peace, Perfect Peace" he wrote while on vacation, having heard a sermon from Isaiah 26:3. The speaker pointed out that in the original Hebrew the phrase "perfect peace" is *Shâlom, Shâlom*, meaning "double peace" or "multiplied peace." That afternoon Bickersteth visited a dying relative and quoted Isaiah's words. Taking paper and pen, he jotted down this poem and read it to the man on the spot.

Peace, perfect peace, in this dark world of sin?
The blood of Jesus whispers peace within.

Peace, perfect peace, by thronging duties pressed?
To do the will of Jesus, this is rest.

Peace, perfect peace, with sorrows surging round?
On Jesus' bosom naught but calm is found.

Peace, perfect peace, with loved ones far away?
In Jesus' keeping we are safe, and they.

Peace, perfect peace, our future all unknown?
Jesus we know, and He is on the throne.

Peace, perfect peace, death shadowing us and ours?
Jesus has vanquished death and all its powers.

It is enough: earth's struggles soon shall cease,
And Jesus call us to Heaven's perfect peace.

*You will keep him in perfect peace, whose mind
is stayed on You, because he trusts in You.*

—Isaiah 26:3

The Eighty-fourth Psalm

In the seventeenth century, a sturdy band of Presbyterians arose in Scotland who refused to acknowledge the king as head of the church. Only Christ, they said, could claim that title. When they signed a covenant to that effect, they were hunted down like dogs. On **January 26, 1681**, two brave Covenanters, Isabel Alison and Marion Harvie, were hanged in Edinburgh. In their last moments, these women sang Psalm 84 from the Scottish Psalter to the mournful tune of "Martyrs."

How lovely is Thy dwelling place,
O Lord of hosts, to me!
The tabernacles of Thy grace
How pleasant, Lord, they be!

For in Thy courts one day excels
A thousand; rather in
My God's house will I keep a door,
Than dwell in tents of sin.

For God the Lord's a sun and shield;
He'll grace and glory give;
And will withhold no good from them
That uprightly do live.

O Thou that art the Lord of hosts,
That man is truly blest,
Who by assured confidence
On Thee alone doth rest.

How lovely is Your tabernacle, O LORD of hosts! My soul longs, yes, even faints for the courts of the LORD.

—Psalm 84:1–2

The Lord Hath Helped Me Hitherto

A handful of gifted nineteenth-century hymnists were translators. Instead of penning their own new pieces, they gave us treasures in English from the Latin and German hymnals. Today is the birthday of one such man, August Crull, who was born into a lawyer's family on **January 27, 1845**, in Rostock, Germany. As a young man, Crull sailed to America to enroll in Concordia College, where he later became professor of German. The 1916 edition of the Concordia yearbook was dedicated to him, saying, "We, the class of 1916, gratefully dedicate this book to our revered teacher, Professor August Crull, who taught at our institution, patiently and faithfully, for forty-two years." Crull was a major force in developing the Lutheran hymnal in America, and it's because of his efforts that many great German hymns are now sung in English. This is his rendition of a hymn based on 1 Samuel 7:12 by the German hymnist Countess Ämilie Juliane.

> The Lord hath helped me hitherto
> By His surpassing favor;
> His mercies every morn were new,
> His kindness did not waver.
> God hitherto hath been my Guide,
> Hath pleasures hitherto supplied,
> And hitherto hath helped me.
>
> Help me henceforth, O God of grace,
> Help me on each occasion,
> Help me in each and every place,
> Help me through Jesus' passion;
> Help me in life and death, O God,
> Help me through Jesus' dying blood;
> Help me as Thou hast helped me!

Then Samuel took a stone and set it up between Mizpah and Shen, and called its name Ebenezer, saying, "Thus far the LORD has helped us."

—1 Samuel 7:12

Now the Day Is Over

I learned this hymn during my college years because the church I attended sang it every Sunday at the close of the evening service. When I began pastoring years later, I found a wonderful rendition of it on a cassette and often played it at the close of day. Now I frequently sing it quietly in my heart when my day's work is over. It's an evening prayer, written by the eccentric British pastor Sabine Baring-Gould, who was born on **January 28, 1834**.

Now the day is over,
Night is drawing nigh,
Shadows of the evening
Steal across the sky.

Jesus, give the weary
Calm and sweet repose;
With Thy tenderest blessing
May mine eyelids close.

Grant to little children
Visions bright of Thee;
Guard the sailors tossing
On the deep, blue sea.

Through the long night watches
May Thine angels spread
Their white wings above me,
Watching round my bed.

When the morning wakens,
Then may I arise
Pure, and fresh, and sinless
In Thy holy eyes.

He who keeps you will not slumber.

—Psalm 121:3

Since Jesus Came into My Heart

Rufus McDaniel, born **January 29, 1850**, began preaching as a teenager and served the Lord faithfully in ministry throughout Ohio, dying in Dayton at age ninety. This hymn, one of about a hundred that he penned, was written in 1914 following the untimely death of his son.

What a wonderful change in my life has been wrought
Since Jesus came into my heart!
I have light in my soul for which long I had sought,
Since Jesus came into my heart!

I'm possessed of a hope that is steadfast and sure,
Since Jesus came into my heart!
And no dark clouds of doubt now my pathway obscure,
Since Jesus came into my heart!

There's a light in the valley of death now for me,
Since Jesus came into my heart!
And the gates of the City beyond I can see,
Since Jesus came into my heart!

I shall go there to dwell in that City, I know,
Since Jesus came into my heart!
And I'm happy, so happy, as onward I go,
Since Jesus came into my heart!

Since Jesus came into my heart,
Since Jesus came into my heart,
Floods of joy o'er my soul like the sea billows roll,
Since Jesus came into my heart.

Though I walk through the valley of the shadow of
death, I will fear no evil; for You are with me.

—Psalm 23:4

O Worship the King

Charles Grant, chairman of the East India Company, was a devout British Christian whose two sons were chips off the old block. In 1790, when Charles came home to serve in Parliament, his boys, Robert and Charles, came with him and entered law school. Both young men were admitted to the bar on the same day, **January 30, 1807**, and both became prominent political leaders. In 1838, Robert passed away at the age of fifty-nine while serving as governor of Bombay. He left behind twelve unpublished hymns, which his brother Charles later found and published. Among them was this great anthem, based on Psalm 104.

O worship the King, all glorious above,
O gratefully sing His power and His love;
Our Shield and Defender, the Ancient of Days,
Pavilioned in splendor, and girded with praise.

O tell of His might, O sing of His grace,
Whose robe is the light, whose canopy space,
His chariots of wrath the deep thunderclouds form,
And dark is His path on the wings of the storm.

Thy bountiful care, what tongue can recite?
It breathes in the air, it shines in the light;
It streams from the hills, it descends to the plain,
And sweetly distills in the dew and the rain.

Frail children of dust, and feeble as frail,
In Thee do we trust, nor find Thee to fail;
Thy mercies how tender, how firm to the end,
Our Maker, Defender, Redeemer, and Friend.

O LORD, how manifold are Your works! In wisdom You have made them all.

—Psalm 104:24

The Sands of Time Are Sinking

As a boy, Charles Haddon Spurgeon lived with his grandparents, who offered him a farthing for every hymn he memorized. He committed to memory almost all of Watts's hymns and many others. When he later became a gospel preacher, there wasn't an auditorium in England large enough for the crowds wanting to hear him, and his sermons were peppered with hymn quotations. He could punch home any truth with the rhythm and rhyme of a memorized hymn. But Spurgeon worked himself to exhaustion, and by age fifty-seven he was worn out. On Sunday morning, June 7, 1891, he stood for what would be the final time in London's Metropolitan Tabernacle and gave out his last hymn. It was Anne Cousin's "The Sands of Time Are Sinking." Shortly afterward, Spurgeon collapsed and was taken to the French Riviera in hopes of a recovery. There he died on **January 31, 1892**, in the Hotel Beau Rivage. When his body was returned to London to lie in state at the Metropolitan Tabernacle, sixty thousand people filed past the olive-wood coffin. At his funeral, the vast congregation stood and opened the service by singing "The Sands of Time Are Sinking."

The sands of time are sinking, the dawn of Heaven breaks;
The summer morn I've sighed for—the fair, sweet morn awakes:
Dark, dark hath been the midnight, but dayspring is at hand,
And glory, glory dwelleth in Immanuel's land.

I've wrestled on towards Heaven, against storm and wind and tide,
Now, like a weary traveler that leaneth on his guide,
Amid the shades of evening, while sinks life's lingering sand,
I hail the glory dawning from Immanuel's land.

I shall sleep sound in Jesus, filled with His likeness rise,
To love and to adore Him, to see Him with these eyes:
'Tween me and resurrection but Paradise doth stand;
Then—then for glory dwelling in Immanuel's land.

The world and its desires pass away, but the man who does the will of God lives forever.

—1 John 2:17 NIV

A Child of the King

In 1876, Hattie Buell traveled to the Thousand Island Park in New York, eager for a time of Bible conference teaching and preaching. On Sunday morning, she listened as the speaker talked of being an heir of God and a joint heir of Christ. "Christian friends," he cried, "we are the children of the King!" Hattie Buell left the meeting and almost immediately wrote "A Child of the King." It was published on **February 1, 1877**, in *The Northern Christian Advocate*.

My Father is rich in houses and lands,
He holdeth the wealth of the world in His hands!
Of rubies and diamonds, of silver and gold,
His coffers are full, He has riches untold.

My Father's own Son, the Savior of men,
Once wandered on earth as the poorest of them;
But now He is pleading our pardon on high,
That we may be His when He comes by and by.

I once was an outcast stranger on earth,
A sinner by choice, and an alien by birth,
But I've been adopted, my name's written down,
An heir to a mansion, a robe and a crown.

A tent or a cottage, why should I care?
They're building a palace for me over there;
Though exiled from home, yet still may I sing:
All glory to God, I'm a child of the King.

I'm a child of the King, A child of the King:
With Jesus my Savior, I'm a child of the King.

We are children of God, and if children, then heirs—heirs of God and joint heirs with Christ.

—Romans 8:16–17

My Country, 'Tis of Thee

Samuel Francis Smith was a Baptist preacher, pastor, college professor, hymnist, linguist, writer, and missionary statesman. He lived to a ripe old age and accomplished much for God's kingdom before passing away suddenly in a train that was about to leave the Boston station en route to a preaching appointment. Despite his lifetime of service, he's best remembered for a hymn he wrote as a second-year seminary student—"America," commonly known as "My Country, 'Tis of Thee." To pick up extra money, Smith had taken on some translation work for the Christian composer Lowell Mason. One of the hymns was a German patriotic song. The words piqued Smith's interest, and he started writing a patriotic song of his own. Within a half hour on the evening of **February 2, 1831**, he had jotted down the words to "America." It was first sung by the Juvenile Choir of Boston's Park Street Congregational Church on July 4, 1831.

> My country, 'tis of thee,
> Sweet land of liberty,
> Of thee I sing;
> Land where my fathers died,
> Land of the pilgrims' pride,
> From every mountainside
> Let freedom ring!
>
> Our father's God, to Thee,
> Author of liberty,
> To Thee we sing.
> Long may our land be bright
> With freedom's holy light;
> Protect us by Thy might,
> Great God, our King.

Blessed is the nation whose God is the LORD.
—Psalm 33:12

I Am Thine, O Lord

Today is the birthday of two composers. Felix Mendelssohn, the German musician who wrote the melody to "Hark! The Herald Angels Sing," was born on this day in 1809. And gospel songwriter William Doane was born on **February 3, 1832**. Doane was a businessman in Cincinnati until sidelined by heart trouble. Afterward he devoted his life to gospel music, writing two thousand tunes. His best compositions were for Fanny Crosby's hymns. One day, as Fanny visited William in his Ohio home, the two old friends fell to talking about the joy of God's presence. By bedtime Fanny had written this hymn, and soon afterward Doane wrote the music.

I am Thine, O Lord, I have heard Thy voice,
And it told Thy love to me;
But I long to rise in the arms of faith
And be closer drawn to Thee.

Consecrate me now to Thy service, Lord,
By the power of grace divine;
Let my soul look up with a steadfast hope,
And my will be lost in Thine.

O, the pure delight of a single hour
That before Thy throne I spend,
When I kneel in prayer, and with Thee, my God,
I commune as friend with friend!

Draw me nearer, nearer, blessèd Lord,
To the cross where Thou hast died.
Draw me nearer, nearer, nearer, blessèd Lord,
To Thy precious, bleeding side.

Draw near to God and He will draw near to you.

—James 4:8

Take My Life and Let It Be

The great Christian worker Frances Ridley Havergal wrote this hymn on **February 4, 1874**, and later gave this explanation about it: "I went for a little visit of five days [to the home of a friend]. There were ten persons in the house, some unconverted . . . some converted, but not rejoicing Christians. He gave me the prayer, 'Lord, give me all in this house.' And He just did. Before I left the house everyone had got a blessing. The last night of my visit I was too happy to sleep, and passed most of the night in praise and renewal of my own consecration, and these little couplets formed themselves and chimed in my heart, one after another till they finished with 'ever, only, all, for Thee.'"

Take my life, and let it be consecrated, Lord, to Thee.
Take my moments and my days; let them flow in ceaseless
   praise.
Take my hands, and let them move at the impulse of Thy love.
Take my feet, and let them be swift and beautiful for Thee.

Take my voice, and let me sing always, only, for my King.
Take my lips, and let them be filled with messages from Thee.
Take my silver and my gold; not a mite would I withhold.
Take my intellect, and use every power as Thou shalt choose.

Take my will, and make it Thine; it shall be no longer mine.
Take my heart, it is Thine own; it shall be Thy royal throne.
Take my love, my Lord, I pour at Thy feet its treasure store.
Take myself, and I will be ever, only, all for Thee.

Consecrate yourselves therefore, and be
holy, for I am the LORD your God.
—Leviticus 20:7

All the Way My Savior Leads Me

Today is the anniversary of Fanny Crosby's first hymn. Blinded at infancy, Fanny grew up to be a renowned poet. In early 1864, her pastor, Rev. Peter Stryker, suggested she visit the famous hymn publisher William Bradbury. On February 2, 1864, she met Bradbury in his office in New York. "Fanny," he said, "I thank God that we have at last met; for I think you can write hymns." Fanny, age forty-four, took up the challenge, and three days later, on **February 5, 1864**, she gave him the first of the approximately eight thousand hymns that she would compose. While that first hymn, "We Are Going to a Home Beyond the Skies," is seldom sung today, my favorite Crosby hymn, written in 1875, is still sung around the world—"All the Way My Savior Leads Me."

All the way my Savior leads me;
What have I to ask beside?
Can I doubt His tender mercy,
Who through life has been my Guide?
Heav'nly peace, divinest comfort,
Here by faith in Him to dwell!
For I know, whate'er befall me,
Jesus doeth all things well;
For I know, whate'er befall me,
Jesus doeth all things well.

All the way my Savior leads me
O the fullness of His love!
Perfect rest to me is promised
In my Father's house above.
When my spirit, clothed immortal,
Wings its flight to realms of day
This my song through endless ages:
Jesus led me all the way;
This my song through endless ages:
Jesus led me all the way.

*You will guide me with Your counsel, and
afterward receive me to glory.*

—Psalm 73:24

How Wonderful It Is to Walk with God

In Genesis 5, we read that Enoch walked with God. In Revelation 2, we're told that Jesus walks among His lampstands now, and His lampstands represent His churches, His people. From Genesis to Revelation, the Bible assures us we can walk with our Lord, enjoying constant, unbroken companionship with Him. Just as the disciples hiked the hills of Galilee and strolled the roads of Judea alongside Jesus, we find Him equally near. This hymn by Salvation Army worker Theodore Kitching captures the wonder of the Christ-walk. It first appeared in the Salvation Army's *War Cry* magazine on **February 6, 1915**.

> How wonderful it is to walk with God
> Along the road that holy men have trod;
> How wonderful it is to hear Him say:
> Fear not, have faith, 'tis I who lead the way!
>
> How wonderful it is to talk with God
> When cares sweep o'er my spirit like a flood;
> How wonderful it is to hear His voice,
> For when He speaks the desert lands rejoice!
>
> How wonderful it is to praise my God,
> Who comforts and protects me with His rod;
> How wonderful to praise him every hour,
> My heart attuned to sing His wondrous power!
>
> How wonderful 'twill be to live with God
> When I have crossed death's deep and swelling flood;
> How wonderful to see Him face to face
> When I have fought the fight and won the race!

Enoch walked with God . . .

—Genesis 5:22

[Jesus] walks in the midst of the seven golden lampstands.

—Revelation 2:1

Jesus Loves Even Me

After the railroad disaster that claimed the life of hymnist Philip Bliss, his writings were compiled and published. Included was a letter to his mother, dated **February 7, 1874**: "Dear Mother . . . It seems to us your spirit grows sweeter and your life more even and calm. It is not surprising that it should be so; for haven't you and your friends prayed for it? If we are in Christ may we not all expect to grow more and more like Him? . . . You may be sure we shall pray for you, and I can never forget that you prayed for me and watched over me many years before I could pray for myself." Just as Bliss expressed appreciation to his mother by letter, he did so to his heavenly Father in this hymn, published in 1870.

I am so glad that our Father in Heav'n
Tells of His love in the Book He has giv'n;
Wonderful things in the Bible I see,
This is the dearest, that Jesus loves me.

Though I forget Him, and wander away,
Still He doth love me wherever I stray;
Back to His dear loving arms would I flee,
When I remember that Jesus loves me.

Oh, if there's only one song I can sing,
When in His beauty I see the great King,
This shall my song through eternity be,
"Oh, what a wonder that Jesus loves me!"

I am so glad that Jesus loves me,
Jesus loves me, Jesus loves me.
I am so glad that Jesus loves me,
Jesus loves even me.

We love Him because He first loved us.

—1 John 4:19

There Is Power in the Blood

The writer of Hebrews said, "With His own blood He entered the Most Holy Place once for all, having obtained eternal redemption. For if the blood of bulls and goats . . . sanctifies for the purifying of the flesh, how much more shall the blood of Christ . . . cleanse your conscience from dead works to serve the living God?" (Heb. 9:12–14). That was the message of Lewis Edgar Jones, who was born **February 8, 1865**. After attending the Moody Bible Institute in Chicago, Jones served the Lord in Texas and California, writing gospel songs on the side. He wrote "There Is Power in the Blood" at a camp meeting at Mountain Lake Park, Maryland.

Would you be free from the burden of sin?
There's power in the blood, power in the blood;
Would you o'er evil a victory win?
There's wonderful power in the blood.

Would you be free from your passion and pride?
There's power in the blood, power in the blood;
Come for a cleansing to Calvary's tide;
There's wonderful power in the blood.

Would you do service for Jesus your King?
There's power in the blood, power in the blood;
Would you live daily His praises to sing?
There's wonderful power in the blood.

There is power, power, wonder-working power
In the blood of the Lamb;
There is power, power, wonder-working power
In the precious blood of the Lamb.

In Him we have redemption through His
blood, the forgiveness of sins.

—Ephesians 1:7

Behold the Savior of Mankind

Rev. Samuel Wesley was a rather unpopular pastor in Epworth, England. On **February 9, 1709**, sitting in his room and thinking of how Christ, too, had been rejected, he penned this hymn for the upcoming Good Friday service. That night Wesley's house caught on fire. Samuel and his wife, Susanna, thought they had gotten all the children out, but looking at an upstairs window they were horrified to see five-year-old John still inside. At the last moment, John was rescued, plucked as a brand from the flames. Shortly afterward, someone found a piece of paper lying in the garden. It was Samuel's hymn, blown through an open window and, like John Wesley himself, saved from the fire.

Behold the Savior of mankind
Nailed to the shameful tree!
How vast the love that Him inclined
To bleed and die for thee!

Hark, how He groans, while nature shakes,
And earth's strong pillars bend!
The temple's veil in sunder breaks;
The solid marbles rend.

'Tis done! the precious ransom's paid!
"Receive my soul!" He cries;
See where He bows His sacred head!
He bows His head and dies!

But soon He'll break death's envious chain,
And in full glory shine;
O Lamb of God, was ever pain,
Was ever love, like Thine?

Behold! The Lamb of God who takes away the sin of the world!
—John 1:29

Fairest Lord Jesus

Richard Storrs Willis entered the world on **February 10, 1819.**
He was born in Boston and was the son of a deacon. After attending Boston Latin School and Yale University, he moved to Germany to study music. There he became friends with Felix Mendelssohn. Returning home, Willis became the music critic for the *New York Tribune* and a noted music publisher. He's best remembered, however, for two beautiful melodies often heard in churches around the world—the tune for the Christmas carol "It Came Upon the Midnight Clear" and the melody for the great German Catholic hymn "Fairest Lord Jesus."

Fairest Lord Jesus, ruler of all nature,
O Thou of God and man the Son,
Thee will I cherish, Thee will I honor,
Thou, my soul's glory, joy, and crown.

Fair are the meadows, fairer still the woodlands,
Robed in the blooming garb of spring:
Jesus is fairer, Jesus is purer
Who makes the woeful heart to sing.

Fair is the sunshine, fairer still the moonlight,
And all the twinkling starry host:
Jesus shines brighter, Jesus shines purer
Than all the angels heaven can boast.

Beautiful Savior! Lord of the nations!
Son of God and Son of Man!
Glory and honor, praise, adoration,
Now and forevermore be Thine.

His Son . . . through whom also He made the worlds . . .

—Hebrews 1:2

Guide Me, O Thou Great Jehovah

For Welsh evangelist William Williams, all of Wales was his parish. For forty-three years he traveled over Wales by horseback—over 100,000 miles in all—preaching in every town, village, nook, and cranny. He wrote so many hymns—about eight hundred of them—that he's called "the Charles Wesley of Wales." In 1745, he published a hymn titled "Strength to Pass Through the Wilderness," comparing the Christian life to Israel's journey toward the Promised Land. Today it is known as "Guide Me, O Thou Great Jehovah," and it is one of our greatest guidance hymns. Today is the birthday of William Williams. He was born **February 11, 1717.**

Guide me, O Thou great Jehovah,
Pilgrim through this barren land.
I am weak, but Thou art mighty;
Hold me with Thy powerful hand.
Bread of Heaven, Bread of Heaven,
Feed me till I want no more,
Feed me till I want no more.

Open now the crystal fountain,
Whence the healing stream doth flow;
Let the fire and cloudy pillar
Lead me all my journey through.
Strong Deliverer, strong Deliverer,
Be Thou still my Strength and Shield,
Be Thou still my Strength and Shield.

When I tread the verge of Jordan,
Bid my anxious fears subside;
Death of deaths, and hell's destruction,
Land me safe on Canaan's side.
Songs of praises, songs of praises,
I will ever give to Thee,
I will ever give to Thee.

You are my rock and my fortress; therefore, for
Your name's sake, lead me and guide me.

—Psalm 31:3

The King of Love My Shepherd Is

I'm thankful for Henry Williams Baker on two accounts. The first is his translation of the great Latin hymn by Aurelius Prudentius, "Of the Father's Love Begotten." The second is his wonderful hymn on the Twenty-third Psalm: "The King of Love My Shepherd Is." According to friends, Baker quoted from this latter hymn as he died on **February 12, 1877**.

> The King of love my Shepherd is,
> Whose goodness faileth never,
> I nothing lack if I am His
> And He is mine forever.
>
> Where streams of living water flow
> My ransomed soul He leadeth,
> And where the verdant pastures grow,
> With food celestial feedeth.
>
> Perverse and foolish oft I strayed,
> But yet in love He sought me,
> And on His shoulder gently laid,
> And home, rejoicing, brought me.
>
> In death's dark vale I fear no ill
> With Thee, dear Lord, beside me;
> Thy rod and staff my comfort still,
> Thy cross before to guide me.
>
> And so through all the length of days
> Thy goodness faileth never;
> Good Shepherd, may I sing Thy praise
> Within Thy house forever.

He restores my soul.

—Psalm 23:3

Jesus, Keep Me Near the Cross

On **February 13, 1915**, the *New York Times* carried this headline: "Fanny Crosby, Blind Hymn Writer, Dies." The article said, in part:

> Fanny Crosby, the blind hymn writer, died at her home at 4:30 o'clock in the morning. She had been growing feeble for the last six months and of late was very weak. She would have been ninety-five years old if she had lived until March 24. Fanny Crosby was the author of more than 8,000 hymns which have been sung in the Protestant churches through the world, her contributions being so numerous that a quarter of a century ago, hymnbook makers gave her 200 different pen names in order to make it appear that the hymns were the work of other authors. . . . She composed with great rapidity and always had her verses complete in her mind before committing them to paper. Many years ago Phillips Brooks gave her seventy-five topics and asked her to write verses based on them. She composed every one of the hymns before a line of any of them was placed on paper.

The newspaper went on to list her best-known hymns, including this one—"Jesus, Keep Me Near the Cross."

Jesus, keep me near the cross,
There a precious fountain—
Free to all, a healing stream,
Flows from Calvary's mountain.

Near the cross I'll watch and wait,
Hoping, trusting ever,
Till I reach the golden strand
Just beyond the river.

In the cross, in the cross,
Be my glory ever,
Till my raptured soul shall find
Rest beyond the river.

The message of the cross is foolishness to those who are perishing,
but to us who are being saved it is the power of God.

—1 Corinthians 1:18

Mansion Over the Hilltop

Ira Forest Stanphill was born on Valentine's Day, **February 14, 1914**, in the town of Bellview, New Mexico. By age ten, he was playing several instruments, and as a teenager he began writing and composing hymns. For many years, he traveled as a singing evangelist, preaching across America and around the world. His most popular gospel song is this one, based on our Lord's promise that in the Father's house are many mansions. We love it, not only because it reassures us of our heavenly home, but because it enjoins a simple and joyful life—"a cottage below"—as we're on our way to heaven.

I'm satisfied with just a cottage below,
A little silver and a little gold;
But in that city where the ransomed will shine,
I want a gold one that's silver lined.

Tho' often tempted, tormented and tested,
And like the prophet, my pillow a stone;
And tho' I find here no permanent dwelling,
I know He'll give me a mansion my own.

Don't think me poor or deserted or lonely,
I'm not discouraged, I'm heaven bound;
I'm but a pilgrim in search of the city,
I want a mansion, a harp and a crown.

I've got a mansion just over the hilltop,
In that bright land where we'll never grow old;
And some day yonder we will never more wander,
But walk on streets that are purest gold

In My Father's house are many mansions; if
it were not so, I would have told you.

—John 14:2

May the Mind of Christ My Savior

Who says young and old can't agree about music? Kate Wilkinson, born in 1859, was a venerable Anglican layperson of whom little is known except that she wrote the words to "May the Mind of Christ My Savior." Arthur Cyril Barham-Gould was a young twentieth-century composer who put Kate's words to music with the hymn tune "St. Leonards," composed in 1925. Two years later, in 1927, he was ordained into the Church of England. Kate passed away in 1928, but Arthur served as vicar of an Anglican church in the Kensington area of London until his death on **February 15, 1953**. Their hymn has become a beloved prayer for all who labor in the kingdom.

May the mind of Christ, my Savior,
Live in me from day to day,
By His love and power controlling
All I do and say.

May the Word of God dwell richly
In my heart from hour to hour,
So that all may see I triumph
Only through His power.

May the peace of God my Father
Rule my life in everything,
That I may be calm to comfort
Sick and sorrowing.

May His beauty rest upon me,
As I seek the lost to win,
And may they forget the channel,
Seeing only Him.

Let this mind be in you which was also in Christ Jesus.

—Philippians 2:5

Rise Up, O Men of God

Today is the birthday of two great hymns. "Now the Day Is Over" by Sabine Baring-Gould was published in *The Church Times* on **February 16, 1867**. And on **February 16, 1911**, the hymn "Rise Up, O Men of God!" appeared in *The Continent*, a Presbyterian journal in Chicago. Its author, William P. Merrill, later wrote: "Nolan R. Best, then editor of *The Continent*, happened to say to me that there was urgent need of a brotherhood hymn. . . . This suggestion lingered in my mind, and just about that time (1911) I came upon an article by Gerald Stanley Lee, entitled, 'The Church of Strong Men.' I was on one of the Lake Michigan steamers going back to Chicago for a Sunday at my own church when suddenly this hymn came up, almost without conscious thought or effort."

Rise up, O men of God!
Have done with lesser things.
Give heart and mind and soul and strength
To serve the King of kings.

Rise up, O men of God!
The kingdom tarries long.
Bring in the day of brotherhood
And end the night of wrong.

Rise up, O men of God!
The church for you doth wait,
Her strength unequal to her task;
Rise up and make her great!

Lift high the cross of Christ!
Tread where His feet have trod.
As brothers of the Son of Man,
Rise up, O men of God!

Blessed is the man whose strength is in You.

—Psalm 84:5

O God, Thou Faithful God

Some of our richest hymns are personal, poignant prayers, which are as appropriate for personal devotions as for public performance. Take this hymn, for example. It acknowledges God's ever-flowing faithfulness, then requests "a healthy frame" and "a conscience free from blame." It asks God's help for doing our work with "zeal and joyfulness." Its author, the German-Polish hymnist Johann Heermann, served the Lord earnestly despite personal problems (on several occasions he lost all his worldly possessions), recurring medical issues (he suffered serious eye and nose infections), and the disruptions of the Thirty Years' War. He died **February 17, 1647**. This hymn, which has eight stanzas in the original, gives us the key to Heermann's zeal. Try singing it to the tune "Nan Danket" ("Now Thank We All Our God").

O God, Thou faithful God,
Thou fountain ever flowing,
Without whom nothing is,
All perfect gifts bestowing,
Grant me a healthy frame,
And give me, Lord, within,
A conscience free from blame,
A soul unhurt by gain.

And grant me, Lord, to do,
With ready heart and willing,
Whate'er Thou shalt command,
My calling here fulfilling;
And do it when I ought,
With zeal and joyfulness,
And bless the work I've wrought,
For Thou must give success.

*Every good gift and every perfect gift is from above,
and comes down from the Father of lights, with whom
there is no variation or shadow of turning.*

—James 1:17

Be Still, My Soul

Eric Liddell was the Scottish runner whose story is told in the movie *Chariots of Fire*. After winning the men's 400-meter race at the 1924 Paris Olympics, he left as a missionary to China. In 1943, during the Japanese invasion of China, Eric was imprisoned in the Weihsien Internment Camp along with numbers of missionary children. There he served with enormous courage until sidelined by a brain tumor. On Sunday, **February 18, 1945**, as he lay dying in the camp hospital, he had his nurse pass a note out the window, asking the camp's Sunday school band to play his favorite hymn, "Be Still, My Soul" ("Finlandia"), which they did. Three days later, he was with the Lord.

> Be still, my soul: the Lord is on thy side.
> Bear patiently the cross of grief or pain.
> Leave to thy God to order and provide;
> In every change, He faithful will remain.
> Be still, my soul: thy best, thy heavenly Friend
> Through thorny ways leads to a joyful end.
>
> Be still, my soul: thy God doth undertake
> To guide the future, as He has the past.
> Thy hope, thy confidence let nothing shake;
> All now mysterious shall be bright at last.
> Be still, my soul: the waves and winds still know
> His voice who ruled them while He dwelt below.
>
> Be still, my soul: the hour is hastening on
> When we shall be forever with the Lord.
> When disappointment, grief and fear are gone,
> Sorrow forgot, love's purest joys restored.
> Be still, my soul: when change and tears are past
> All safe and blessèd we shall meet at last.

*Be still, and know that I am God; I will
be exalted among the nations.*

—Psalm 46:10

The Lord's Prayer

America's first Protestant foreign missionary was Adoniram Judson. He and a group of fellow students at Andover Seminary became inflamed for missions in the early 1800s, sparking a revival that led to the establishment of several American mission boards. On February 5, 1812, Adoniram married an indomitable young lady named Ann Hasseltine, and the next day they were commissioned as missionaries. They set sail aboard the *Caravan* on **February 19, 1812**. Space won't permit the telling of their tragic but triumphant story (everyone should read a biography of Judson), but one of the lesser-known aspects of Judson's ministry is that he wrote a handful of hymns, some of them during a torturous imprisonment. His son, Dr. Edward Judson, later commented on one of them—"The Lord's Prayer"—saying: "It illustrates the nature of the subjects which occupied the thoughts of the missionary during this long protracted agony. It is comprised in fewer words than the original Greek, and contains only two more than the common translation."

> Our Father, God, who art in heaven,
> All hallowed be Thy name;
> Thy kingdom come, Thy will be done
> In earth and heaven the same.
>
> Give us this day our daily bread;
> And, as we those forgive
> Who sin against us, so may we
> Forgiving grace receive.
>
> Into temptation lead us not;
> From evil set us free;
> The kingdom, power, and glory, Lord,
> Ever belong to Thee.

For Yours is the kingdom and the power
and the glory forever. Amen.

—Matthew 6:13

The Love of God

Recently I visited Forest Lawn Memorial Cemetery in Glendale, California, to view the world's largest oil painting, a breathtaking panorama of Calvary. It's housed in a special theater there, surrounded by three hundred acres of graves. There's probably no other place on earth where so many world-famous people are congregated, all just beneath the sod. Among the graves at Forest Lawn is that of a lowly German-born American named Frederick M. Lehman, who died on **February 20, 1953**. He is the author of today's hymn, "The Love of God," which he wrote in 1917 while sitting on an empty lemon box in a packing house where he worked in Pasadena.

The love of God is greater far
Than tongue or pen can ever tell;
It goes beyond the highest star,
And reaches to the lowest hell;
The guilty pair, bowed down with care,
God gave His Son to win;
His erring child He reconciled,
And pardoned from his sin.

Could we with ink the ocean fill,
And were the skies of parchment made,
Were every stalk on earth a quill,
And every man a scribe by trade,
To write the love of God above,
Would drain the ocean dry.
Nor could the scroll contain the whole,
Though stretched from sky to sky.

O love of God, how rich and pure! How measureless and strong!
It shall forevermore endure, the saints' and angels' song.

Now may the Lord direct your hearts into the love of God.

—2 Thessalonians 3:5

Calvary Covers It All

Walter Taylor grew up in a rough Pittsburgh gang; but on **February 21, 1896**, he gave his heart wholly to Christ. Sometime afterward, he also gave his heart in marriage to his sweetheart, Ethelwyn. The couple eventually took over the reins of the famed Pacific Garden Mission of Chicago, where they were affectionately called "Ma" and "Pa" Taylor. Ma Taylor regularly played the piano and organ at the mission, and she counseled those needing spiritual help. One day a man named Charles Crawford spoke in chapel, saying, "In spite of the fact that my record was black as midnight before conversion . . . Calvary covers it all." Inspired by his words, Ethelwyn wrote this beloved hymn.

> Far dearer than all that the world can impart
> Was the message came to my heart.
> How that Jesus alone for my sin did atone,
> And Calvary covers it all.
>
> How matchless the grace, when I looked in the face
> Of this Jesus, my crucified Lord;
> My redemption complete I then found at His feet,
> And Calvary covers it all.
>
> How blessed the thought, that my soul by Him bought,
> Shall be His in the glory on high;
> Where with gladness and song, I'll be one of the throng
> And Calvary covers it all.
>
> *Calvary covers it all,*
> *My past with its sin and stain;*
> *My guilt and despair Jesus took on Him there,*
> *And Calvary covers it all.*

Blessed are those whose lawless deeds are forgiven, and whose sins are covered.

—Romans 4:7

I'll Praise My Maker While I've Breath

These verses by Isaac Watts were on the mind of the dying John Wesley in 1791. Wesley had stayed remarkably well all his life, and at age eighty boasted he was as vigorous as a twenty-five-year-old. But in 1790, he admitted, "I am now an old man, decayed from head to foot." On **February 22, 1791**, as the eighty-eight-year-old Wesley preached for the last time at his City Road Chapel, he ended with Watts's hymn "I'll Praise My Maker While I've Breath." A few days later, lying on his deathbed, he astonished his friends by suddenly singing the same hymn in a strong voice. As he died, his voice became too weak to sing, but he was heard saying, "I'll praise . . . I'll praise. . . ."

> I'll praise my Maker while I've breath,
> And when my voice is lost in death,
> Praise shall employ my nobler powers;
> My days of praise shall ne'er be past,
> While life, and thought, and being last,
> Or immortality endures.
>
> Happy the one whose hopes rely
> On Israel's God: He made the sky,
> And earth, and seas, with all their train:
> His truth for ever stands secure;
> He saves th'oppressed, He feeds the poor,
> And none shall find His promise vain.
>
> I'll praise Him while He lends me breath,
> And when my voice is lost in death,
> Praise shall employ my nobler powers;
> My days of praise shall ne'er be past,
> While life, and thought, and being last,
> Or immortality endures.

Praise the LORD! Praise the LORD, O my soul!
While I live I will praise the LORD.

—Psalm 146:1–2

I Know That My Redeemer Lives

One of history's great composers, George Frederick Handel, was born **February 23, 1685**. He was a musical prodigy, performing to acclaim at age seven and composing music by age nine. As a young man, he wrote operas, oratorios, and cantatas in both Germany and Italy before settling in England in 1712. Today he's best known for his spectacular oratorio *Messiah*, but he also gave the church tunes for several popular hymns, including the Christmas carol "While Shepherds Watched Their Flocks by Night." In Britain, his "Gopsal" is the preferred tune for "Rejoice the Lord Is King." And Handel's majestic melody "Bradford" is the musical setting for Charles Wesley's triumphant Easter hymn "I Know That My Redeemer Lives."

I know that my Redeemer lives,
And ever prays for me;
A token of His love He gives,
A pledge of liberty.

I find Him lifting up my head,
He brings salvation near,
His presence makes me free indeed,
And He will soon appear.

Jesus, I hang upon Thy Word;
I steadfastly believe
Thou wilt return and claim me, Lord
And to Thyself receive.

The bliss of those that fully dwell,
Fully in Thee believe,
'Tis more than angel tongues can tell,
Or angel minds conceive.

For I know that my Redeemer lives, and He shall stand at last on the earth.

—Job 19:25

All Creatures of Our God and King

Pietro di Bernardone, a rich cloth merchant in Assisi, Italy, was enamored with all things French, so he named his son Francesco, or Francis. But on **February 24, 1208**, as Francis sat in church listening to a reading of Matthew 10, he decided to abandon his dad's wealth and become a radical disciple of Jesus Christ. He began traveling and preaching, and even the birds and fish seemed to listen attentively to him. He's known today as St. Francis of Assisi, and he's the author of my favorite hymn, *Cantico di Fratre Sole* ("Canticle to Brother Sun"), which is known to us by its English paraphrase: "All Creatures of Our God and King."

All creatures of our God and King,
Lift up your voices, let us sing: Alleluia, alleluia!
Thou burning sun with golden beams,
Thou silver moon that gently gleams,
O praise Him, O praise Him, Alleluia, alleluia, alleluia!

Thou rushing wind that art so strong,
Ye clouds that sail in heaven along, O praise Him, Alleluia!
Thou rising morn, in praise rejoice,
Ye lights of evening, find a voice,
O praise Him, O praise Him, Alleluia, alleluia, alleluia!

Let all things their Creator bless,
And worship Him in humbleness, O praise Him, Alleluia!
Praise, praise the Father, praise the Son,
And praise the Spirit, Three in One,
O praise Him, O praise Him, Alleluia, alleluia, alleluia!

Praise Him, sun and moon . . . fire and hail, snow and clouds . . . mountains . . . cattle . . . creeping things and flying fowl . . . all peoples. . . . Let them praise the name of the LORD.

—from Psalm 148

Saved, Saved, Saved!

This exuberant hymn owes much of its appeal to its calliope-like melody that would be at home on carnival carousals. Not surprisingly, it was composed by a young man who had just come to faith in Christ. Roger Hickman was born in 1888 in Missouri and was saved at age twenty. This composition, one of his earliest, was matched with Oswald J. Smith's poem "Saved!" and first sung in the 1919 Toronto Gospel Crusade of evangelist Paul Rader. In later years, Hickman chaired the music department at Baptist Bible Institute in Lakeland, Florida, and he went on to write over one hundred gospel songs and tunes before his death on **February 25, 1968**.

Saved! saved! saved! my sins are all forgiv'n;
Christ is mine! I'm on my way to Heav'n;
Once a guilty sinner, lost, undone,
Now a child of God, saved thro' His Son.

Saved! saved! saved! by grace and grace alone;
Oh, what wondrous love to me was shown,
In my stead Christ Jesus bled and died,
Bore my sins, for me was crucified.

Saved! saved! saved! oh, joy beyond compare!
Christ my life, and I His constant care;
Yielding all and trusting Him alone,
Living now each moment as His own.

Saved! I'm saved thro' Christ, my all in all;
Saved! I'm saved, whatever may befall;
He died upon the cross for me,
He bore the awful penalty;
And now I'm saved eternally—
I'm saved! saved! saved!

So they said, "Believe on the Lord Jesus
Christ, and you will be saved."

—Acts 16:31

Have Thine Own Way, Lord

George Stebbins was born on **February 26, 1846**, and spent the first twenty-three years of his life on a farm in western New York. Moving to Chicago and then to Boston, he became acquainted with D. L. Moody and Ira Sankey, and he spent the next twenty-five years working with them in evangelism. He became the last surviving member of the Moody evangelistic team, living until 1945 and almost reaching his one-hundredth birthday. His *Memoirs and Reminiscences* is a historical goldmine from the era of gospel music. Though a noted soloist and choir director, he's best remembered for writing melodies to hymns such as "There Is a Green Hill Far Away," "Take Time to Be Holy," "Saved by Grace, " and Adelaide Pollard's invitational hymn, "Have Thine Own Way, Lord."

Have Thine own way, Lord! Have Thine own way!
Thou art the Potter, I am the clay.
Mold me and make me after Thy will,
While I am waiting, yielded and still.

Have Thine own way, Lord! Have Thine own way!
Search me and try me, Master today!
Wash me just now, Lord, wash me just now,
As in Thy presence humbly I bow.

Have Thine own way, Lord! Have Thine own way!
Wounded and weary, help me I pray!
Power, all power, surely is Thine!
Touch me and heal me, Savior divine!

Have Thine own way, Lord! Have Thine own way!
Hold o'er my being absolute sway.
Fill with thy Spirit till all shall see
Christ only, always, living in me!

As the clay is in the potter's hand, so are you in My hand.

—Jeremiah 18:6

He Hideth My Soul

William J. Kirkpatrick, born in Pennsylvania on **February 27, 1838**, became a prolific composer of gospel tunes and a noted music publisher. He penned the tunes to many of Fanny Crosby's hymns, including "He Hideth My Soul." As we approach the Lenten season, take a moment to study this beloved Crosby/Kirkpatrick song. Notice that Jesus Christ is a wonderful Savior who hides our souls in the cleft of the rock, takes our burdens away, holds us up, gives us strength for the day, and crowns each moment with numberless blessings. He hides us safely in the cleft of the rock and covers us there with His hand.

A wonderful Savior is Jesus my Lord,
A wonderful Savior to me;
He hideth my soul in the cleft of the rock,
Where rivers of pleasure I see.

A wonderful Savior is Jesus my Lord,
He taketh my burden away;
He holdeth me up, and I shall not be moved,
He giveth me strength as my day.

With numberless blessings each moment He crowns,
And filled with His fullness divine,
I sing in my rapture, oh, glory to God
For such a Redeemer as mine!

He hideth my soul in the cleft of the rock
That shadows a dry, thirsty land;
He hideth my life with the depths of His love,
And covers me there with His hand,
And covers me there with His hand.

I will put you in the cleft of the rock, and
will cover you with My hand.

—Exodus 33:22

Our Heavenly Father, Hear

We often need to speak up for Christian ideas and ideals, even though they run counter to the popular culture. British newspaper publisher James Montgomery never feared using his newspaper to champion social reforms and to advance the cause of missions. He was twice imprisoned for his views, but prayer kept him strong. Here's his hymn on the Lord's Prayer, written **February 28, 1835**. Sing it to the tune of "A Charge to Keep," "Rise Up, O Men of God," or "Breathe on Me, Breath of God."

> Our Heav'nly Father, hear
> The prayer we offer now.
> Thy name be hallowed far and near;
> To Thee all nations bow.
>
> Thy kingdom come; Thy will
> On earth be done in love
> As saints and seraphim fulfill
> Thy holy will above.
>
> Our daily bread supply
> While by Thy word we live.
> The guilt of our iniquity
> Forgive as we forgive.
>
> From dark temptation's power,
> From Satan's wiles, defend.
> Deliver in the evil hour
> And guide us to the end.
>
> Thine shall forever be
> Glory and power divine;
> The scepter, throne, and majesty
> Of heaven and earth are Thine.

Our Father in heaven, hallowed be Your name.

—Matthew 6:9

The Lord, He Is Our Sun and Shield

Benjamin Keach, born **February 29, 1640**, became a Christian at fifteen and began preaching at eighteen. When the Act of Uniformity passed in 1662, he was seized for his Baptist preaching and put in the pillory in the open market. Keach afterward became pastor of a small church that met privately in London. When the laws changed, the church moved into a building of its own, and Keach introduced a new and controversial practice—the singing of hymns (as opposed to only the metrical Psalms). Baptists were opposed to hymns at this time, but Keach led his church to sing a hymn at Lord's Supper services and, later, on days of thanksgiving. Finally, about 1690, the church voted (with a few dissenters) to sing hymns every Sunday. The next year, Keach published a book advocating the singing of hymns and another book of three hundred hymns for congregational use, including "The Lord, He Is Our Sun and Shield." It was brave young Benjamin Keach who paved the way for Isaac Watts, the man who popularized British hymn singing a generation later.

The Lord, He is our sun and shield.
Our buckler and safeguard,
And hence we stand and will not yield,
Though enemies press hard.

Let foes strike at us as they please,
On the head or the heart;
This precious shield which we do use
Secures us every part.

From sin, from Satan, and the world
No art we need to fear,
Since Thou art such a shield to us,
O God and Savior dear!

For the LORD God is a sun and shield; the LORD will give grace and glory; no good thing will He withhold from those who walk uprightly.

—Psalm 84:11

Ye Servants of God,
Your Master Proclaim

As John and Charles Wesley evangelized England in the 1700s and established the Methodist movement, they faced a firestorm of criticism, opposition, and discouragement, and so did their followers. At the same time, England itself was facing invasion by France. Many citizens thought that, in challenging the established church, the Wesleys were disloyal and unpatriotic in a time of national crisis. On **March 1, 1744**, as the French fleet gathered in Dunkirk, Charles rushed to the press a selection of thirty-three songs titled "Hymns for Times of Trouble." The best known of these is Wesley's famous "Ye Servants of God, Your Master Proclaim."

> Ye servants of God, your Master proclaim,
> And publish abroad His wonderful name;
> The name all victorious of Jesus extol:
> His kingdom is glorious and rules over all.
>
> When devils engage, the billows arise,
> And horribly rage, and threaten the skies:
> Their fury shall never our steadfastness shock,
> The weakest believer is built on a rock.
>
> God ruleth on high, almighty to save,
> And still He is nigh, His presence we have;
> The great congregation His triumph shall sing,
> Ascribing salvation to Jesus, our King.
>
> Then let us adore and give Him His right,
> All glory and power, all wisdom and might;
> All honor and blessing with angels above,
> And thanks never ceasing and infinite love.

The LORD of hosts is with us; the God of Jacob is our refuge.

—Psalm 46:7

Give to the Winds Thy Fears

When thinking of the Wesley brothers, we usually consider Charles the hymnist and John the preacher. But Charles preached widely, and John tried his hand at writing a few hymns. To be honest, John did his best work when translating the hymns of others, especially those of the remarkable German Pietist Paul Gerhardt. Today on the anniversary of John Wesley's death, **March 2, 1791**, here's his translation of one of Gerhardt's greatest hymns, "Give to the Winds Thy Fears."

> Give to the winds thy fears,
> Hope and be undismayed.
> God hears thy sighs and counts thy tears,
> God shall lift up thy head.
>
> Through waves and clouds and storms,
> He gently clears thy way.
> Wait thou His time; so shall this night
> Soon end in joyous day.
>
> Still heavy is thy heart?
> Still sinks thy spirit down?
> Cast off the world, let fear depart,
> Bid every care begone.
>
> Far, far above thy thought,
> His counsel shall appear,
> When fully He the work hath wrought,
> That caused thy needless fear.
>
> Let us in life, in death,
> Thy steadfast truth declare,
> And publish with our latest breath
> Thy love and guardian care.

For God has not given us a spirit of fear, but of power and of love and of a sound mind.

—2 Timothy 1:7

Prince of Peace, Control My Will

Someone once defined anxiety as a small trickle of fear that cuts a channel in the brain into which all other thoughts drain. That's certainly true for me. My tendency to worry constantly drives me to the Prince of Peace whose presence and promises alone can settle my will, emotions, and innermost disposition. Sometimes it helps to have a prayer like "Prince of Peace, Control My Will." It appeared anonymously in the **March 3, 1858**, edition of the *Church of England Magazine* and was immediately set to music by William Bradbury. Make it your prayer today and let the Prince of Peace rule your mind and heart.

Prince of Peace, control my will;
Bid the struggling heart be still;
Bid my fears and doubtings cease,
Hush my spirit into peace.

Thou hast bought me with Thy blood,
Opened wide the gate to God;
Peace I ask, but peace must be,
Lord, in being one with Thee.

May Thy will, not mine, be done;
May Thy will and mine be one;
Chase these doubtings from my heart,
Now Thy perfect peace impart.

Savior, at Thy feet I fall,
Thou my life, my God, my all;
Let Thy happy servant be
One forevermore with Thee!

His name will be called . . . Prince of Peace.

—Isaiah 9:6

Moment by Moment

"Never a trial that He is not there, / Never a burden that He doth not bear, / Never a sorrow that He doth not share, / Moment by moment, I'm under His care." Those bolstering words were written by Major Daniel Whittle after a visit to the 1893 Chicago World's Fair. As Whittle walked around seeing the sights, his friend said, "I do not like the hymn 'I Need Thee Every Hour' very well because I need Him every moment of the day." Soon Whittle had composed "Moment by Moment." Major Whittle was only sixty-one when he passed away in Northfield, Massachusetts, on **March 4, 1901**, but he left behind a rich legacy of gospel songs, including other favorites such as "There Shall Be Showers of Blessing" and "The Banner of the Cross."

Dying with Jesus, by death reckoned mine;
Living with Jesus, a new life divine;
Looking to Jesus till glory doth shine,
Moment by moment, O Lord, I am Thine.

Never a trial that He is not there,
Never a burden that He doth not bear,
Never a sorrow that He doth not share,
Moment by moment, I'm under His care.

Never a heartache, and never a groan,
Never a teardrop and never a moan;
Never a danger but there on the throne,
Moment by moment He thinks of His own.

Moment by moment I'm kept in His love;
Moment by moment I've life from above;
Looking to Jesus till glory doth shine;
Moment by moment, O Lord, I am Thine.

Christ lives in me; and the life which I now live
in the flesh I live by faith in the Son of God,
who loved me and gave Himself for me.

—Galatians 2:20

Marvelous Grace of Our Loving Lord

I don't think his name was ever mentioned in the church where I grew up, and until I began researching hymns, I'd never heard of him. But fame has little to do with influence. I've sung Daniel Towner's tunes all my life, and his music is a part of my heritage. He was born **March 5, 1850**, in Rome, Pennsylvania, and he studied under his musician father. Daniel devoted his life to music ministry in local churches and at Moody Bible Institute, writing the tunes to such favorites as "Trust and Obey," "Anywhere with Jesus," "At Calvary," "My Anchor Holds," "Only a Sinner Saved by Grace," "Saved by the Blood of the Crucified One," and this hymn by Julia Johnston about God's "marvelous, infinite, matchless grace."

Marvelous grace of our loving Lord,
Grace that exceeds our sin and our guilt!
Yonder on Calvary's mount outpoured—
There where the blood of the Lamb was spilt.

Sin and despair, like the seawaves cold,
Threaten the soul with infinite loss;
Grace that is greater—yes, grace untold—
Points to the refuge, the mighty cross.

Marvelous, infinite, matchless grace,
Freely bestowed on all who believe!
You that are longing to see His face,
Will you this moment His grace receive?

Grace, grace, God's grace,
Grace that will pardon and cleanse within;
Grace, grace, God's grace,
Grace that is greater than all our sin.

For by grace you have been saved through faith, and
that not of yourselves; it is the gift of God.

—Ephesians 2:8

Send the Light

Charles Gabriel, an Iowan, began working at Grace Methodist Episcopal Church in San Francisco in 1890. One of his first tasks was to compose a hymn for the church's Missionary Day. His "Send the Light" was sung on **March 6, 1890**, and its popularity propelled Gabriel to national prominence as a songwriter. Today we remember him as the author of such favorites as "I Stand Amazed in the Presence" and "O That Will Be Glory for Me." He was also the composer of the music for "His Eye Is on the Sparrow" and "Since Jesus Came into My Heart." A contemporary of his said, "Mr. Gabriel's music is nothing if not melodious. Even a comparatively commonplace theme under his pen receives some touch that gives it a perennial freshness." It's always a fresh, melodious heart that sends the light.

There's a call comes ringing over the restless wave,
"Send the light! Send the light!"
There are souls to rescue there are souls to save,
Send the light! Send the light!

We have heard the Macedonian call today,
"Send the light! Send the light!"
And a golden offering at the cross we lay,
Send the light! Send the light!

Let us not grow weary in the work of love,
"Send the light! Send the light!"
Let us gather jewels for a crown above,
Send the light! Send the light!

Send the light, the blessèd Gospel light;
Let it shine from shore to shore!
Send the light, the blessèd Gospel light;
Let it shine forevermore!

In Him was life, and the life was the light of men.

—John 1:4

Take My Hand

Today's hymn is a seldom-sung prayer from a nearly forgotten hymnist, but her story is worth telling and her hymn is worth singing. Julie von Hausmann was born on **March 7, 1826**, in Latvia, in the Baltics. Though she was the fifth of six sisters, her siblings were considerably older or younger than she, so Julie was often alone. In quiet hours, she recorded her thoughts in poetry and prayer. In later years, as she traveled in European locales searching for relief from headaches, her poems were published and became well-known. Her most popular hymn, originally written in German, is "Take My Hand." According to some reports, she penned it following the death of her fiancé, with whom she was planning a career of missionary service. In her later years, Julie traveled through Germany, France, Switzerland, and Estonia, living with relatives and writing her devotional poetry, which was widely published in its day.

> O take my hand, dear Father, and lead Thou me,
> Till at my journey's ending I dwell with Thee.
> Alone I cannot wander one single day,
> So do Thou guide my footsteps on life's rough way.
>
> O cover with Thy mercy my poor, weak heart,
> Lest I in joy or sorrow from Thee depart.
> Permit Thy child to linger here at Thy feet,
> Thy goodness blindly trusting with faith complete.
>
> Though oft Thy power but faintly may stir my soul,
> With Thee, my Light in darkness, I reach the goal.
> Take then my hand, dear Father, and lead Thou me,
> Till at my journey's ending I dwell with Thee.

For I, the LORD your God, will hold your right hand, saying to you, "Fear not, I will help you."

—Isaiah 41:13

Jesus Shall Reign Where'er the Sun

After his college years, Isaac Watts returned home at the age of twenty and for the next two years wrote many of the famous hymns that later earned him the title "Father of English Hymnody." Watts preached his first sermon on his twenty-fourth birthday, and shortly afterward he became assistant pastor of the Independent Church in Mark Lane, London. In 1701, Watts was called as senior pastor at Mark Lane and was ordained on **March 8, 1702**. Watts, a very short man, was odd looking, poor of health, and a lifelong bachelor. But his seven hundred hymns are an enduring testimony to his zealous message that "Jesus shall reign where'er the sun does his successive journeys run."

Jesus shall reign where'er the sun
Does his successive journeys run;
His kingdom stretch from shore to shore,
Till moons shall wax and wane no more.

To Him shall endless prayer be made,
And praises throng to crown His head;
His Name like sweet perfume shall rise
With every morning sacrifice.

People and realms of every tongue
Dwell on His love with sweetest song;
And infant voices shall proclaim
Their early blessings on His name.

The saints shall flourish in His days,
Dressed in the robes of joy and praise.
Peace, like a river, from His throne
Shall flow to nations yet unknown.

*From the rising of the sun to its going down,
the Lord's name is to be praised.*

—Psalm 113:3

Blessed Assurance

Happy birthday to Phoebe Knapp, born **March 9, 1839**. Joseph and Phoebe Knapp were among the wealthiest of New York's glittering social scene. Joseph was founder of the Metropolitan Life Insurance Company, and the Knapp mansion was one of New York's premier social settings. They were active Christians, and Phoebe took keen interest in the ministry of gospel music. After Joseph's death, she moved into the Savoy Hotel and had an organ installed in her room on which she composed gospel tunes. One day, hymnist Fanny Crosby, a close friend, walked into the room. Phoebe played one of her compositions and asked, "What does this tune say?" Clapping her hands, Fanny said, "Why, that says, 'Blessed assurance, Jesus is mine.'" Fanny immediately wrote the words, giving birth to her most famous hymn.

> Blessèd assurance, Jesus is mine!
> O what a foretaste of glory divine!
> Heir of salvation, purchase of God,
> Born of His Spirit, washed in His blood.
>
> Perfect submission, perfect delight,
> Visions of rapture now burst on my sight;
> Angels descending bring from above
> Echoes of mercy, whispers of love.
>
> Perfect submission, all is at rest,
> I in my Savior am happy and blest,
> Watching and waiting, looking above,
> Filled with His goodness, lost in His love.
>
> *This is my story, this is my song,*
> *Praising my Savior, all the day long;*
> *This is my story, this is my song,*
> *Praising my Savior, all the day long.*

Let us draw near with a true heart in full assurance of faith.

—Hebrews 10:22

All Praise to Thee, My God, This Night

A hundred years ago, this hymn was considered one of the four greatest in the Anglican church, the others being "Hark! The Herald Angels Sing," "Rock of Ages," and "Lo, He Comes with Clouds Descending." This was an evening hymn, part of a trilogy written by Thomas Ken. It's been said that his three hymns—a morning hymn, an evening hymn, and a midnight hymn—conferred a greater benefit on the world than if he had founded three hospitals. On **March 10, 1711**, realizing death was near, Bishop Ken spent the evening destroying papers and files that might in any way injure others. Afterward he took to his bed, and on March 19, he passed away. Two days later, twelve poor men carried him to his grave just as the sun was rising in the east.

> All praise to Thee, my God, this night,
> For all the blessings of the light!
> Keep me, O keep me, King of kings,
> Beneath Thine own almighty wings.
>
> Forgive me, Lord, for Thy dear Son,
> The ill that I this day have done,
> That with the world, myself, and Thee,
> I, ere I sleep, at peace may be.
>
> When in the night I sleepless lie,
> My soul with heavenly thoughts supply;
> Let no ill dreams disturb my rest,
> No powers of darkness me molest.
>
> Praise God, from Whom all blessings flow;
> Praise Him, all creatures here below;
> Praise Him above, ye heavenly host;
> Praise Father, Son, and Holy Ghost.

I will both lie down in peace, and sleep; for You alone, O LORD, make me dwell in safety.

—Psalm 4:8

O Zion, Haste

Mary Ann Thomson was born in London on December 5, 1834, and died in Philadelphia on **March 11, 1923**. She was a gifted writer, the wife of a prominent librarian and literary expert in Pennsylvania. She and her husband, John, were leaders in Philadelphia's Church of the Annunciation (Episcopal). Mrs. Thomson wrote this hymn during the illness of a child. "One night," she said, "while I was sitting up with one of my children, who was ill with typhoid fever, I thought I should like to write a missionary hymn." She started "O Zion, Haste" that night, but it took three years to finish. It became one of the most used missionary hymns of all time.

> O Zion, haste, thy mission high fulfilling,
> To tell to all the world that God is light,
> That He who made all nations is not willing
> One soul should perish, lost in shades of night.
>
> Behold how many thousands still are lying
> Bound in the darksome prison house of sin,
> With none to tell them of the Savior's dying,
> Or of the life He died for them to win.
>
> Proclaim to every people, tongue, and nation
> That God, in Whom they live and move, is love;
> Tell how He stooped to save His lost creation,
> And died on earth that we might live above.
>
> Give of thy sons to bear the message glorious;
> Give of thy wealth to speed them on their way;
> Pour out thy soul for them in prayer victorious;
> O Zion, haste to bring the brighter day.
>
> *Publish glad tidings, tidings of peace;*
> *Tidings of Jesus, redemption, and release.*

The king's business required haste.

—1 Samuel 21:8

Commit Whatever Grieves Thee

Someone recently asked for my favorite hymn writer, and I couldn't answer; but near the top would be the great Lutheran hymnist Paul Gerhardt, who was born **March 12, 1607**. Gerhardt lived a century after Martin Luther, when the flames of the Reformation were dying down. His hymns helped fuel the Pietist revival that kept the church singing. Gerhardt was born near Luther's Wittenberg but spent much of his life in Berlin. Of all the hymns of Paul Gerhardt, the one I wanted to choose for this book is his hymn of encouragement "Commit Whatever Grieves Thee." (For another translation of this same hymn, see March 2, "Give to the Winds Thy Fears"). I've memorized the first verse and have found it eminently useful to anyone to whom I have occasion to quote it.

Commit whatever grieves thee
Into the gracious hands
Of Him Who never leaves thee,
Who Heav'n and earth commands.
Who points the clouds their courses,
Whom winds and waves obey,
He will direct thy footsteps
And find for thee a way.

Thy hand is never shortened,
All things must serve Thy might;
Thine every act is blessing,
Thy path is purest light.
Thy work no man can hinder,
Thy purpose none can stay,
Since Thou to bless Thy children
Wilt always find a way.

Cast your burden on the LORD, and He shall sustain you; He shall never permit the righteous to be moved.

—Psalm 55:22

O Sacred Head, Now Wounded

March 13, 1804, is the birthday of the Presbyterian pastor and professor James W. Alexander, a Virginian whose career alternated
between teaching at Princeton University and pastoring in New
Jersey and New York. His most lasting claim to fame, however,
was in translating from Latin into English some of the medieval
hymns of Bernard of Clairvaux, most notably "O Sacred Head,
Now Wounded." St. Bernard (1091–1153) had written seven passion hymns, each addressed to one of the wounded parts of the
Lord's crucified body (feet, knees, hands, side, chest, heart, and
head). This is Professor Alexander's 1830 translation of Bernard's
hymn addressed to Christ's wounded head.

> O sacred Head, now wounded,
> With grief and shame weighed down,
> Now scornfully surrounded
> With thorns, Thine only crown:
> How pale Thou art with anguish,
> With sore abuse and scorn!
> How does that visage languish,
> Which once was bright as morn!
>
> What language shall I borrow
> To thank Thee, dearest Friend,
> For this, Thy dying sorrow,
> Thy pity without end?
> O make me Thine forever,
> And should I fainting be,
> Lord, let me never, never
> Outlive my love for Thee.

*Then Jesus came out, wearing the crown of thorns and the
purple robe. And Pilate said to them, "Behold the Man!"*

—John 19:5

I Saw the Cross of Jesus

George Müller was a rascal, a prodigal, and a jailbird who eventually became a pastor, a global evangelist, and the founder of a massive complex of orphanage houses in Bristol, England. With no obvious sources of income, Müller housed and fed his orphans through prayer and on a basis of sheer faith. When he died at age ninety-two, the entire city of Bristol closed down. On **March 14, 1898,** over two thousand orphans, many of them weeping as though they had lost a father, marched in his funeral procession. A hundred carriages followed the hearse and thousands of people lined the route to Arnos Vale Cemetery. Müller's influence remains to this day, and every Christian should read his remarkable biography. There is even a hymn attributed to him. Though we can't be certain of its authorship, it certainly expresses Müller's own testimony and may well have come from his hand. It was first published in a collection of poems in 1861.

I saw the cross of Jesus,
When burdened with my sin;
I sought the cross of Jesus
To give me peace within;
I brought my sins to Jesus,
He cleansed me by His blood;
And in the cross of Jesus
I found my peace with God.

I clasp the cross of Jesus
In every trying hour,
My sure and certain refuge,
My never failing tower;
In every fear and conflict,
I more than conqu'ror am;
Living, I'm safe—or dying—
Thro' Christ the risen Lamb.

. . . by Him to reconcile all things to Himself . . .
having made peace through the blood of His cross.

—Colossians 1:20

Stand Up and Bless the Lord

James Montgomery (1771–1854) was a Moravian orphan who grew up to be a prominent British journalist. Today he is best remembered as a hymnist and the author of the Christmas carol "Angels from the Realms of Glory." His compositions are a treasure trove for modern worshipers. (I especially like his hymn based on Psalm 46, which begins: "God is our Refuge and Defense; / In trouble our unfailing Aid; / Secure in His omnipotence, / What foe can make our souls afraid?") On **March 15, 1824**, Montgomery introduced a hymn he'd written for the Red Hill Wesleyan Sunday School Anniversary in his town of Sheffield, England. It began, "Stand up and bless the Lord, / Ye children of His choice." When the hymn was published the next year, Montgomery changed the word "children" to "people," making it applicable to every Christian.

> Stand up and bless the Lord
> Ye people of His choice;
> Stand up and bless the Lord your God
> With heart and soul and voice.
>
> Though high above all praise,
> Above all blessing high,
> Who would not fear His holy Name,
> And laud and magnify?
>
> God is our Strength and Song,
> And His salvation ours;
> Then be His love in Christ proclaimed
> With all our ransomed powers.
>
> Stand up and bless the Lord;
> The Lord your God adore;
> Stand up and bless His glorious Name;
> Henceforth forevermore.

Stand up and bless the LORD your God forever and ever!
—Nehemiah 9:5

If Thou But Suffer God to Guide Thee

I can't tell you how much I love this hymn by Georg Neumark, who was born in central Germany on **March 16, 1621**. At age twenty, Neumark left home for the University of Königsberg. Along the way, he was waylaid and robbed, leaving him destitute and depressed for several weeks. Then an unexpected door opened, and Neumark was hired as a tutor in a wealthy home. That became the occasion for his writing this great hymn, *Wer Nur Den Lieben Gott Lässt Walten*. Three years later, Neumark finally made it to Königsberg, and he went on to have a successful career in the literary world. But he's best remembered for his youthful hymn about God's unfailing guidance, which, in its older English rendering, is titled "If Thou But Suffer God to Guide Thee."

If thou but suffer God to guide thee
And hope in Him through all thy ways,
He'll give thee strength, whate'er betide thee,
And bear thee through the evil days.
Who trusts in God's unchanging love
Builds on the rock that naught can move.

Be patient and await His leisure
In cheerful hope, with heart content
To take whatever thy Father's pleasure
And His discerning love hath sent,
Nor doubt our inmost wants are known
To Him who chose us for His own.

Sing, pray, and keep His ways unswerving,
Perform thy duties faithfully,
And trust His Word: though undeserving,
Thou yet shalt find it true for thee.
God never yet forsook in need
The soul that trusted Him indeed.

*The LORD will guide you continually, and
satisfy your soul in drought.*

—Isaiah 58:11

Savior, Thy Dying Love

This hymn appeared in the **March 17, 1864**, edition of the *Watchman and Reflector*, a Christian magazine published in Boston. Its author, Sylvanus Phelps, pastored the First Baptist Church of New Haven. Originally the first lines of the hymn said, "Something, my God, for Thee, / Something for Thee. . . ." Phelps later rewrote the poem, and it was set to music by gospel composer Robert Lowry. Years later, on his seventieth birthday, Phelps received a letter from Lowry, saying, "It is worth living seventy years even if nothing comes of it but one such hymn as 'Savior! Thy Dying Love Thou Gavest Me.' . . . Happy is the man who can produce one song which the world will keep on singing after its author shall have passed away."

Savior, Thy dying love Thou gavest me.
Nor should I aught withhold, dear Lord, from Thee.
In love my soul would bow, my heart fulfill its vow,
Some offering bring Thee now, something for Thee.

O'er the blest mercy seat, pleading for me,
My feeble faith looks up, Jesus, to Thee.
Help me the cross to bear, Thy wondrous love declare,
Some song to raise, or prayer, something for Thee.

Give me a faithful heart, likeness to Thee.
That each departing day henceforth may see
Some work of love begun, some deed of kindness done,
Some wanderer sought and won, something for Thee.

All that I am and have, Thy gifts so free,
In joy, in grief, through life, O Lord, for Thee!
And when Thy face I see, my ransomed soul shall be
Through all eternity, something for Thee.

He died for all, that those who live should live no longer for themselves, but for Him who died for them and rose again.

—2 Corinthians 5:15

Leaning on Thee

Charlotte Elliott, born **March 18, 1789**, became permanently disabled as a young woman. One day, while trying to cope with her illness, she wrote out a set of four life resolutions. The first was to rededicate herself "to walk very humbly, watchfully, and circumspectly before God." The second was to pray three times daily: "To devote my morning prayer chiefly to my own peculiar wants, dangers, and difficulties. My noonday prayer to the recollection of others—all who ought to be remembered by me; and my evening prayer more specially to praise than the other two, that I may lie down with more of holy love, and joy, and peace than I have ever known, and experience 'the joy of the Lord' to be indeed my strength." Her third resolution was for purity, gentleness, quietness, calmness, and other virtues; and the fourth was for a "cheerful submission to the will of God as to the measure of health and usefulness which He sees fit to grant me." It's not surprising that Miss Elliott produced a flood of poems, hymns, and books, especially for the bereaved, the ill, the dying, the deaf, the disturbed, and the distraught. Her most famous hymn is "Just As I Am." But here are three verses of another useful hymn, published under the title "Written for One Not Likely to Recover."

> Leaning on Thee, my Guide, my Friend,
> My gracious Savior, I am blest;
> Though weary, Thou dost condescend
> To be my rest.
>
> Leaning on Thee, with childlike faith,
> To Thee the future I confide;
> Each step of life's untrodden path
> Thy love will guide.
>
> Leaning on Thee, no fear alarms;
> Calmly I stand on death's dark brink.
> I feel the everlasting arms.
> I cannot sink.

Lean on the God of Israel; the LORD of hosts is His name.

—Isaiah 48:2

The Doxology

In the days before hymns were accepted in England, Thomas Ken, an Anglican priest and British educator, longed for his students to sing praises to God, even if it had to be done privately. In 1674, he wrote and published a book for his students titled *Manual of Prayers for the Use of the Scholars of Winchester College*. Included were original hymns for morning and for evening prayers. Each of these songs ended with the words, "Praise God from whom all blessings flow." Thomas Ken passed away on **March 19, 1711**, but his doxology—one of the first hymns in the English language—is still sung and loved around the world.

Awake, my soul, and with the sun
Thy daily stage of duty run;
Shake off dull sloth, and joyful rise,
To pay thy morning sacrifice.

Wake, and lift up thyself, my heart,
And with the angels bear thy part,
Who all night long unwearied sing
High praise to the eternal King.

Direct, control, suggest, this day,
All I design, or do, or say,
That all my powers, with all their might,
In Thy sole glory may unite.

Praise God, from Whom all blessings flow;
Praise Him, all creatures here below;
Praise Him above, ye heavenly host;
Praise Father, Son, and Holy Ghost.

Every day I will bless You, and I will
praise Your name forever and ever.

—Psalm 145:2

Still, Still with Thee

Harriet Beecher Stowe is best known in American history for *Uncle Tom's Cabin*, her antislavery novel that was published on **March 20, 1852**. It sold a million copies and became, with the exception of the Bible, the best-selling book of the nineteenth century. It also helped hasten the Civil War, and Abraham Lincoln reportedly said upon meeting Stowe, "So this is the little lady who made this big war." But Harriet's hatred of slavery was the result of her love for Jesus Christ, and she often expressed her love for the Lord through song. Her best-known hymn speaks of the pleasures of starting the day with the Lord—"when the bird waketh and the shadows flee"—and Harriet lived what she wrote. She habitually rose at 4:30 in the morning, and there in her quiet hour as purple morning broke, she enjoyed the "sweet consciousness" of His presence.

Still, still with Thee, when purple morning breaketh,
When the bird waketh, and the shadows flee;
Fairer than morning, lovelier than daylight,
Dawns the sweet consciousness, I am with Thee.

Alone with Thee, amid the mystic shadows,
The solemn hush of nature newly born;
Alone with Thee in breathless adoration,
In the calm dew and freshness of the morn.

Still, still with Thee, as to each newborn morning,
A fresh and solemn splendor still is given,
So does this blessèd consciousness, awaking,
Breathe each day nearness unto Thee and Heaven.

*Now in the morning, having risen a long while
before daylight, He went out and departed to
a solitary place; and there He prayed.*

—Mark 1:35

How Tedious and Tasteless

This unusual hymn was written by John Newton, the old slave trader who was converted on **March 21, 1747**, after surviving a deadly storm at sea. "I began to pray," he later wrote, "to think of that Jesus that I had so often derided; I recollected His death; a death for sins not His own, but, as I remembered, for the sake of those who put their trust in Him." For the rest of his life, Newton (author of "Amazing Grace") observed March 21 as his own special holiday.

Newton's hymn "How Tedious and Tasteless" is sung to the tune "Green Fields," adapted from a composition by Johann Sebastian Bach, who was born on **March 21, 1685**, in the small town of Eisenach in central Germany. J. S. Bach was a musical prodigy who became one of the greatest composers in the history of Western music. Fueled by his Lutheran faith, he signed his compositions with the initials SDG—*Soli Deo Gloria* ("To God alone be the glory").

How tedious and tasteless the hours
When Jesus I no longer see;
Sweet prospects, sweet birds and sweet flowers,
Have all lost their sweetness to me;
The midsummer sun shines but dim,
The fields strive in vain to look gay.
But when I am happy in Him,
December's as pleasant as May.

His Name yields the richest perfume,
And sweeter than music His voice;
His presence disperses my gloom,
And makes all within me rejoice.
I should, were He always thus nigh,
Have nothing to wish or to fear;
No mortal as happy as I,
My summer would last all the year.

Let me hear your voice; for your voice is
sweet, and your face is lovely.

—Song of Solomon 2:14

Up from the Grave He Arose!

In early church history, Christians longed to celebrate Easter each year, but when? On what day? Most churches celebrated the Sunday closest to the Jewish Passover, but sometimes they didn't know whether to choose the Sunday before or after. This was debated at the famous Council of Nicaea, held in AD 325. There it was decided Easter would fall on the Sunday after the first full moon following the Spring equinox. Easter, then, would occur between March 22 and April 25, which means **March 22** is the earliest possible date on the church calendar for celebrating Resurrection Sunday. In honor of the upcoming season, here is Robert Lowry's classic Easter hymn "Up from the Grave He Arose," published in 1874.

Low in the grave He lay, Jesus my Savior,
Waiting the coming day, Jesus my Lord!
Up from the grave He arose,
With a mighty triumph o'er His foes,
He arose a Victor from the dark domain,
And He lives forever, with His saints to reign.
He arose! He arose!
Hallelujah! Christ arose!

Death cannot keep its Prey, Jesus my Savior;
He tore the bars away, Jesus my Lord!
Up from the grave He arose,
With a mighty triumph o'er His foes,
He arose a Victor from the dark domain,
And He lives forever, with His saints to reign.
He arose! He arose!
Hallelujah! Christ arose!

"Don't be alarmed," he said. "You are looking for Jesus the Nazarene, who was crucified. He has risen! He is not here. See the place where they laid him. But go, tell his disciples and Peter, 'He is going ahead of you into Galilee. There you will see him, just as he told you.'"

—Mark 16:6–7 NIV

The Hallelujah Chorus

When his friends saw him on the streets, they shook their heads. It appeared George Frederick Handel had passed his prime, that his musical genius had worn itself out. But then he received a package of compiled Scriptures from Charles Jennens, and his passion was reborn. Shutting himself in his house on August 22, 1741, Handel began putting Scripture to music. By September 14, he had written the great oratorio known as *Messiah*. It was first performed in Dublin on April 13, 1742, during Handel's tour of Ireland. Its London debut was **March 23, 1743**, at Covent Garden, and when the majestic "Hallelujah Chorus" burst forth, the audience was stunned to see King George II stand to his feet. Following the king's lead, they also stood, starting a tradition that lasts to this day.

Hallelujah! Hallelujah!
Hallelujah! Hallelujah! Hallelujah!
Hallelujah! Hallelujah!
Hallelujah! Hallelujah! Hallelujah!
For the Lord God Omnipotent reigneth.
Hallelujah! Hallelujah!
Hallelujah! Hallelujah!
For the Lord God Omnipotent reigneth.
Hallelujah! Hallelujah!
Hallelujah! Hallelujah!
The kingdom of this world is become
The kingdom of our Lord,
And of His Christ, and of His Christ;
And He shall reign for ever and ever,
And He shall reign for ever and ever,
And He shall reign for ever and ever,
And He shall reign for ever and ever!
King of kings! And Lord of lords!
Hallelujah! Hallelujah! Hallelujah! Hallelujah! Hallelujah!

Then I heard what sounded like a great multitude, like the roar of rushing waters and like loud peals of thunder, shouting: "Hallelujah! For our Lord God Almighty reigns!"

—Revelation 19:6 NIV

Redeemed, How I Love to Proclaim It!

Happy birthday, Aunt Fanny! America's most prolific hymnist was born in the little community of Southeast, in Putnam County, New York, on **March 24, 1820**. Christened Frances Jane Crosby, her earliest days were tragic. Her father, John, died when she was only an infant. When she was six weeks old, she was blinded for life through the malpractice of a quack doctor. Her distraught mother, Mercy, had to go to work to provide for the family, and Fanny's grandmother became her primary caregiver. No one would have dreamed that the little blind girl would become one of the most beloved personalities of nineteenth-century Christianity. During the course of her feisty ninety-four years, she wrote over eight thousand hymns, including this great song of testimony, "Redeemed, How I Love to Proclaim It!"

Redeemed, how I love to proclaim it!
Redeemed by the blood of the Lamb;
Redeemed through His infinite mercy,
His child and forever I am.

Redeemed, and so happy in Jesus,
No language my rapture can tell;
I know that the light of His presence
With me doth continually dwell.

I think of my blessèd Redeemer,
I think of Him all the day long:
I sing, for I cannot be silent;
His love is the theme of my song.

Redeemed, redeemed,
Redeemed by the blood of the Lamb;
Redeemed, redeemed,
His child, and forever, I am.

Christ has redeemed us from the curse of the law, having become a curse for us.

—Galatians 3:13

Crown Him with Many Crowns

One of our most rousing and majestic hymns, "Crown Him with Many Crowns," has a fascinating history that demonstrates the power of hymnody to unite us. The original stanzas were written by Matthew Bridges, who embraced Roman Catholic doctrine. In response, Godfrey Thring, a staunch Anglican, wrote additional verses from a Protestant perspective. In the beginning, then, we had dueling versions of this hymn. As time went by, churches began singing the best verses from both hymns, and the hymn as we know and love it today includes stanzas from both authors! Today is Thring's birthday—**March 25, 1823**.

Crown Him with many crowns, the Lamb upon His throne.
Hark! How the heavenly anthem drowns all music but its own.
Awake, my soul, and sing of Him who died for thee,
And hail Him as thy matchless King through all eternity.

Crown Him the Lord of life, who triumphed o'er the grave,
And rose victorious in the strife for those He came to save.
His glories now we sing, who died and rose on high,
Who died eternal life to bring and lives that death may die.

Crown Him the Lord of love, behold His hands and side,
Those wounds, yet visible above, in beauty glorified.
No angel in the sky can fully bear that sight,
But downward bends his wondering eye at mysteries so bright.

Crown Him the Lord of Heaven, enthroned in worlds above,
Crown Him the King to whom is given the wondrous name of
    Love.
Crown Him with many crowns, as thrones before Him fall;
Crown Him, ye kings, with many crowns, for He is King of all.

His eyes were like a flame of fire, and on
His head were many crowns.

—Revelation 19:12

He Leadeth Me

Today is the anniversary of "He Leadeth Me," which was penned on **March 26, 1862**, by a newly graduated seminary student named Joseph Gilmore. Gilmore was bringing the midweek sermon at the First Baptist Church of Philadelphia that evening. His text was Psalm 23, but he didn't get past the phrase "He leadeth me." Gilmore later wrote, "Those words took hold of me as they had never done before. . . . It was the darkest hour of the Civil War. I did not refer to that fact . . . but it may subconsciously have led me to realize that God's leadership is the one significant fact in human experience." After the service, he gathered with friends in a nearby home, and there he scribbled down the words to this great hymn of guidance.

He leadeth me, O blessèd thought!
O words with heav'nly comfort fraught!
Whate'er I do, where'er I be
Still 'tis God's hand that leadeth me.

Lord, I would place my hand in Thine,
Nor ever murmur nor repine;
Content, whatever lot I see,
Since 'tis my God that leadeth me.

And when my task on earth is done,
When by Thy grace the vict'ry's won,
E'en death's cold wave I will not flee,
Since God through Jordan leadeth me.

He leadeth me, He leadeth me,
By His own hand He leadeth me;
His faithful follower I would be,
For by His hand He leadeth me.

He leads me beside the still waters.

—Psalm 23:2

Come, Ye Thankful People, Come

After the publication of *Then Sings My Soul*, my book of hymn stories, someone asked why I didn't focus on the composers of the music. "Those hymns wouldn't have been great without the powerful music that accompanies them," said my reader. Well, today is the birthday of three composers. Peter Lutkin, who wrote the thrilling music to "The Lord Bless You and Keep You," was born **March 27, 1858**. Emma Ashford, composer of the music to "They Who Seek the Throne of Grace," was born on **March 27, 1850**. And George Elvey was born **March 27, 1816**, in Canterbury, England. He was a boy singer at Canterbury Cathedral, and later he became choir director there as well as organist at St. George's Chapel in Windsor. He composed the tunes to "Crown Him with Many Crowns" and "Come, Ye Thankful People, Come."

Come, ye thankful people, come, raise the song of harvest home;
All is safely gathered in, ere the winter storms begin.
God our Maker doth provide for our wants to be supplied;
Come to God's own temple, come, raise the song of harvest home.

All the world is God's own field, fruit unto His praise to yield;
Wheat and tares together sown unto joy or sorrow grown.
First the blade and then the ear, then the full corn shall appear;
Lord of harvest, grant that we wholesome grain and pure may be.

For the Lord our God shall come, and shall take His harvest home;
From His field shall in that day all offenses purge away,
Giving angels charge at last in the fire the tares to cast;
But the fruitful ears to store in His garner evermore.

Even so, Lord, quickly come, bring Thy final harvest home;
Gather Thou Thy people in, free from sorrow, free from sin,
There, forever purified, in Thy garner to abide;
Come, with all Thine angels come, raise the glorious harvest home.

O LORD my God, I will give thanks to You forever.

—Psalm 30:12

The Longer I Serve Him

According to Deuteronomy 28:47, our life's purpose is to serve the Lord with joy and gladness of heart. America's gospel music man, Bill Gaither, has been doing that for years. Born **March 28, 1936**, in Alexandria, Indiana, Bill formed his first singing group in 1956, while a student at Anderson College. It was called the Bill Gaither Trio, being made up of his sister, his brother, and himself. In 1962, Bill married Gloria Sickal, and for several years Bill and Gloria juggled musical pursuits with busy teaching jobs. Then in 1967, they plunged full-time into gospel music and went on to enrich the world with some of today's best-loved Christian songs, including "The King Is Coming," "Because He Lives," "Something Beautiful," "He Touched Me," "There's Something About That Name," "Let's Just Praise the Lord," and this one, "The Longer I Serve Him."

Since I started for the Kingdom,
Since my life He controls,
Since I gave my heart to Jesus,
The longer I serve Him,
The sweeter He grows.

Ev'ry need He is supplying,
Plenteous grace He bestows;
Ev'ry day my way gets brighter,
The longer I serve Him,
The sweeter He grows.

The longer I serve Him, the sweeter He grows,
The more that I love Him, more love He bestows;
Each day is like heaven, my heart overflows,
The longer I serve Him, the sweeter He grows.

Not lagging in diligence, fervent in spirit, serving the Lord.

—Romans 12:11

In Age and Feebleness Extreme

Charles Wesley, the Sweet Singer of Methodism, started writing verses immediately upon his conversion and during his lifetime composed over six thousand hymns—probably more than anyone else in history. His associate, Henry Moore, described him this way: "When he was nearly eighty he rode a little horse, grey with age. . . . As he jogged leisurely along, he jotted down any thoughts that struck him. He kept a card in his pocket for this purpose, on which he wrote his hymn in shorthand. Not infrequently he has come to our house in City Road, and, having left the pony in the garden in front, he would enter, crying out, 'Pen and ink! Pen and ink!' These being supplied, he wrote the hymn he had been composing." Despite the incredible quantity of his hymns, there remained a depth of quality that astounds us today in hymns such as "And Can It Be," "O for a Thousand Tongues," "Rejoice, the Lord Is King," the Easter anthem "Christ the Lord Is Risen Today," and the Christmas carol "Hark! The Herald Angels Sing." In addition, Charles joined his brother John in traveling from one end of Britain to the other as open-air evangelists and founders of the Methodist movement.

Charles composed his last hymn on Saturday, **March 29, 1788**, the day he died. In January of that year, he'd found himself too weak for even short rides. In February, he'd been confined to bed. He was in no pain and showed no signs of specific illness; he was just worn out physically. On March 29, he composed this one-verse hymn, "In Age and Feebleness Extreme," and, too weak to write it down, dictated it to his wife, Sally. He slipped into unconsciousness. As his daughter Sarah held his hand, the great Charles Wesley caught a smile from God and dropped into eternity.

In age and feebleness extreme,
Who shall a helpless worm redeem?
Jesus, my only hope Thou art,
Strength of my failing flesh and heart:
O could I catch one smile from Thee,
And drop into eternity!

Now also when I am old and grayheaded, O God, do not forsake me, until I declare Your strength to this generation, Your power to everyone who is to come.

—Psalm 71:18

Stand Up, Stand Up for Jesus

On Tuesday, **March 30, 1858**, Rev. Dudley Tyng, age twenty-nine, addressed a mass gathering of men in Philadelphia, exhorting them to serve the Lord with all their hearts. "I would rather that this right arm were amputated at the trunk," he said, "than that I should come short of my duty to you in delivering God's message." A week later in a freak accident, Tyng's arm was caught in the cogs of a corn thresher and he was fatally injured. His dying words were, "Let us all stand up for Jesus." The following Sunday, Tyng's friend and fellow clergyman, George Duffield, preached from Ephesians 6:14, ending his sermon by reciting this poem he'd written for the occasion:

> Stand up, stand up for Jesus, ye soldiers of the cross;
> Lift high His royal banner, it must not suffer loss.
> From victory unto victory His army shall He lead,
> Till every foe is vanquished, and Christ is Lord indeed.
>
> Stand up, stand up for Jesus, the trumpet call obey;
> Forth to the mighty conflict, in this His glorious day.
> Ye that are brave now serve Him against unnumbered foes;
> Let courage rise with danger, and strength to strength oppose.
>
> Stand up, stand up for Jesus, stand in His strength alone;
> The arm of flesh will fail you, ye dare not trust your own.
> Put on the Gospel armor, each piece put on with prayer;
> Where duty calls or danger, be never wanting there.
>
> Stand up, stand up for Jesus, the strife will not be long;
> This day the noise of battle, the next the victor's song.
> To him who overcometh a crown of life shall be;
> They with the King of Glory shall reign eternally.

Stand therefore, having girded your waist with truth, having put on the breastplate of righteousness.

—Ephesians 6:14

Glorious Things of Thee Are Spoken

When Franz Joseph Haydn was born on **March 31, 1732**, no one imagined he would become one of history's great composers. He grew up in a small village in lower Austria, and his parents were quite poor. But as a six-year-old, Franz showed such musical promise that he was sent to a nearby town for training. Two years later he became a choirboy in Vienna. When his voice changed, he found himself out of work and penniless, a seventeen-year-old street musician who lived hand-to-mouth. But he felt God had called him to a ministry of music, writing, "I know that God has favored me, and recognize it thankfully." Each morning, he awakened and prayed on his knees before beginning the day's composing. He began most of his scores with the words *In Nomini Jesu* ("In the name of Jesus") and ended them with *Laus Deo* ("Praise God") or *Soli Deo Gloria* ("To God alone be glory"). Many of his compositions are now used as hymn tunes, including the German national anthem, which doubles as the melody of this well-known John Newton hymn.

Glorious things of thee are spoken,
Zion, city of our God!
He, whose Word cannot be broken,
Formed thee for His own abode.
On the Rock of Ages founded,
What can shake thy sure repose?
With salvation's walls surrounded,
Thou may'st smile at all thy foes.

Round each habitation hovering,
See the cloud and fire appear!
For a glory and a cov'ring
Showing that the Lord is near.
Thus deriving from our banner
Light by night and shade by day;
Safe they feed upon the manna
Which He gives them when they pray.

Glorious things are spoken of you, O city of God!
—Psalm 87:3

At Calvary

Keep praying for prodigals! William Newell was a prodigal who caused spasms of anxiety for his dad. But the Lord answered prayer, and young William eventually became a beloved professor at Moody Bible Institute. With this hymn, William Newell put his testimony in writing, saying, "Years I spent in vanity and pride. . . ." He went on to become a popular conference speaker, author, and Bible commentator, but he never lost the wonder of what God can do with a prodigal. Today you can find his simple gravestone in the cemetery of Holy Trinity Episcopal Church in Fruitland, Florida:

Newell
William Reed
Born: May 22, 1868
Died: **April 1, 1956**
His Message: Romans 8:1
THERE IS THEREFORE NOW NO CONDEMNATION
TO THOSE WHO ARE IN CHRIST JESUS

Years I spent in vanity and pride,
Caring not my Lord was crucified,
Knowing not it was for me He died on Calvary.

Now I've given to Jesus everything,
Now I gladly own Him as my King,
Now my raptured soul can only sing of Calvary!

Oh, the love that drew salvation's plan!
Oh, the grace that brought it down to man!
Oh, the mighty gulf that God did span at Calvary!

Mercy there was great, and grace was free;
Pardon there was multiplied to me;
There my burdened soul found liberty at Calvary.

There is therefore now no condemnation
to those who are in Christ Jesus.

—Romans 8:1

Brethren, We Have Met to Worship

I often think of the third line in this hymn as I go about the Lord's work, especially in my preaching: "All is vain unless the Spirit of the Holy One comes down." Thankfully, the Holy Spirit *does* come down and our work is "not in vain in the Lord" (1 Cor. 15:58). The words of this old hymn are usually attributed to George Atkins, of whom little is known. The hymn's tune, "Holy Manna," was composed by William Moore and registered in the district of West Tennessee on **April 2, 1825**. It's one of eighteen tunes known to be written by Moore, but little else is known about him. "Holy Manna," however, is enough to ensure him a place in the history of American gospel music.

> Brethren, we have met to worship and adore the Lord our God;
> Will you pray with all your power, while we try to preach the Word?
> All is vain unless the Spirit of the Holy One comes down;
> Brethren, pray, and holy manna will be showered all around.
>
> Brethren, see poor sinners round you slumbering on the brink of woe;
> Death is coming, hell is moving, can you bear to let them go?
> See our fathers and our mothers, and our children sinking down;
> Brethren, pray, and holy manna will be showered all around.
>
> Sisters, will you join and help us? Moses' sister aided him;
> Will you help the trembling mourners who are struggling hard with sin?
> Tell them all about the Savior, tell them that He will be found;
> Sisters, pray, and holy manna will be showered all around.
>
> Let us love our God supremely, let us love each other, too;
> Let us love and pray for sinners, till our God makes all things new.
> Then He'll call us home to Heaven, at His table we'll sit down;
> Christ will gird Himself and serve us with sweet manna all around.

Therefore, my beloved brethren, be steadfast, immovable, always abounding in the work of the Lord, knowing that your labor is not in vain in the Lord.

—1 Corinthians 15:58

O Happy Band of Pilgrims

Joseph the Hymnographer was born into a Christian home in Sicily about the year AD 810. When he was fifteen, he traveled to Thessalonica and entered a monastery where his keen spirit and humble piety impressed his superiors. He was transferred to Constantinople, and there he preached in the public squares and engaged in iconoclastic disputes. Space doesn't permit a full summary of his life, which included a six-year period of slavery in Crete following his capture by Arab bandits, but it's enough to say that Joseph the Hymnographer, as his name suggests, is chiefly remembered for his hymns. He died peacefully in the 880s, and his commemoration day in the Greek Church is **April 3**.

> O happy band of pilgrims,
> If onward you will tread,
> With Jesus as your Fellow,
> To Jesus as your Head.
>
> O happy if you labor,
> As Jesus did for men;
> O happy if you hunger
> As Jesus hungered then.
>
> The faith by which you see Him,
> The hope in which you yearn,
> The love that through all troubles
> To Him alone will turn.
>
> O happy band of pilgrims,
> Look upward to the skies,
> Where such a light affliction
> Shall win you such a prize.

Beloved, I beg you as sojourners and pilgrims, abstain from fleshly lusts which war against the soul.

—1 Peter 2:11

'Tis So Sweet to Trust in Jesus

Whatever problem you're facing today, the Lord can bear it for you. You simply have to "take Him at His Word" and "rest upon His promises." That's what sustained Louisa Stead through years of missionary service and personal tragedy, including the accidental drowning of her husband (which reportedly led to her writing this hymn). Later, while working in South Africa, she met and married Robert Wodehouse. The two returned to America in 1895 for health reasons, but after attending a large conference in New York, they felt compelled to offer themselves as missionaries once again. On **April 4, 1901**, they arrived in Rhodesia (Zimbabwe), ready to invest their remaining days in overseas missions, borne along by the truth of Louisa's song.

'Tis so sweet to trust in Jesus,
Just to take Him at His word;
Just to rest upon His promise,
Just to know "Thus saith the Lord!"

O how sweet to trust in Jesus,
Just to trust His cleansing blood;
Just in simple faith to plunge me
'Neath the healing, cleansing flood!

I'm so glad I learned to trust Thee,
Precious Jesus, Savior, Friend;
And I know that Thou art with me,
Wilt be with me to the end.

Jesus, Jesus, how I trust Him!
How I've proved Him o'er and o'er!
Jesus, Jesus, precious Jesus!
O for grace to trust Him more!

As for God, His way is perfect; the word of the Lord
is proven; He is a shield to all who trust in Him.

—2 Samuel 22:31

All Things Bright and Beautiful

Today is the birthday of Ludwig (Louis) Spohr, the German musician and violin virtuoso, who was born on **April 5, 1784**. Spohr composed several popular hymn tunes. His best-known melody is titled "Gerald," which is most often associated with Charles Wesley's song of aspiration, "I Want a Principle Within." But many people also use "Gerald" as the tune for this Irish children's hymn, written by Cecil F. Alexander and published in 1848 in her book *Hymns for Little Children*.

All things bright and beautiful,
All creatures great and small,
All things wise and wonderful:
The Lord God made them all.

Each little flower that opens,
Each little bird that sings,
He made their glowing colors,
He made their tiny wings.

The purple-headed mountains,
The river running by,
The sunset and the morning
That brightens up the sky.

The cold wind in the winter,
The pleasant summer sun,
The ripe fruits in the garden,
He made them every one.

He gave us eyes to see them,
And lips that we might tell
How great is God Almighty,
Who has made all things well.

Our help is in the name of the Lord,
who made heaven and earth.

—Psalm 124:8

All My Heart with Joy Is Springing

Here's a humbling thought: sometimes we do more good by advancing the work of others than by pushing our own efforts. Today marks the death of Benjamin Hall Kennedy, who passed away on **April 6, 1889**. Kennedy authored a number of hymns that are nearly forgotten. His translations of the hymns of others, however, have stood the test of time. He discovered a number of great German hymns and rendered them into English where they became classics, including the powerful faith hymn of Joachim Magdeburg, "Who Trusts in God, a Strong Abode"; Johann Schwedler's hymn "Ask Ye What Great Thing I Know"; and this Paul Gerhardt Christmas carol, "All My Heart with Joy Is Springing."

> All my heart with joy is springing,
> While in air everywhere
> Angel choirs are singing.
> Hear them to the shepherds telling:
> "Christ is born! On this morn
> God with man is dwelling."
>
> Come ye now, and kneel before Him;
> Mortals all, great and small,
> Worship and adore Him:
> Love your King, whose love invites you:
> Lo, His star from afar
> To His dwelling lights you.
>
> Ye who strive with fierce temptation,
> Sorrow-stung, conscience-wrung,
> Here is consolation:
> For the woes which men inherit
> Christ can feel, Christ will heal
> Every wounded spirit.

Ask, and you will receive, that your joy may be full.

—John 16:24

At the Cross

From historical references in Luke's Gospel, we can date the Lord's death to a Passover between the years of AD 27 and 34. Scripture also indicates Jesus was slain on a Friday. Passover Friday occurred in the years 30 and 33, with the most likely date being **April 7, 30**. Thousands of songs have commemorated this event. One of the greatest is an Isaac Watts hymn known by two titles. When sung to the more traditional tune of "Martyrdom," it's listed as "Alas! And Did My Savior Bleed?" In 1885, Ralph E. Hudson wrote a livelier tune ("Hudson") and added a refrain. This version is known as "At the Cross."

Alas! and did my Savior bleed
And did my Sovereign die?
Would He devote that sacred head
For such a worm as I?

Was it for crimes that I had done
He groaned upon the tree?
Amazing pity! grace unknown!
And love beyond degree!

But drops of grief can ne'er repay
The debt of love I owe:
Here, Lord, I give myself away
'Tis all that I can do.

At the cross, at the cross where I first saw the light,
And the burden of my heart rolled away,
It was there by faith I received my sight,
And now I am happy all the day!

When they had come to the place called
Calvary, there they crucified Him.

—Luke 23:33

Softly and Tenderly

When the body of slain civil rights leader Martin Luther King Jr. was returned to Atlanta for burial, his friends at the Southern Christian Leadership Conference wanted his body taken from the church in a wagon pulled by two Georgia mules, signifying King's concern for the "least of these." They found a suitable wagon in an antique store in West End, but it was closed. Unable to find the owner, they simply "borrowed" it. On **April 8, 1968**, mourners at Ebenezer Baptist Church sang "Softly and Tenderly," then King's body was borne away on the wagon. Watching on television, the owner of the antique store didn't recognize his wagon, but when he stopped by his shop and found it missing, he put two and two together. He didn't mind, and today the wagon stands in the visitor center of the Martin Luther King Jr. National Historic Site in Atlanta.

Softly and tenderly Jesus is calling,
Calling for you and for me;
See, on the portals He's waiting and watching,
Watching for you and for me.

Why should we tarry when Jesus is pleading,
Pleading for you and for me?
Why should we linger and heed not His mercies,
Mercies for you and for me?

Time is now fleeting, the moments are passing,
Passing from you and from me;
Shadows are gathering, deathbeds are coming,
Coming for you and for me.

Come home, come home,
Ye who are weary, come home;
Earnestly, tenderly, Jesus is calling,
Calling, O sinner, come home!

Inasmuch as you did it to one of the least of these My brethren, you did it to Me.

—Matthew 25:40

When the Roll Is Called Up Yonder

The week of Sunday, **April 9, 1922**, a small item appeared in the *New York Times*: "Mrs. Gertrude Merritt, who until her conversion eleven years ago was known as 'Chinatown Gertie,' died on Sunday in her home in Cherry Street." Gertie had been one of the most notorious characters in New York. From age fourteen, she was a drug addict, prostitute, and underground figure who eluded police in the heart of Chinatown's underworld. After accepting Christ as Savior, she became a passionate worker for Him in the Bowery. During her funeral at the Midnight Mission, Superintendent Tom Noonan said, "This is going to be a different funeral. We have come here to rejoice." The mourners spontaneously decided to sing one of Gertie's favorite hymns, and the whole crowd burst out in a joyful rendition of "When the Roll Is Called Up Yonder."

When the trumpet of the Lord shall sound, and time shall be no
  more,
And the morning breaks, eternal, bright and fair;
When the saved of earth shall gather over on the other shore,
And the roll is called up yonder, I'll be there.

On that bright and cloudless morning when the dead in Christ
  shall rise,
And the glory of His resurrection share;
When His chosen ones shall gather to their home beyond the
  skies,
And the roll is called up yonder, I'll be there.

Let us labor for the Master from the dawn till setting sun,
Let us talk of all His wondrous love and care;
Then when all of life is over, and our work on earth is done,
And the roll is called up yonder, I'll be there.

When the roll is called up yonder,
When the roll is called up yonder,
When the roll is called up yonder,
When the roll is called up yonder I'll be there.

We . . . would prefer to be away from the
body and at home with the Lord.

—2 Corinthians 5:8 NIV

Tell Me the Story of Jesus

As a boy, John R. Sweney was so gifted musically that he began giving lessons. As a young man he became a popular composer. For a quarter century, he served as professor of music at the Philadelphia Military Academy, writing classical compositions still heard today. But he's best remembered for the great hymn tunes that he began writing after turning his life over to the Lord Jesus in 1871. He wrote the music to many of Fanny Crosby's hymns, such as "Tell Me the Story of Jesus," and is remembered as one of the great composers of the gospel song era. He died on **April 10, 1899**, in Chester, Pennsylvania.

Tell me the story of Jesus,
Write on my heart every word.
Tell me the story most precious,
Sweetest that ever was heard.

Tell how the angels in chorus,
Sang as they welcomed His birth.
"Glory to God in the highest!
Peace and good tidings to earth."

Tell of the cross where they nailed Him,
Writhing in anguish and pain.
Tell of the grave where they laid Him,
Tell how He liveth again.

Tell me the story of Jesus,
Write on my heart every word.
Tell me the story most precious,
Sweetest that ever was heard.

God anointed Jesus of Nazareth with the Holy Spirit and with power, who went about doing good and healing all who were oppressed by the devil, for God was with Him. And we are witnesses.

—Acts 10:38–39

O God, Our Help in Ages Past

In the years prior to 1719, London pastor Isaac Watts decided to undertake the formidable task of converting the Psalms of David into Christian hymns. The resulting volume was titled *The Psalms of David Imitated in the Language of the New Testament*. In a letter on **April 11, 1728**, Watts explained, "In my opinion, the Psalms ought to be translated in such a manner for Christian worship, in order to show the hidden glories of that divine posey [verse or poem]." As a result, we have some of our greatest hymns couched in the language of the Psalms but full of references to Jesus and fit for Christian worship. "Jesus Shall Reign" was based on Psalm 72. Watts paraphrased Psalm 98 in "Joy to the World." And his rendition of Psalm 90 goes like this:

> O God, our help in ages past,
> Our hope for years to come,
> Our shelter from the stormy blast,
> And our eternal home.
>
> Under the shadow of Thy throne
> Thy saints have dwelt secure;
> Sufficient is Thine arm alone,
> And our defense is sure.
>
> Before the hills in order stood,
> Or earth received her frame,
> From everlasting Thou art God,
> To endless years the same.

LORD, You have been our dwelling place in all generations. Before the mountains were brought forth, or ever You had formed the earth and the world, even from everlasting to everlasting, You are God.

—Psalm 90:1–2

Come, Thou Almighty King

Today is the birthday of two great hymn composers. Arthur Henry Messiter, born **April 12, 1834**, spent much of his life as the organist of Trinity Church in New York City. He's the composer of the tune "Marion" ("Rejoice, Ye Pure in Heart").

Felice de Giardini was born in Italy on **April 12, 1716**. Much of his life was spent in Milan and Turin, where he was renowned as a violinist and composer; but he died virtually penniless in Moscow in 1796. He gave us the majestic "Italian Hymn," which is the setting for "Come, Thou Almighty King."

Come, Thou almighty King,
Help us Thy name to sing, help us to praise!
Father all glorious, o'er all victorious,
Come and reign over us, Ancient of Days!

Come, Thou Incarnate Word,
Gird on Thy mighty sword, our prayer attend!
Come, and Thy people bless, and give Thy Word success,
Spirit of holiness, on us descend!

Come, Holy Comforter,
Thy sacred witness bear in this glad hour!
Thou, who almighty art, now rule in every heart,
And ne'er from us depart, Spirit of power!

To Thee, great One in Three,
Eternal praises be, hence evermore;
Thy sovereign majesty may we in glory see,
And to eternity love and adore!

Blessing and honor and glory and power be to Him who sits on the throne, and to the Lamb, forever and ever!

—Revelation 5:13

God of Wonders

Oh, to experience the revivals we read about in stirring accounts of yesteryear! The revivals of the past ignited the church with fresh fire, transformed societies from the inside out, and propelled new generations into lifelong ministry. For Swedish Pastor Nils Frykman, revival was testimony to our mighty God working mighty wonders. This old hymn, published on **April 13, 1877**, was written on an evening the previous year when a revival swept over a group meeting in a Swedish farmhouse. Watching people weep and rejoice at the same time, Frykman took out his pen and composed this hymn on the spot.

> Our mighty God works mighty wonders—
> What joy, to see them all around!
> Men's idols fall before His thunders,
> Their altars crumbling to the ground.
> He breaks the fetters, frees the slaves,
> His fallen children still He saves.
>
> His mighty Word goes forth to conquer,
> Its power destroys the forts of doubt.
> The warriors bold yield up their armor
> To Him who will not cast them out.
> They cleansing find in Jesus' blood
> And laud and magnify our God.
>
> O God, be praised! The day is nearing,
> When to our ears a voice shall come,
> "Look up, the Lord is now appearing,
> To gather all His loved ones home!"
> O blessèd day of jubilee!
> For thee I wait! I wait for thee!

Revive me, O LORD, for Your name's sake!

—Psalm 143:11

The Regions Beyond

Today is the anniversary of the baptisms of two very different hymn composers. John Wainwright, a church organist in Manchester, England, was baptized on **April 14, 1723**. He penned the music to the Christmas carol "Christians, Awake, Salute the Happy Morn." Over 150 years later, Margaret Simpson was born in Louisville, Kentucky. Her father, Albert B. Simpson, was a prominent Presbyterian pastor who went on to establish the Christian and Missionary Alliance. Because Margaret was a frail baby, she was baptized privately in the church's manse on **April 14, 1878**. But she lived and prospered and later composed the music to many of her father's hymns, including this great missionary song, "The Regions Beyond."

To the regions beyond I must go, I must go
Where the story has never been told;
To the millions that never have heard of His love,
I must tell the sweet story of old.

To the hardest of places He calls me to go,
Never thinking of comfort or ease;
The world may pronounce me a dreamer, a fool,
Enough if the Master I please.

Oh, you that are spending your leisure and powers
In those pleasures so foolish and fond;
Awake from your selfishness, folly and sin,
And go to the regions beyond.

To the regions beyond I must go, I must go,
Till the world, all the world,
His salvation shall know.

---

*We shall be greatly enlarged by you in our sphere,
to preach the gospel in the regions beyond.*

—2 Corinthians 10:15–16

What If It Were Today?

Lelia Naylor was born **April 15, 1862**, in the mountains on the Ohio and West Virginia border, just as her father was leaving to fight in the Civil War. She married Charles Morris when she was nineteen, and the two joined the Methodist Episcopal Church, where Lelia sang in the choir. One day at her sewing machine, Lelia began composing a song, and it became the first of over one thousand gospel hymns that flowed from her pen. She typically wrote her hymns while doing housework or chores, diverting to the piano as needed. Her hymns include "Can the World See Jesus in You?" "I've Anchored My Soul in the Haven of Rest," "Let Jesus Come into Your Heart," "Nearer, Still Nearer," "Sweeter As the Years Go By," and this rousing hymn about the second coming.

Jesus is coming to earth again; what if it were today?
Coming in power and love to reign; what if it were today?
Coming to claim His chosen Bride, all the redeemed and
  purified,
Over this whole earth scattered wide; what if it were today?

Satan's dominion will then be o'er, O that it were today!
Sorrow and sighing shall be no more, O that it were today!
Then shall the dead in Christ arise, caught up to meet Him in
  the skies,
When shall these glories meet our eyes? What if it were today?

Faithful and true would He find us here if He should come
  today?
Watching in gladness and not in fear, if He should come today?
Signs of His coming multiply; morning light breaks in eastern
  sky.
Watch, for the time is drawing nigh; what if it were today?

Glory, glory! Joy to my heart 'twill bring.
Glory, glory! When we shall crown Him King.
Glory, glory! Haste to prepare the way;
Glory, glory! Jesus will come some day.

"Surely I am coming quickly." Amen. Even so, come, Lord Jesus!
—Revelation 22:20

How Great Thou Art

As missionaries laboring in Poland in the 1920s, Stuart K. Hine and his wife came across a Russian version of a Swedish poem by Carl Boberg. Set to a Swedish folk tune, it extolled God's greatness and glorified Him for the wonders of His creation. Later, inspired by his travels and experiences in the Carpathian Mountains, Stuart composed his own original verses, and he also developed his own arrangement of the melody. The result is our beloved hymn "How Great Thou Art." While the composer of the original folk tune that inspired Hine's arrangement is unknown to us, the tune itself first appeared in the Swedish publication *Sanningsvittnet* on this day, **April 16, 1891**. The words and music of "How Great Thou Art" are a perfect match, especially as they swell to the worshipful crescendo, "Then sings my soul, my Savior God to Thee. . . ."

O Lord my God, when I in awesome wonder,
Consider all the worlds Thy hands have made;
I see the stars, I hear the rolling thunder,
Thy power throughout the universe displayed.

And when I think that God, His Son not sparing,
Sent Him to die, I scarce can take it in;
That on the cross, my burden gladly bearing,
He bled and died to take away my sin.

When Christ shall come, with shout of acclamation,
And take me home, what joy shall fill my heart.
Then I shall bow, in humble adoration,
And there proclaim, my God, how great Thou art.

Then sings my soul, My Savior God, to Thee;
How great Thou art, how great Thou art!
Then sings my soul, My Savior God, to Thee:
How great Thou art, how great Thou art!

Great is the LORD, and greatly to be praised;
and His greatness is unsearchable.

—Psalm 145:3

O Father, Thy Kingdom Is Come

"How Great Thou Art" is only one of the great Swedish hymns sprinkled through our hymnbooks. One of the greatest Swedish writers was Karolina W. Sandell-Berg, who is known as the "Fanny Crosby of Sweden." She wrote two of my favorite hymns, "Children of the Heavenly Father" and "Day by Day." Less well known is Lina's hymn "O Father, Thy Kingdom Is Come." On **April 17, 1869**, two Swedish missionaries were killed in an area of what is now Ethiopia. Later, another missionary died, several others became sick, and the final remaining missionary in that area was massacred. The news affected Lina deeply, and that's what inspired her to write this moving missionary hymn.

> O Father, Thy kingdom is come upon earth,
> Thou rulest in all Thy creation;
> Thou sendest Thy witnesses, telling Thy worth,
> To call and entreat every nation,
> With news of Thy mighty salvation,
> With news of Thy mighty salvation.
>
> They lift up a light amid shadows of fear,
> And love is Thy banner above them;
> No trouble shall touch them, no foes that appear
> Shall e'er from their loyalty move them;
> 'Tis Thou dost uphold and approve them,
> 'Tis Thou dost uphold and approve them.
>
> They go in Thy strength, and they speak in Thy Name,
> With power of Thy promise forth faring,
> And during the battle the victory claim,
> Their trust in Thy strength is their daring,
> Salvation to all men declaring,
> Salvation to all men declaring.

Your kingdom come. Your will be done on earth as it is in heaven.

—Luke 11:2

O God of Bethel

The funeral of missionary David Livingstone brought London to a standstill. His body rested in a simple casket covered by a wreath of flowers from Queen Victoria. Westminster Abbey was filled with statesmen, explorers, Christian leaders, and family members. The hymn of the hour was "O God of Bethel." According to the 1893 book by Charles Robinson, *Annotations Upon Popular Hymns*, "Dr. Philip Doddridge wrote this hymn to be sung after a sermon on 'Jacob's Vow,' Genesis 28:20–22, which he preached on January 16, 1737. This hymn was found among the effects of David Livingstone, the one which sustained his heart through the wilderness journeys over Africa, and which, as his favorite, was sung at his funeral beneath the arches of Westminster Abbey, **April 18, 1874**."

O God of Bethel, by Whose hand
Thy people still are fed,
Who through this weary pilgrimage
Hast all our fathers led.

Through each perplexing path of life
Our wandering footsteps guide;
Give us each day our daily bread,
And raiment fit provide.

O spread Thy covering wings around
Till all our wanderings cease,
And at our Father's loved abode
Our souls arrive in peace.

Such blessings from Thy gracious hand
Our humble prayers implore;
And Thou shalt be our chosen God,
And portion evermore.

Behold, I am with you and will keep you wherever you go . . . I will not leave you.

—Genesis 28:15

In Heavenly Love Abiding

April 19, 1823, is the birthday of the insightful and inspiring British hymnist Anna Laetitia Waring. She was born in the south of Wales. I have a volume of her poems that I enjoy very much. Her best-known hymn is "In Heavenly Love Abiding," which I've most often sung to the tune "Seasons," composed by Felix Mendelssohn. But it is sometimes sung to a much-loved tune named "Aurelia" ("The Church's One Foundation"), composed by Charles Wesley's grandson, the noted organist Samuel S. Wesley, who died on **April 19, 1876**.

> In heavenly love abiding, no change my heart shall fear.
> And safe in such confiding, for nothing changes here.
> The storm may roar without me, my heart may low be laid,
> But God is round about me, and can I be dismayed?
>
> Wherever He may guide me, no want shall turn me back.
> My Shepherd is beside me, and nothing can I lack.
> His wisdom ever waking, His sight is never dim.
> He knows the way He's taking, and I will walk with Him.
>
> Green pastures are before me, which yet I have not seen.
> Bright skies will soon be o'er me, where darkest clouds have
>   been.
> My hope I cannot measure, my path to life is free;
> My Savior has my treasure, and He will walk with me.

*As the Father loved Me, I also have loved you; abide in My love.
If you keep My commandments, you will abide in My love, just as
I have kept My Father's commandments and abide in His love.*

—John 15:9–10

The Rock That Is Higher Than I

The psalmist David understood what it was to fret and fear; in Psalm 61:2, he cried, "From the end of the earth I will cry to You, when my heart is overwhelmed; lead me to the rock that is higher than I." Those words inspired a popular hymn during the financial panic of 1871. It was written by Erastus Johnson, who was born in a logging camp along Maine's Penobscot River on **April 20, 1826**. Erastus had a colorful life as a schoolteacher, gold miner, and oilman. While he was attending a YMCA convention in Carlisle, Pennsylvania, news came of large bank failures across the country. Many of the business leaders at the convention were worried. Erastus wrote this hymn on the spot, and William Fischer, who was leading the convention music, immediately composed the tune to which it is still sung.

> Oh! sometimes the shadows are deep,
> And rough seems the path to the goal,
> And sorrows, sometimes how they sweep
> Like tempests down over the soul.
>
> Oh! sometimes how long seems the day,
> And sometimes how weary my feet!
> But toiling in life's dusty way,
> The Rock's blessèd shadow, how sweet!
>
> Then near to the Rock let me keep
> If blessings or sorrows prevail,
> Or climbing the mountain way steep,
> Or walking the shadowy vale.
>
> *O then to the Rock let me fly*
> *To the Rock that is higher than I*
> *O then to the Rock let me fly*
> *To the Rock that is higher than I!*

Lead me to the rock that is higher than I.
For you have been a shelter for me.

—Psalm 61:2–3

Holy, Holy, Holy

April 21, 1783, marks the birth of Anglican hymnist and missionary Reginald Heber, author of the majestic anthem "Holy, Holy, Holy." Early in his ministry, Heber labored in the village of Hodnet, England, preaching in the village church and enjoying the relaxed pace of life. He wrote several hymns, but hymn singing was still frowned upon by the established church. So Heber stored his hymns in an old family trunk. In 1823, his superiors assigned Heber to oversee the Anglican work in India. He labored there for three years before suffering a stroke and dying at age forty-three. His widow later came across his poems in the trunk. "Holy, Holy, Holy" was published in 1861, thirty-five years after Heber's death.

Holy, holy, holy! Lord God Almighty!
Early in the morning our song shall rise to Thee;
Holy, holy, holy, merciful and mighty!
God in three Persons, blessèd Trinity!

Holy, holy, holy! All the saints adore Thee,
Casting down their golden crowns around the glassy sea;
Cherubim and seraphim falling down before Thee,
Who was, and is, and evermore shall be.

Holy, holy, holy! though the darkness hide Thee,
Though the eye of sinful man Thy glory may not see;
Only Thou art holy; there is none beside Thee,
Perfect in power, in love and purity.

Holy, holy, holy! Lord God Almighty!
All Thy works shall praise Thy name in earth and sky and sea;
Holy, holy, holy, merciful and mighty!
God in three Persons, blessèd Trinity!

Holy, holy, holy, Lord God Almighty, who
was and is and is to come!

—Revelation 4:8

In the Secret of His Presence

On **April 22, 1900**, as missionary J. Hudson Taylor preached at West Presbyterian Church in New York City from Mark 11:23, he said: "God has often placed me in positions in China where I had to put great trust in Him. In fact, I *had* to trust in Him, for there was no one else to whom I could look for help, and He never once failed me. He has always provided for me in His own way and time. I have been robbed in the interior of China of every cent I had, but I have never yet gone to bed hungry. Nearly half a century ago, I formed the China Inland Mission, and from the day of its inception . . . we have never lacked for any good thing. Verily, we have taken no thought of the morrow." According to Hudson Taylor, this poem by Ellen Goreh was the favorite hymn of his missionaries across China. Until researching this book, I'd never run across it before; but the words meet a need just now in my life. Perhaps they will in yours too.

> In the secret of His presence how my soul delights to hide!
> Oh, how precious are the lessons which I learn at Jesus' side!
> Earthly cares can never vex me, neither trials lay me low;
> For when Satan comes to tempt me, to the secret place I go.
>
> When my soul is faint and thirsty, 'neath the shadow of His wing
> There is cool and pleasant shelter, and a fresh and crystal spring;
> And my Savior rests beside me, as we hold communion sweet:
> If I tried, I could not utter what He says when thus we meet.
>
> Would you like to know the sweetness of the secret of the Lord?
> Go and hide beneath His shadow: this shall then be your
> reward;
> And whene'er you leave the silence of that happy meeting
> place,
> You must mind and bear the image of the Master in your face.

Trust in the LORD with all your heart, and lean not on your own understanding. In all your ways acknowledge Him, and He shall direct your paths.

—Proverbs 3:5–6

Now Thank We All Our God

The best time to thank God is *now*, whatever the circumstances or problems. "*Now* thank we all our God . . . " This old German hymn was penned by Pastor Martin Rinkhart during the Thirty Years' War. These were days of unimaginable suffering. At times Rinkhart was the town's only pastor, and he conducted about 4,500 funerals of those who died of war and plague. Sometimes he buried forty or fifty people a day. Rinkhart was born on **April 23, 1586**, in Saxony, and died just before Christmas in 1649. The German title of this hymn is "Nun danket alle Gott," and the first stanza is one of pure thanksgiving. The second stanza is a prayer, and the third is a doxology.

Now thank we all our God, with heart and hands and voices,
Who wondrous things has done, in whom His world rejoices;
Who, from our mother's arms, has blessed us on our way
With countless gifts of love, and still is ours today.

O may this bounteous God through all our life be near us,
With ever joyful hearts and blessèd peace to cheer us;
And keep us in His grace, and guide us when perplexed,
And free us from all ills in this world and the next.

All praise and thanks to God the Father now be given;
The Son, and Him who reigns with them in highest heaven;
The one eternal God, whom earth and heaven adore;
For thus it was, is now, and shall be evermore.

In everything give thanks; for this is the
will of God in Christ Jesus for you.
—1 Thessalonians 5:18

When We All Get to Heaven

One of my favorite hymns, "My Faith Has Found a Resting Place"—along with the gospel songs "More About Jesus," "When We All Get to Heaven," "Singing I Go Along Life's Road," "Sunshine in My Soul," "Sweeter As the Years Go By," and "Will There Be Any Stars in My Crown?"—was written by "the Sunshine Hymnist," Eliza Edmunds Hewitt, of Philadelphia. She spent much of her life bedridden with a spinal injury after being attacked at school by one of her students. During her prolonged convalescence, Eliza discovered the joy of writing hymns. She got to heaven on **April 24, 1920**.

> Sing the wondrous love of Jesus,
> Sing His mercy and His grace.
> In the mansions bright and blessèd
> He'll prepare for us a place.
>
> While we walk the pilgrim pathway,
> Clouds will overspread the sky;
> But when traveling days are over,
> Not a shadow, not a sigh.
>
> Onward to the prize before us!
> Soon His beauty we'll behold;
> Soon the pearly gates will open;
> We shall tread the streets of gold.
>
> *When we all get to heaven,*
> *What a day of rejoicing that will be!*
> *When we all see Jesus,*
> *We'll sing and shout the victory!*

And there shall be no more curse, but the throne of God and of the Lamb shall be in it, and His servants shall serve Him.

—Revelation 22:3

My God, Thee Will I Praise

John Leopold was a tailor in Augsburg, Germany, during the six-teenth century. His heart was evidently hungry, for when he heard the Anabaptists preaching the gospel of Christ, he gave himself wholeheartedly to their message and joined the church. Later he became a teacher and a preacher himself. Since the Anabaptists were an outlawed Protestant sect, this resulted in his arrest by civil authorities. Leopold was condemned to death for his faith. When told that the sword would soon take him from life to death, he replied, "No, gentlemen of Augsburg, but if God wills, from death to life." John Leopold was executed on **April 25, 1528**. He's the author of an early Anabaptist hymn of prayer titled "My God, Thee Will I Praise."

> My God, Thee will I praise
> When my last hour shall come,
> And then my voice I'll raise
> Within the heavenly home.
> O Lord, most merciful and kind,
> Now strengthen my weak faith,
> And give me peace of mind.
>
> To Thee in very deed
> My spirit I commend,
> Help me in all my need,
> And let me ne'er offend.
> Give to my flesh Thy Strength,
> That I with Thee may stand
> A conqueror at length.

For I am hard-pressed between the two, having a desire to depart and be with Christ, which is far better.

—Philippians 1:23

When Time Seems Short

This hymn was written on Saturday, **April 26, 1862**, as Dr. George Washington Bethune prepared his sermon for the next day. The Princeton-trained Bethune was a respected Reformed Dutch pastor, author, and hymnist. He was traveling in Florence, Italy, in an effort to restore his health, but he had agreed to give Sunday's message at a local church. His text was Matthew 9:2. He preached his message on April 27 in Florence, then suddenly collapsed and died, leaving this as his final and remarkably appropriate hymn.

When time seems short, and death is near,
And I am pressed by doubt and fear,
And sins, an overflowing tide,
Assail my peace on every side,
This thought my refuge still shall be,
I know my Savior died for me.

His name is Jesus, and He died—
For guilty sinners crucified;
Content to die, that He might win
Their ransom from the death of sin.
No sinner worse than I can be,
Therefore I know He died for me.

I read God's holy Word, and find
Great truths which far transcend my mind
And little do I know beside
Of thought so high and deep and wide.
This is my best theology—
I know the Savior died for me.

When Jesus saw their faith, He said to the paralytic,
"Son, be of good cheer; your sins are forgiven you."

—Matthew 9:2

Calvary

William M. Darwood came from England to America at age thirteen and was saved at nineteen. He began preaching immediately and went on to become a celebrated New York City pastor. But Darwood was grieved by the erosion of solid doctrine in the pulpits of his day. "My brethren are making a sad mistake," he said. "What the world needs more than anything else is the truth as it is in Christ Jesus. . . . It is not what the ministers think, or what someone else thinks, which they must preach, but Jesus, for only in Him is salvation and rest of soul to be found." In the spring of 1913, Darwood's health began to fail, but he kept reading and studying God's Word to the last week of his life. On the evening of **April 27, 1914**, a friend entered his sickroom and greeted him. "Well, my brother," Darwood cheerfully replied, "I am very glad to see you." He smiled and was gone. Here is Darwood's hymn on the great subject of Calvary.

On Calv'ry's brow my Savior died,
'Twas there my Lord was crucified;
'Twas on the cross He bled for me,
And purchased there my pardon free.

'Mid rending rocks and dark'ning skies,
My Savior bows His head and dies;
The op'ning veil reveals the way
To heaven's joys and endless day.

O Jesus, Lord, how can it be,
That Thou shouldst give Thy life for me,
To bear the cross and agony
In that dread hour on Calvary!

O Calvary! dark Calvary!
Where Jesus shed His blood for me;
O Calvary! blest Calvary!
'Twas there my Savior died for me.

For Jews request a sign, and Greeks seek after
wisdom; but we preach Christ crucified.

—1 Corinthians 1:22–23

Lord, Speak to Me

Today is the birthday of one of my favorite hymns, written by one of my favorite hymnists. When I first began pastoring thirty years ago, I often listened to "Lord, Speak to Me" on an old tape recorded by vocalists Robert Hale and Dean Wilder. To this day, I often pray the first verse before standing to preach, and the final verse is a life prayer of mine. This prayer was penned on **April 28, 1872**, at Winter-dyne, Bewdley, England, by the British Bible teacher and hymnist Frances Ridley Havergal. It was published later that year under the title "A Worker's Prayer," accompanied by the words of Romans 14:7.

Lord, speak to me that I may speak
In living echoes of Thy tone;
As Thou has sought, so let me seek
Thine erring children lost and lone.

O teach me, Lord, that I may teach
The precious things Thou dost impart;
And wing my words, that they may reach
The hidden depths of many a heart.

O fill me with Thy fullness, Lord,
Until my very heart o'erflow
In kindling thought and glowing word,
Thy love to tell, Thy praise to show.

O use me, Lord, use even me,
Just as Thou wilt and when and where;
Until Thy blessèd face I see,
Thy rest, Thy joy, Thy glory share.

For none of us lives to himself, and no one dies to himself.

—Romans 14:7

All Glory, Laud and Honor

"All Glory, Laud and Honor" is an ancient Latin hymn. Written around AD 820 by the imprisoned Theodulph, Bishop of Orleans, it was translated into English by John Neale in 1851. The tune is an old European melody titled "St. Theodulph," which gives the hymn a note of celebration and joy as well as warmth and poignancy. The composer, Melchior Teschner, was born in Prussia on **April 29, 1584**, and devoted his life to the ministry of music and pastoring.

All glory, laud and honor,
To Thee, Redeemer, King,
To whom the lips of children
Made sweet hosannas ring.

Thou art the King of Israel,
Thou David's royal Son,
Who in the Lord's name comest,
The King and blessèd One.

The people of the Hebrews
With palms before Thee went;
Our praise and prayer and anthems
Before Thee we present.

Thou didst accept their praises;
Accept the prayers we bring,
Who in all good delightest,
Thou good and gracious King.

Blessed is He who comes in the name of the
LORD! Hosanna in the highest!

—Matthew 21:9

Safe in the Arms of Jesus

"On **April 30, 1868**," wrote Fanny Crosby in her memoirs, "Dr. W. H. Doane came into my house and said, 'I have exactly forty minutes before my train leaves for Cincinnati. Here is a melody. Can you write words for it?' I replied that I would see what I could do. Then followed a space of twenty minutes during which I was wholly unconscious of all else except the work I was doing. At the end of that time I recited the words to 'Safe in the Arms of Jesus.' Mr. Doane copied them, and had time to catch his train."

Safe in the arms of Jesus, safe on His gentle breast,
There by His love o'ershaded, sweetly my soul shall rest.
Hark! 'tis the voice of angels, borne in a song to me.
Over the fields of glory, over the jasper sea.

Safe in the arms of Jesus, safe from corroding care,
Safe from the world's temptations, sin cannot harm me there.
Free from the blight of sorrow, free from my doubts and fears;
Only a few more trials, only a few more tears!

Jesus, my heart's dear Refuge, Jesus has died for me;
Firm on the Rock of Ages, ever my trust shall be.
Here let me wait with patience, wait till the night is o'er;
Wait till I see the morning break on the golden shore.

Safe in the arms of Jesus, safe on His gentle breast,
There by His love o'ershaded, sweetly my soul shall rest.

Hold me up, and I shall be safe, and I shall
observe Your statutes continually.

—Psalm 119:117

Leaning on the Everlasting Arms

No one did more to promote gospel songs throughout the South than Presbyterian educator and music teacher Anthony Showalter, who was born **May 1, 1858**, in Cherry Grove, Virginia. One day Showalter received two letters from former pupils, both of whose wives had just passed away. Looking for a verse to comfort them, he found Deuteronomy 33:27, which talks about the undergirding of God's everlasting arms. As Showalter pondered the verse, the words "Leaning, leaning, safe and secure from all alarms" came to mind. Soon he'd written the melody and refrain for this hymn. His friend Elisha Hoffman later supplied the verses.

What a fellowship, what a joy divine,
Leaning on the everlasting arms;
What a blessedness, what a peace is mine,
Leaning on the everlasting arms.

O how sweet to walk in this pilgrim way,
Leaning on the everlasting arms;
O how bright the path grows from day to day,
Leaning on the everlasting arms.

What have I to dread, what have I to fear,
Leaning on the everlasting arms;
I have blessèd peace with my Lord so near,
Leaning on the everlasting arms.

Leaning, leaning, safe and secure from all alarms;
Leaning, leaning, leaning on the everlasting arms.

The eternal God is your refuge, and
underneath are the everlasting arms.

—Deuteronomy 33:27

Praise Him, Praise Him

On **May 2, 1911**, the irrepressible hymnist Fanny Crosby was honored at a celebration at New York's Carnegie Hall. On stage, a choir of two hundred voices sang her hymns while Miss Crosby, age ninety-one, listened and glowed with joy. Finally, she was assisted onstage, at first appearing frail and feeble. But when she stood to speak, using only a chair back for support, she told the crowd she expected to live until 103. "When I was taken from the carriage into the hotel today," she said, "I heard someone say: 'Get her a rolling chair.' But I spoke right up and said, 'I don't need any rolling chair. I can walk on my own feet. My strength is in the Lord.'" I can't find a listing of the songs sung that evening, but almost certainly the crowd rang out one of Fanny's most popular hymns, which was the theme of her life: "Praise Him, Praise Him!"

> Praise Him! Praise Him! Jesus, our blessèd Redeemer!
> Sing, O Earth, His wonderful love proclaim!
> Hail Him! hail Him! highest archangels in glory;
> Strength and honor give to His holy name!
> Like a shepherd, Jesus will guard His children,
> In His arms He carries them all day long:
>
> Praise Him! Praise Him! Jesus, our blessèd Redeemer!
> For our sins He suffered, and bled, and died.
> He our Rock, our hope of eternal salvation,
> Hail Him! hail Him! Jesus the Crucified.
> Sound His praises! Jesus who bore our sorrows,
> Love unbounded, wonderful, deep and strong.
>
> Praise Him! Praise Him! Jesus, our blessèd Redeemer!
> Heav'nly portals loud with hosannas ring!
> Jesus, Savior, reigneth forever and ever.
> Crown Him! Crown Him! Prophet and Priest and King!
> Christ is coming! over the world victorious,
> Pow'r and glory unto the Lord belong.
>
> *Praise Him! Praise Him!*
> *Tell of His excellent greatness.*
> *Praise Him! Praise Him!*
> *Ever in joyful song!*

Praise Him for His mighty acts; praise Him according to His excellent greatness!

—Psalm 150:2

Jesus, Savior, Pilot Me

I first heard this hymn as a graduate student at Wheaton College when it was sung one evening at the church I was attending. "Jesus, Savior, Pilot Me" was written by Edward Hopper, who served as pastor of the Church of Sea and Land in New York City, where he ministered to mariners sailing into the port of New York from all over the world. The hymn first appeared without attribution in the **May 3, 1871**, issue of *The Sailors Magazine*. A Philadelphia composer wrote the music, and for many years the parishioners of the Church of Sea and Land numbered it as one of their favorite hymns. Only years later did Hopper confess he was its author.

Jesus, Savior, pilot me
Over life's tempestuous sea;
Unknown waves before me roll,
Hiding rock and treacherous shoal.
Chart and compass come from Thee;
Jesus, Savior, pilot me.

As a mother stills her child,
Thou canst hush the ocean wild;
Boisterous waves obey Thy will,
When Thou sayest to them, "Be still!"
Wondrous Sovereign of the sea,
Jesus, Savior, pilot me.

When at last I near the shore,
And the fearful breakers roar
'Twixt me and the peaceful rest,
Then, while leaning on Thy breast,
May I hear Thee say to me,
"Fear not, I will pilot thee."

He guides them to their desired haven. Oh, that men would give thanks to the LORD.

—Psalm 107:30–31

Peace, Troubled Soul

Abraham Lincoln's funeral train passed through the nation's heartland, arriving in Springfield, Illinois, where the casket was carried to the State House and placed in Representative Hall. The casket lid was removed, and thousands of mourners passed by quietly and looked down on the silent, upturned face of the slain president. The long procession included old friends, crippled soldiers fresh from the battlefields, little children, liberated slaves, and fellow politicians. At ten o'clock on **May 4, 1865**, as a 250-voice choir sang "Peace, Troubled Soul," the lid of the casket was shut forever, and the remains of the sixteenth president were borne outside and placed in a hearse bound for Oak Ridge Cemetery. "Peace, Troubled Soul," by Samuel Ecking, is usually sung to the tune "When I Survey the Wondrous Cross."

> Peace, troubled soul, thou need'st not fear;
> Thy great Provider still is near;
> Who fed thee last, will feed thee still:
> Be calm, and sink into His will.
>
> The Lord, who built the earth and sky,
> In mercy stoops to hear thy cry;
> His promise all may freely claim;
> Ask and receive in Jesus' Name.
>
> Without reserve give Christ your heart,
> Let Him His righteousness impart;
> Then all things else He'll freely give;
> With Him you all things shall receive.
>
> Thus shall the soul be truly blest,
> That seeks in God His only rest;
> May I that happy person be,
> In time and in eternity.

For you shall go out with joy, and be led out with peace.

—Isaiah 55:12

In the Cross of Christ I Glory

In past eras, many of our great Christian composers have been organists. Ithamar Conkey, for example, who was born into a Scottish family on **May 5, 1815**, in Shutesbury, Massachusetts, became a church organist and music director at Central Baptist Church in Norwich, Connecticut. One Sunday in 1849, as his pastor was preaching a series on "Words on the Cross," the congregation sang John Bowring's hymn "In the Cross of Christ I Glory," but the tune didn't match the words. Because of rainy weather, only one choir member showed up that day for the service. Conkey wrote a beautiful new melody for Bowring's words and named it "Rathbun," in honor of Mrs. Beriah S. Rathbun, his one faithful choir member.

> In the cross of Christ I glory,
> Towering o'er the wrecks of time;
> All the light of sacred story
> Gathers round its head sublime.
>
> When the woes of life o'ertake me,
> Hopes deceive, and fears annoy,
> Never shall the cross forsake me,
> Lo! it glows with peace and joy.
>
> When the sun of bliss is beaming
> Light and love upon my way,
> From the cross the radiance streaming
> Adds more luster to the day.
>
> Bane and blessing, pain and pleasure,
> By the cross are sanctified;
> Peace is there that knows no measure,
> Joys that through all time abide.

But God forbid that I should boast except in the cross of our Lord Jesus Christ, by whom the world has been crucified to me, and I to the world.

—Galatians 6:14

What Wondrous Love Is This

Sometimes a hymn brings back memories and holds a cherished place in our lives, even if we didn't realize its significance at the time. When I was in high school, I traveled to Nashville to stay with a friend who was a student at Free Will Baptist Bible College. We attended a program of some sort at which the college choir sang this song. I remember it because they had produced a cassette tape of the program, and I listened to it over and over. It was a period of searching in my life, and this hymn settled into my consciousness. I've never forgotten it. The hymn's author is uncertain, but the haunting melody was written by a Southern music teacher named William Walker who was born **May 6, 1809.**

What wondrous love is this, O my soul, O my soul!
What wondrous love is this, O my soul!
What wondrous love is this that caused the Lord of bliss
To bear the dreadful curse for my soul, for my soul,
To bear the dreadful curse for my soul.

When I was sinking down, sinking down, sinking down,
When I was sinking down, sinking down,
When I was sinking down beneath God's righteous frown,
Christ laid aside His crown for my soul, for my soul,
Christ laid aside His crown for my soul.

To God and to the Lamb, I will sing, I will sing,
To God and to the Lamb, I will sing,
To God and to the Lamb who is the great "I Am,"
While millions join the theme, I will sing, I will sing,
While millions join the theme, I will sing.

To Him who loved us and washed us from our sins in His own blood . . . to Him be glory and dominion forever and ever. Amen.

—Revelation 1:5–6

I Could Not Do Without Thee

Hymnist Frances Ridley Havergal had an irrepressible personality, and the radiance of her life, writings, and hymns will never be extinguished. Her secret is contained in this lesser-known hymn, written **May 7, 1873**.

I could not do without Thee,
I cannot stand alone,
I have no strength or goodness,
No wisdom of my own;
But Thou, beloved Savior,
Art all in all to me,
And weakness will be power
If leaning hard on Thee.

I could not do without Thee,
For, oh, the way is long,
And I am often weary,
And sigh replaces song:
How could I do without Thee?
I do not know the way;
Thou knowest, and Thou leadest,
And wilt not let me stray.

I could not do without Thee,
For years are fleeting fast,
And soon in solemn oneness
The river must be passed;
But Thou wilt never leave me,
And though the waves roll high,
I know Thou wilt be near me,
And whisper, "It is I."

I can do all things through Christ who strengthens me.

—Philippians 4:13

My Mother's Bible

On **May 8, 1914**, a resolution was passed by both houses of the United States Congress. When it was signed the next day by President Woodrow Wilson, Mother's Day became a national observance. A glance at older hymnals shows many gospel songs devoted to the theme of "mother"—a practice now neglected. In honor of Mother's Day, here is a once-popular song by M. B. Williams, "My Mother's Bible."

There's a dear and precious Book, though it's worn and faded
   now,
Which recalls those happy days of long ago,
When I stood at mother's knee,
With her hand upon my brow,
And I heard her voice in gentle tones and low.

As she read the stories o'er of those mighty men of old,
Of Joseph and of Daniel and their trials,
Of little David bold,
Who became a king at last,
Of Satan and his many wicked wiles.

Then she read of Jesus' love, as He blessed the children dear,
How He suffered, bled and died upon the tree;
Of His heavy load of care,
Then she dried my flowing tears
With her kisses as she said it was for me.

Well, those days are past and gone, but their memory lingers
   still
And the dear old Book each day has been my guide;
And I seek to do His will,
As my mother taught me then,
And ever in my heart His Words abide.

Blessed Book, precious Book,
On thy dear old tearstained leaves I love to look;
Thou art sweeter day by day,
As I walk the narrow way
That leads at last to that bright home above.

From childhood you have know the Holy Scriptures.

—2 Timothy 3:15

Just As I Am

On **May 9, 1822**, Dr. Caesar Malan of Switzerland visited Charlotte Elliott, an embittered invalid in Brighton, England. Because of her poor health, Charlotte had become rude and irritable. Dr. Malan spoke to her about her spiritual needs. "I am miserable," Charlotte confessed. "I want to be saved. I want to come to Jesus; but I don't know how." That's when Malan gave her his famous reply, which later became the basis for the greatest invitational hymn of all time. "Why not come just as you are?" he asked. Charlotte *did* come just as she was, and later she wrote this hymn about it.

> Just as I am, without one plea,
> But that Thy blood was shed for me,
> And that Thou bidst me come to Thee,
> O Lamb of God, I come, I come.
>
> Just as I am, and waiting not
> To rid my soul of one dark blot,
> To Thee whose blood can cleanse each spot,
> O Lamb of God, I come, I come.
>
> Just as I am, though tossed about
> With many a conflict, many a doubt,
> Fightings and fears within, without,
> O Lamb of God, I come, I come.
>
> Just as I am, poor, wretched, blind;
> Sight, riches, healing of the mind,
> Yea, all I need in Thee to find,
> O Lamb of God, I come, I come.

He said to them, "Come and see . . ."
—John 1:39

"Come, follow Me."
—Matthew 19:21

Sing Praise to God Who Reigns Above

I don't hear this hymn sung much nowadays, but it should be. It's joyful, triumphant, and easy to sing, with a rolling German melody that dates from 1556. I've always loved it. The words were published in 1675 by Johann J. Schütz, a Lutheran attorney in Frankfurt. But we wouldn't have this great hymn if it hadn't been for a British translator named Frances Elizabeth Cox, who was born **May 10, 1812**, in Oxford. Her life's mission was to translate some of the great German hymns into the English language, and her magnum opus, *Hymns from the German,* is still in print after over one hundred years. It's best-known entry: "Sing Praise to God Who Reigns Above."

Sing praise to God who reigns above, the God of all creation,
The God of power, the God of love, the God of our salvation.
With healing balm my soul He fills and every faithless murmur stills:
To God all praise and glory!

What God's almighty power hath made His gracious mercy keepeth,
By morning glow or evening shade His watchful eye ne'er sleepeth;
Within the kingdom of His might, Lo! all is just and all is right:
To God all praise and glory!

The Lord is never far away, but through all grief distressing,
An ever present help and stay, our peace and joy and blessing.
As with a mother's tender hand, God gently leads the chosen band:
To God all praise and glory!

Thus, all my toilsome way along, I sing aloud Thy praises,
That earth may hear the grateful song my voice unwearied raises.
Be joyful in the Lord, my heart, both soul and body bear your part:
To God all praise and glory!

Sing praises to God, sing praises! Sing praises to our King, sing praises!

—Psalm 47:6

What Will It Be to Dwell Above?

Joseph Swain, an orphaned teenager, grew alarmed one day about his spiritual condition and procured a Bible. As he read it, he decided to give his heart to Jesus. He was baptized by Dr. John Rippon on **May 11, 1783**, at age eighteen, and he began preaching for the Baptists. Swain loved the hymns of Isaac Watts, and he began writing hymns for his own church in London. Though Swain died in his mid-thirties, he left behind a church full of converts and a songbook full of hymns. Try Swain's hymn about heaven to the tune of "Faith of Our Fathers."

> What will it be to dwell above,
> And with the Lord of glory reign,
> Since the blest knowledge of His love
> So brightens all this dreary plain?
> No heart can think, no tongue can tell,
> What joy 'twill be with Christ to dwell.
>
> When sin no more obstructs the sight,
> And flesh and sense deceive no more,
> When we shall see the Prince of light,
> And all His works of grace explore,
> What heights and depths of love divine
> Will there through endless ages shine!
>
> And God has fixed the happy day,
> When the last tear shall dim our eyes;
> When He will wipe these tears away,
> And fill our hearts with glad surprise;
> To hear His voice, and see His face,
> And know the fullness of His grace!

And thus we shall always be with the Lord.

—1 Thessalonians 4:17

Thou, Whose Almighty Word

John Marriott was a highly intelligent but self-effacing British clergyman. He wrote a handful of hymns but was too modest to publish or even quote them. Six weeks after Marriott's death, Thomas Mortimer, a fellow Anglican pastor, recited this poem publicly for the first time at a meeting of the London Missionary Society on **May 12, 1825**, in Great Queen Street Chapel, London. The poem was soon set to music and became a beloved British missionary hymn.

Thou, whose almighty Word
Chaos and darkness heard,
And took their flight;
Hear us, we humbly pray,
And, where the Gospel's day
Sheds not its glorious ray,
Let there be light!

Spirit of truth and love,
Life giving, holy Dove,
Speed forth Thy flight;
Move on the water's face
Bearing the lamp of grace,
And, in earth's darkest place,
Let there be light!

Blessèd and holy Three,
Glorious Trinity,
Wisdom, love, might!
Boundless as ocean's tide,
Rolling in fullest pride,
Through the world far and wide,
Let there be light!

Then God said, "Let there be light"; and there was light.

—Genesis 1:3

Revive Us Again

Birthday greetings go out today to the author of this hymn, Dr. William Paton Mackay, a Scottish physician born **May 13, 1839**. His mother raised him on her knees, praying earnestly for his soul; but as a young man Mackay was a prodigal. One day, while making his rounds in the hospital, he witnessed the dying moments of an injured workman and was impressed with the man's love for his Bible. To his shock, Mackay realized that it was his own Bible—the one his mother had given him and which he had sold years before—that had comforted the man in his dying hour. His name was still inscribed in his mother's hand. "Sufficient to say," he later testified, "that the regained possession of my Bible was the cause of my conversion."

> We praise Thee, O God! For the Son of Thy love,
> For Jesus who died, and is now gone above.
>
> We praise Thee, O God! For Thy Spirit of light,
> Who hath shown us our Savior, and scattered our night.
>
> All glory and praise to the Lamb that was slain,
> Who hath borne all our sins, and hath cleansed every stain.
>
> All glory and praise to the God of all grace,
> Who hast brought us, and sought us, and guided our ways.
>
> Revive us again; fill each heart with Thy love;
> May each soul be rekindled with fire from above.
>
> *Hallelujah! Thine the glory.*
> *Hallelujah! Amen.*
> *Hallelujah! Thine the glory.*
> *Revive us again.*

Will You not revive us again, that Your people may rejoice in You?

—Psalm 85:6

Praise the Savior, Ye Who Know Him

One of my all-time favorites, "Praise the Savior, Ye Who Know Him," is by Thomas Kelly, an Irish minister who wrote nearly eight hundred hymns. Kelly was a zealous evangelist, a socially gracious man, and a gifted musician and poet. His best-known hymn is "Look, Ye Saints, the Sight Is Glorious." But "Praise the Savior" is a great hymn that combines worship with consecration in a comforting way. At age eighty-five, Kelly suffered a stroke. He passed away the following year, on **May 14, 1855**. At his deathbed, someone quoted Psalm 23, saying, "The Lord is my Shepherd." Kelly summoned enough strength to respond with his dying words: "The Lord is my Everything."

Praise the Savior, ye who know Him!
Who can tell how much we owe Him?
Gladly let us render to Him
All we are and have.

Jesus is the name that charms us,
He for conflict fits and arms us;
Nothing moves and nothing harms us
While we trust in Him.

Trust in Him, ye saints, forever,
He is faithful, changing never;
Neither force nor guile can sever
Those He loves from Him.

Then we shall be where we would be,
Then we shall be what we should be,
Things that are not now, nor could be,
Soon shall be our own.

We who first trusted in Christ should be to the praise of His glory.

—Ephesians 1:12

Majestic Sweetness Sits Enthroned

We can rise above handicaps! Thomas Hastings, an albino from a poor family, battled speech impediments and eye problems throughout life. He received little formal training, yet he taught himself the rudiments of music and as a teen began directing his church choir. As a young man he was such a popular singing school instructor that twelve churches in New York City wanted him to lead their music. During his life, Hastings penned fifty volumes of church music, including a thousand hymn tunes and hundreds of hymn texts. He's sometimes credited with being the greatest force in shaping the development of church music in America. He's best remembered for his melodies to "Rock of Ages," "From Every Stormy Wind That Blows," and "Majestic Sweetness Sits Enthroned." Hastings died in his eighties in New York City on **May 15, 1872**.

Majestic sweetness sits enthroned
Upon the Savior's brow;
His head with radiant glories crowned,
His lips with grace o'erflow,
His lips with grace o'erflow.

To Christ, the Lord, let every tongue
Its noblest tribute bring;
When He's the subject of the song,
Who can refuse to sing?
Who can refuse to sing?

His hand a thousand blessings pours
Upon my guilty head:
His presence gilds my darkest hours,
And guards my sleeping bed,
And guards my sleeping bed.

To Him I owe my life and breath
And all the joys I have;
He makes me triumph over death
And saves me from the grave,
And saves me from the grave.

The LORD reigns, He is clothed with majesty.

—Psalm 93:1

Wonderful Words of Life

The custom of singing at the bedside of dying Christians is an old and powerful tradition. For example, consider the deathbed of Rev. William Nast. Nast was born in Germany but became an effective Methodist preacher in America during an era when itinerate evangelists were scorned. Nast had to sometimes duck during sermons as hecklers threw rotten eggs at him. But during his sunset years, Nast found himself acclaimed as the Patriarch of German Methodism, and he was in great demand throughout the United States. People flocked to hear him, and children were named for him, as were schools and colleges. At age ninety-two, William Nast fell ill. On **May 16, 1899**, a group of Methodist deaconesses gathered by his bed to sing Philip Bliss's simple song "Wonderful Words of Life." Nast responded with "Amen!" and "Hallelujah!" He then said, "Come Lord Jesus," and was called home.

> Sing them over again to me, wonderful words of life,
> Let me more of their beauty see, wonderful words of life;
> Words of life and beauty teach me faith and duty.
>
> Christ, the blessèd One, gives to all wonderful words of life;
> Sinner, list to the loving call, wonderful words of life;
> All so freely given, wooing us to heaven.
>
> Sweetly echo the gospel call, wonderful words of life;
> Offer pardon and peace to all, wonderful words of life;
> Jesus, only Savior, sanctify forever.
>
> *Beautiful words, wonderful words, wonderful words of life,*
> *Beautiful words, wonderful words, wonderful words of life.*

Lord, to whom shall we go? You have the words of eternal life.

—John 6:68

MAY 16

Come, Christians, Join to Sing

This is a very singable hymn. The words roll joyfully off the tongue because of the elegant but simple Spanish melody arranged by David Evans. A Welsh musician, Evans started life in the coal industry, but he eventually became a church organist in London and then a long-tenured professor of music at University College, Cardiff. He was considered the most outstanding musician in Wales during his lifetime and was the author of several compositions, hymn tunes, and volumes related to music. He died in the impossible-to-pronounce Welsh mining town of Rhosllannerchrugog on **May 17, 1948**.

Come, Christians, join to sing
Alleluia! Amen!
Loud praise to Christ our King;
Alleluia! Amen!
Let all, with heart and voice,
Before His throne rejoice;
Praise is His gracious choice.
Alleluia! Amen!

Come, lift your hearts on high,
Alleluia! Amen!
Let praises fill the sky;
Alleluia! Amen!
He is our Guide and Friend;
To us He'll condescend;
His love shall never end.
Alleluia! Amen!

Make a joyful shout to the LORD, all you lands! Serve the LORD with gladness; come before His presence with singing. Know that the LORD, He is God.

—Psalm 100:1–3

This Is My Father's World

As a young man, Maltbie Davenport Babcock gained renown as an athlete, scholar, and musician. He entered the Presbyterian ministry and eventually became a prominent pastor in New York. Imagine the shock when his parishioners opened the *New York Times* to read this headline: "The Rev. Dr. Babcock Committed Suicide." That was sensational journalism, but it wasn't the whole story. While on a trip to the Holy Land, Babcock contracted some kind of brain fever. En route home, he was hospitalized in Naples, Italy. According to accounts, moans were heard coming from his locked room. When hospital personnel broke in, Babcock said meekly, "I have swallowed corrosive sublimate." Those were his last words, but there were also blood stains in the bed where he had apparently, in delirium, severed his arteries. And so he died at age forty-three on **May 18, 1901**. His congregation defended his memory, and he is honored to this day, especially whenever we sing one of the hymns that were published after his death, such as this one.

> This is my Father's world, and to my listening ears
> All nature sings, and round me rings the music of the spheres.
> This is my Father's world: I rest me in the thought
> Of rocks and trees, of skies and seas;
> His hand the wonders wrought.
>
> This is my Father's world, the birds their carols raise,
> The morning light, the lily white, declare their Maker's praise.
> This is my Father's world: He shines in all that's fair;
> In the rustling grass I hear Him pass;
> He speaks to me everywhere.
>
> This is my Father's world. O let me ne'er forget
> That though the wrong seems oft so strong, God is the ruler yet.
> This is my Father's world: the battle is not done:
> Jesus Who died shall be satisfied,
> And earth and Heav'n be one.

For the world is Mine, and all its fullness.

—Psalm 50:12

Do You Know How Many Stars?

You've probably never heard this hymn, but it's a delightful poem you can teach your children or grandchildren. It was written by the nineteenth-century German pastor Johann Wilhelm Hey, who died **May 19, 1854**. He was a beloved preacher in his time and the author of a little book of poems for children, *Febeln für Kinder*, published in Hamburg in 1833. This poem was later set to a German melody and is popular among German children to this day.

Do you know how many stars
There are shining in the sky?
Do you know how many clouds
Every day go floating by?
God, the Lord, their number knoweth,
For each one His care He showeth,
Of the bright and boundless host,
Of the bright and boundless host.

Do you know how many birdies
In the sunshine sing each day?
Do you know how many fishes
In the sparkling water play?
God, the Lord, who dwells in Heaven,
Name and life to each has given,
In His love they live and move,
In His love they live and move.

Do you know how many children
Go to little beds at night,
And without a care or sorrow
Wake again with morning light?
God in Heav'n each name can tell,
Knows us, too, and loves us well,
He's our best and dearest Friend,
He's our best and dearest Friend.

He counts the number of the stars; He calls them all by name.

—Psalm 147:4

My Jesus, I Love Thee

Don't underestimate how God can use teenagers. Isaac Watts began writing his great hymns at age eighteen. John Milton wrote a wonderful hymn when he was fifteen: "Let us with a gladsome mind / Praise the Lord for He is Kind." The composer E. J. Hopkins, who wrote the music to "For the Beauty of the Earth," was appointed church organist at age sixteen. The popular praise song "We Are Standing on Holy Ground" was written by Geron Davis when he was nineteen. "Work for the Night Is Coming" was composed by an eighteen-year-old, as was the gospel song "Whosoever Meaneth Me." And this great hymn of prayer, "My Jesus, I Love Thee," was written by a sixteen-year-old named William Ralph Featherstone. Today marks the anniversary of his homegoing on **May 20, 1873**.

> My Jesus, I love Thee, I know Thou art mine;
> For Thee all the follies of sin I resign.
> My gracious Redeemer, my Savior art Thou;
> If ever I loved Thee, my Jesus, 'tis now.
>
> I love Thee because Thou has first lovèd me,
> And purchased my pardon on Calvary's tree.
> I love Thee for wearing the thorns on Thy brow;
> If ever I loved Thee, my Jesus, 'tis now.
>
> I'll love Thee in life, I will love Thee in death,
> And praise Thee as long as Thou lendest me breath;
> And say when the death dew lies cold on my brow,
> If ever I loved Thee, my Jesus, 'tis now.

He said to Him, "Yes, Lord; You know that I love You."

—John 21:16

Where Shall My Wondering Soul Begin?

Charles Wesley was converted on **May 21, 1738**, and his journal entry for that day says, "I began an hymn upon my conversion, but I was persuaded to break off for fear of pride. Mr. Bray, coming, encouraged me to proceed in spite of Satan. I prayed Christ to stand by me, and finished the hymn." For the next fifty-seven years, Charles averaged writing three hymns a week. We aren't sure which hymn Charles wrote on May 21, but most experts think it was "Where Shall My Wondering Soul Begin?"—probably the first of Wesley's 6,500 hymns!

> Where shall my wondering soul begin?
> How shall I all to heaven aspire?
> A slave redeemed from death and sin,
> A brand plucked from eternal fire,
> How shall I equal triumphs raise,
> Or sing my great Deliverer's praise?
>
> O how shall I the goodness tell,
> Father, which Thou to me hast showed?
> That I, a child of wrath and hell,
> I should be called a child of God,
> Should know, should feel my sins forgiven,
> Blessed with this antepast [foretaste] of Heaven!
>
> For you the purple current flowed
> In pardons from His wounded side,
> Languished for you the eternal God,
> For you the Prince of glory died:
> Believe, and all your sin's forgiven;
> Only believe, and yours is Heaven!

. . . being justified freely by His grace through the redemption that is in Christ Jesus.

—Romans 3:24

Onward, Christian Soldiers

On Sunday, **May 22, 1910**, as part of the festivities of the World Sunday School Convention meeting in Washington, D.C., it was arranged for "Onward, Christian Soldiers" to be sung around the world. Translators had worked for months rendering the words into a hundred languages. Children in churches and on mission fields everywhere marched through the streets singing this song. In one day "Onward, Christian Soldiers" became a worldwide hymn and a global call to worship. Some have since criticized this hymn for its military themes. But if you're like me, your love for this song reaches back to vacation Bible school days, as we marched to our classes singing, "Onward, Christians soldiers, marching as to war, / With the cross of Jesus going on before."

> Onward, Christian soldiers, marching as to war,
> With the cross of Jesus going on before.
> Christ, the royal Master, leads against the foe;
> Forward into battle see His banners go!
>
> At the sign of triumph Satan's host doth flee;
> On then, Christian soldiers, on to victory!
> Hell's foundations quiver at the shout of praise;
> Brothers lift your voices, loud your anthems raise.
>
> Like a mighty army moves the church of God;
> Brothers, we are treading where the saints have trod.
> We are not divided, all one body we,
> One in hope and doctrine, one in charity.
>
> *Onward, Christian soldiers, marching as to war,*
> *With the cross of Jesus going on before.*

Take the helmet of salvation, and the sword of the Spirit, which is the word of God.

—Ephesians 6:17

Did You Think to Pray?

At Columbia International University, I was taught to begin each day with my "quiet time"—a half hour or so spent at my desk in Bible study and prayer. That has become the core habit of my life, and I recommend it to one and all. This old hymn by Mary Kidder makes the same point, asking, "Ere you left your room this morning, / Did you think to pray?" The music is by William O. Perkins, a gifted Bostonian who founded a music academy, published church songbooks, and wrote the music to several popular hymns. Today is his birthday—**May 23, 1831.**

When you met with great temptation,
Did you think to pray?
By His dying love and merit,
Did you claim the Holy Spirit
As your guide and stay?

When your heart was filled with anger,
Did you think to pray?
Did you plead for grace, my brother,
That you might forgive another
Who had crossed your way?

When sore trials came upon you,
Did you think to pray?
When your soul was bowed in sorrow,
Balm of Gilead did you borrow
At the gates of day?

O how praying rests the weary!
Prayer will change the night to day;
So when life seems dark and dreary,
Don't forget to pray.

My voice You shall hear in the morning, O LORD.

—Psalm 5:3

Come, Thou Fount of Every Blessing

Rev. Robert Robinson was apprenticed to a barber and hairdresser when he was fourteen, but everything changed on **May 24, 1752**, when he went to hear a sermon by the great evangelist George Whitefield. During his sermon, Whitefield burst into tears and cried, "Oh, my hearers, the wrath's to come! The wrath's to come!" Those words troubled Robinson for more than three years until he finally gave his heart to Christ on December 10, 1755. Robinson became a preacher of the gospel and the writer of two hymns: "Mighty God, While Angels Bless Thee" and this one, "Come, Thou Fount of Every Blessing." He died at age fifty-four while on a preaching trip in Birmingham.

Come, Thou Fount of every blessing,
Tune my heart to sing Thy grace;
Streams of mercy, never ceasing,
Call for songs of loudest praise.
Teach me some melodious sonnet,
Sung by flaming tongues above.
Praise the mount! I'm fixed upon it,
Mount of Thy redeeming love.

O to grace how great a debtor
Daily I'm constrained to be!
Let Thy goodness, like a fetter,
Bind my wandering heart to Thee.
Prone to wander, Lord, I feel it,
Prone to leave the God I love;
Here's my heart, O take and seal it,
Seal it for Thy courts above.

All my springs are in You.

—Psalm 87:7

Love Lifted Me

This rousing old gospel song was jointly composed by James Rowe and Howard E. Smith. Rowe's daughter later recalled, "Howard E. Smith was a little man whose hands were so knotted with arthritis that you would wonder how he could use them at all, much less play the piano. . . . I can see them now, my father striding up and down humming a bar or two, and Howard E. playing it and jotting it down. Thus was 'Love Lifted Me' composed. That was in Saugatuck, Connecticut, a good many years ago." The year was 1912, and the song was purchased and copyrighted by Charlie D. Tillman. On **May 25, 1915,** Tillman sold the copyright to Robert H. Coleman for $100, and later that year it was published in Coleman's songbook *The Herald*.

I was sinking deep in sin, far from the peaceful shore,
Very deeply stained within, sinking to rise no more;
But the Master of the sea, heard my despairing cry,
From the waters lifted me, now safe am I.

All my heart to Him I give, ever to Him I'll cling,
In His blessèd presence live, ever His praises sing.
Love so mighty and so true, merits my soul's best songs;
Faithful, loving service too, to Him belongs.

Souls in danger, look above, Jesus completely saves;
He will lift you by His love, out of the angry waves.
He's the Master of the sea, billows His will obey,
He your Savior wants to be, be saved today.

Love lifted me! Love lifted me!
When nothing else could help
Love lifted me!
Love lifted me! Love lifted me!
When nothing else could help
Love lifted me!

But Jesus took him by the hand and lifted him up, and he arose.

—Mark 9:27

Jesus, Thy Blood and Righteousness

Several years ago, I rented a car in Berlin and drove to the little town of Herrnhut. There I found the mansion of the famous Count Nicolaus Ludwig von Zinzendorf. It was in shambles, but on a well-tended hillside nearby was Zinzendorf's grave and those of other early Moravians. The story of Zinzendorf's life—his taking in of Christian refugees, founding the settlement of Herrnhut, and launching the modern missions movement—is too long to tell here. But what a story! **May 26, 1700**, is his birthday, so let's remember him today as the author of this hymn. He wrote it in 1739 on board a ship as he traveled home from visiting Moravian mission works in the Caribbean.

Jesus, Thy blood and righteousness
My beauty are, my glorious dress;
'Midst flaming worlds, in these arrayed,
With joy shall I lift up my head.

Lord, I believe Thy precious blood,
Which, at the mercy seat of God,
Forever doth for sinners plead,
For me, e'en for my soul, was shed.

Lord, I believe were sinners more
Than sands upon the ocean shore,
Thou hast for all a ransom paid,
For all a full atonement made.

When from the dust of death I rise
To claim my mansion in the skies,
Ev'n then this shall be all my plea,
Jesus hath lived, hath died, for me.

Jesus . . . who was delivered up because of our offenses,
and was raised because of our justification.

—Romans 4:24–25

He Keeps Me Singing

Luther Burgess Bridgers started preaching as a teenager and enrolled at Asbury College for training. After pastoring several years in Methodist churches, he began holding revivals and evangelistic campaigns. In 1910, he suffered unspeakable tragedy when his wife and three sons perished in a house fire in Harrodsburg, Kentucky. The words and music of this hymn, published that same year, presumably flowed out of Bridgers's recovery from grief. He went on to preach widely throughout the South and across Europe. He remarried in 1914 and spent the rest of his life teaching music and pastoring. Bridgers passed away on **May 27, 1948**.

There's within my heart a melody
Jesus whispers sweet and low,
Fear not, I am with thee, peace, be still,
In all of life's ebb and flow.

All my life was wrecked by sin and strife,
Discord filled my heart with pain,
Jesus swept across the broken strings,
Stirred the slumbering chords again.

Feasting on the riches of His grace,
Resting 'neath His sheltering wing,
Always looking on His smiling face,
That is why I shout and sing.

Jesus, Jesus, Jesus,
Sweetest name I know,
Fills my every longing,
Keeps me singing as I go.

The Lord is my strength and song, and
He has become my salvation.

—Exodus 15:2

Wholly Thine

In researching this book, I've found the *New York Times* archives a rich source of information. For example, an item appeared on October 21, 1916, with the headline: "Mrs. A. S. Hawks Stricken: Famous Hymn Writer Is a Contemporary of Fanny Crosby." The article said that Mrs. Hawks had suffered "ailments incident to old age" and was critically ill. It was over a year later, on January 4, 1918, that her obituary appeared, saying, "Mrs. Annie Sherwood Hawks, author of many famous Gospel hymns, including 'I Need Thee Every Hour,' died at her home here today, in her eighty-fourth year. She had lived here with her daughter . . . a quarter of a century." For the story behind "I Need Thee Every Hour," see the installment for November 20. To commemorate her birthday, **May 28, 1836**, ponder this lesser-known Hawks hymn.

> Thine, most gracious Lord,
> O make me wholly Thine—
> Thine in thought, in word and deed,
> For Thou, O Christ, art mine.
>
> Wholly Thine, my Lord,
> To go when Thou dost call;
> Thine to yield my very self
> In all things, great and small.
>
> Thine, Lord, wholly Thine,
> For ever one with Thee—
> Rooted, grounded in Thy love,
> Abiding, sure and free.
>
> *Wholly Thine, wholly Thine;*
> *Thou hast bought me, I am Thine;*
> *Blessèd Savior, Thou art mine;*
> *Make me wholly Thine.*

I wholly followed the LORD *my God.*

—Joshua 14:8

Safe in Jehovah's Keeping

The old English and German hymns were full of sturdy theology and deep reverence for the majesty and power of the almighty God. When Ira Sankey and Fanny Crosby came along, they introduced a new kind of church music by relaxing the melodies, adding choruses, lightening the messages, and calling them gospel songs. This didn't go over well with everyone. Robert Anderson, for example, thought Crosby's song "Safe in the Arms of Jesus" was "reeking with mere sentiment." He offered his own substitute (see below), and now we have two great hymns!

Anderson was born in Dublin, Ireland, on **May 29, 1841**. He was a noted Christian author, but perhaps his greatest claim to fame was working for Scotland Yard at the time Jack the Ripper was terrorizing London.

Safe in Jehovah's keeping, led by His glorious arm,
God is Himself my refuge, a present help from harm.
Fears may at times distress me, griefs may my soul annoy;
God is my strength and portion, God my exceeding joy.

Safe in Jehovah's keeping, safe in temptation's hour,
Safe in the midst of perils, kept by Almighty power.
Safe when the tempest rages, safe though the night be long;
E'en when my sky is darkest, God is my strength and song.

Safe in Jehovah's keeping,
Led by His glorious arm,
God is Himself my refuge,
A present help from harm.

The fear of man brings a snare, but whoever
trusts in the LORD shall be safe.

—Proverbs 29:25

Praise to the Lord

⁎

The author of this great creation hymn was born on **May 30, 1650**. Though he lived only thirty years, Joachim Neander served faithfully as an endearing pastor and as the author of sixty hymns. In his spare time, he loved to hike through a beautiful valley near Düsseldorf, and after his untimely death from tuberculosis, this valley (or *thal* in German) was named for him—Neander-thal. Ironically, many years later the skeletal remains of an early race of humans were found here and dubbed "Neanderthal man." The discovery gave a temporary boost to supporters of human evolution. How odd that the name of the writer of one of our greatest creation hymns should be attached to a theory he never would have supported.

> Praise to the Lord, the Almighty, the King of creation!
> O my soul, praise Him, for He is thy health and salvation!
> All ye who hear, now to His temple draw near;
> Praise Him in glad adoration.
>
> Praise to the Lord, who o'er all things so wondrously reigneth,
> Shelters thee under His wings, yea, so gently sustaineth!
> Hast thou not seen how thy desires e'er have been
> Granted in what He ordaineth?
>
> Praise to the Lord, O let all that is in me adore Him!
> All that hath life and breath, come now with praises before Him.
> Let the amen sound from His people again,
> Gladly for aye we adore Him.

Praise the Lord! For it is good to sing praises to our God; for it is pleasant, and praise is beautiful.

—Psalm 147:1

O Thou, My Soul

Today is the anniversary of the sermon that launched the modern missionary movement. On **May 31, 1792**, William Carey, a cobbler in England, preached at a Baptist meeting in Nottingham, urging his colleagues to "expect great things from God" and to "attempt great things for God." Carey later sailed for India, becoming the Father of Modern Missions. For seven hard years, he labored without seeing any conversions. Then, in December of 1800, a Hindu man named Krishnu, a carpenter, came to Christ. From his baptism on the last Sunday of 1800 until his death by cholera in 1822, Krishnu Pal served the Lord faithfully. He even wrote a hymn that was widely used around the world—the life-hymn of the first convert of modern missions.

O thou, my soul, forget no more
The Friend who all thy sorrows bore;
Let every idol be forgot;
But, O my soul, forget Him not.

Renounce thy works and ways, with grief,
And fly to this divine relief;
Nor Him forget, who left His throne,
And for thy life gave up His own.

Eternal truth and mercy shine
In Him, and He Himself is thine;
And canst thou, then, with sin beset,
Such charms, such matchless charms, forget?

Oh, no; till life itself depart,
His name shall cheer and warm my heart;
And lisping this, from earth I'll rise,
And join the chorus in the skies.

Bless the LORD, O my soul, and forget not all His benefits.

—Psalm 103:2

I Am Resolved

Let's renew our acquaintance with the word *resolved*. Except for New Year's resolutions, we seldom use this term in daily speech. But being *resolute* means being determined, bold, steady, faithful, and undeterred. That's a good description of James Henry Fillmore, whose birthday we celebrate today (**June 1, 1849**). As a young man he left medical school to become a traveling evangelist, and along the way he wrote gospel songs. On one occasion he wrote a song for the Christian Endeavor Society. He was pleased with the music but later wanted stronger words—words that spoke of our resolution to Christ. His friend Palmer Hartsough wrote the words of "I Am Resolved," fitting them perfectly into Fillmore's music.

I am resolved no longer to linger,
Charmed by the world's delight,
Things that are higher, things that are nobler,
These have allured my sight.

I am resolved to follow the Savior,
Faithful and true each day;
Heed what He sayeth, do what He willeth,
He is the living Way.

I am resolved, and who will go with me?
Come, friends, without delay,
Taught by the Bible, led by the Spirit,
We'll walk the heav'nly way.

I will hasten to Him, hasten so glad and free;
Jesus, greatest, highest, I will come to Thee.
I will hasten, hasten to Him, hasten so glad and free;
Jesus, Jesus, greatest, highest, I will come to Thee.

But Daniel resolved not to defile himself.

—Daniel 1:8 NIV

Ardent Hope of Heavenly Rest

If you thumb through an old hymnal, one published 150 or 200 years ago, you'll likely find an entire section devoted to hymns celebrating the "Christian Sabbath"—Sunday as a day of rest and worship. The first day of the week was a hallowed day to earlier generations, and it was considered a symbol or "type" of heaven—a period of rest, worship, and simple pleasures. Rev. Philip Doddridge, noted pastor and hymnist, preached on this subject on **June 2, 1736**, using as his text Hebrews 4:9. At the close of the sermon he introduced this hymn to be sung. The first verse began, "Lord of the Sabbath, hear our vows" and described the grateful sacrifice of congregational singing. With verse 2, Doddridge got down to his main theme:

Thine earthly Sabbaths, Lord, we love;
But there's a nobler rest above;
To that our laboring souls aspire
With ardent hope and strong desire.

No more fatigue, no more distress
Nor sin nor hell shall reach the place;
No sighs shall mingle with the songs,
Which rise up from immortal tongues.

No rude alarms of raging foes,
No cares to break the long repose;
No midnight shade, no clouded sun,
But sacred, high, eternal noon.

O long-expected day, begin!
Dawn on these realms of woe and sin:
Fain would we leave this weary road,
And sleep in death, to rest with God.

There remains therefore a rest for the people of God.

—Hebrews 4:9

Like a River Glorious

I have long collected clippings, books, hymns, and stories about the effervescent British personality and musician Frances Ridley Havergal. She was only forty-two when she fell ill and died on **June 3, 1879**, and her deathbed scene was remarkable. At one point, she rallied and asked the doctors, "What is the element of danger?" They replied, "You are seriously ill." She said, "I thought so, but if I am going, it is too good to be true!" Later she smiled at her sister and said, "Splendid to be so near the gates of heaven!" When someone in the room quoted Isaiah 41:10 to her incorrectly, she whispered it correctly, and then said, "I am lost in amazement! There hath not failed one word of all His good promises!" Her last word was the first note of a hymn: "He . . . !" Then her face lit up with wonder and she passed to heaven. My favorite Havergal hymn is "Like a River Glorious," published three years before her death.

> Like a river glorious is God's perfect peace,
> Over all victorious in its bright increase;
> Perfect, yet it floweth fuller every day,
> Perfect, yet it groweth deeper all the way.
>
> Hidden in the hollow of His blessed hand,
> Never foe can follow, never traitor stand;
> Not a surge of worry, not a shade of care,
> Not a blast of hurry touch the spirit there.
>
> Every joy or trial falleth from above,
> Traced upon our dial by the Sun of Love;
> We may trust Him fully all for us to do.
> They who trust Him wholly find Him wholly true.
>
> *Stayed upon Jehovah, hearts are fully blest*
> *Finding, as He promised, perfect peace and rest.*

Thus says the LORD: "Behold, I will extend peace to her like a river."

—Isaiah 66:12

Jesus Paid It All

Maybe it was just a boring sermon. For whatever reason, Elvina M. Hall (born **June 4, 1820**) wasn't listening to the preacher. She was sitting up with the choir of the Monument Street Methodist Church in Baltimore, Maryland, composing the words of this hymn and scribbling them onto the flyleaf of the church hymnal. Afterward her choir director, a Baltimore coal merchant named John Grape, saw the words and wrote the music for them. It was first published in 1874 in Philip Bliss's *Gospel Song Book Collection*. Somehow I don't think Elvina's pastor minded that her mind wandered that day.

> I hear the Savior say,
> "Thy strength indeed is small;
> Child of weakness, watch and pray,
> Find in Me thine all in all."
>
> For nothing good have I
> Whereby Thy grace to claim,
> I'll wash my garments white
> In the blood of Calv'ry's Lamb.
>
> And now complete in Him
> My robe His righteousness,
> Close sheltered 'neath His side,
> I am divinely blest.
>
> *Jesus paid it all,*
> *All to Him I owe;*
> *Sin had left a crimson stain,*
> *He washed it white as snow.*

For the wages of sin is death, but the gift of God is eternal life in Christ Jesus our Lord.

—Romans 6:23

The Day Is Past and Gone

It's wonderful to go to bed at night with the Lord protecting us as we sleep. Once during the Civil War, a woman was caught in the Battle of Vicksburg. Fighting raged around her, and a shell struck her house. Her diary entry from **June 5, 1863**, says: "The candles were useless in the dense smoke, and it was many minutes before we could see. Then we found the entire side of the room torn out. The soldiers . . . assisted (us) to board up the breaks with planks to keep out prowlers, and we went to bed in the cellar. . . . This morning the yard is partially ploughed by a couple (of shells) that fell there in the night. . . . As we descend at night to the lower regions, I think of the evening hymn that grandmother taught me when a child: *Lord, keep us safe this night, secure from all our fears; May angels guard us while we sleep, till morning light appears.*" That hymn, "The Day Is Past and Gone," was penned by a Massachusetts hymnist and Baptist preacher named John Leland.*

> The day is past and gone;
> The evening shades appear;
> Oh, may I ever keep in mind,
> The night of death draws near!
>
> Lord, keep me safe this night,
> Secure from all my fears;
> May angels guard me while I sleep,
> Till morning light appears.
>
> And when I early rise,
> To view the unwearied sun,
> May I set out to win the prize,
> And after glory run.

I lay down and slept; I awoke, for the LORD sustained me.

—Psalm 3:5

---

* The identity of this female Civil War diarist is questionable. The journal entry appeared anonymously under the title "A Woman's Diary of the Siege of Vicksburg" in *The Century Illustrated Monthly Magazine—May 1885 to October 1885*, Vol. XXX (New York: The Century Company, 1885), 772.

O Love That Will Not Let Me Go

With regard to today's hymn, George Matheson, the blind Scottish hymnist and pastor, wrote, "My hymn was composed in the manse of Innelan on the evening of the **6th of June, 1882**, when I was 40 years of age. I was alone in the manse at that time. It was the night of my sister's marriage, and the rest of the family were staying overnight in Glasgow. Something happened to me, which was known only to myself, and which caused me the most severe mental suffering. The hymn was the fruit of that suffering. It was the quickest bit of work I ever did in my life. I had the impression of having it dictated to me by some inward voice rather than of working it out myself. I am quite sure that the whole work was completed in five minutes, and equally sure that it never received at my hands any retouching or correction."

O Love that will not let me go,
I rest my weary soul in thee;
I give thee back the life I owe,
That in thine ocean depths its flow
May richer, fuller be.

O Light that followest all my way,
I yield my flickering torch to thee;
My heart restores its borrowed ray,
That in thy sunshine's blaze its day
May brighter, fairer be.

O Cross that liftest up my head,
I dare not ask to fly from thee;
I lay in dust life's glory dead,
And from the ground there blossoms red
Life that shall endless be.

Behold what manner of love the Father has bestowed on us, that we should be called children of God!

—1 John 3:1

The Old Rugged Cross

When asked how he came to write this classic hymn, Rev. George Bennard explained that he had been praying for "a full understanding of the cross" and had spent many hours studying this subject in the Bible. "I saw the Christ of the cross as if I were seeing John 3:16 leave the printed page, take form, and act out the meaning of redemption," he said. From his study, he composed both words and music to this hymn as he traveled through the Midwest on preaching assignments. On the evening of **June 7, 1913**, while preaching in Pokagon, Michigan, Rev. Bennard introduced his hymn and it was first sung. The five-voice choir was composed of Frank Virgil, Olive Marrs, Clara Virgil, William Thaldorf, and Florence Jones (who was also the organist).

On a hill far away stood an old rugged cross,
The emblem of suffering and shame;
And I love that old cross where the dearest and best
For a world of lost sinners was slain.

O that old rugged cross, so despised by the world,
Has a wondrous attraction for me;
For the dear Lamb of God left His glory above
To bear it to dark Calvary.

To the old rugged cross I will ever be true;
Its shame and reproach gladly bear;
Then He'll call me some day to my home far away,
Where His glory forever I'll share.

So I'll cherish the old rugged cross,
Till my trophies at last I lay down;
I will cling to the old rugged cross,
And exchange it some day for a crown.

He was crucified in weakness, yet He lives by the power of God.

—2 Corinthians 13:4

How Firm a Foundation

I live near President Andrew Jackson's home, the Hermitage, and I've found his life an interesting study. Jackson's wife, Rachael, a dedicated Christian, died before he assumed the presidency. Jackson himself wasn't converted until he retired from office, but afterward he developed a love for hymns, especially "How Firm a Foundation." In June of 1845, being very weak, he was laid in his bed at the Hermitage. His daughter-in-law, Sarah Jackson, sat through the night with him, her candle casting restless shadows on his face. She noticed his lips moving, and bending near she heard him repeating the words of this hymn: "When through the deep waters I call thee to go. . . ." Shortly afterward, Jackson died quietly on **June 8, 1845**.

How firm a foundation, ye saints of the Lord,
Is laid for your faith in His excellent Word!
What more can He say than to you He hath said,
You, who unto Jesus for refuge have fled?

In every condition, in sickness, in health;
In poverty's vale, or abounding in wealth;
At home and abroad, on the land, on the sea,
As thy days may demand, shall thy strength ever be.

When through the deep waters I call thee to go,
The rivers of woe shall not thee overflow;
For I will be with thee, thy troubles to bless,
And sanctify to thee thy deepest distress.

The soul that on Jesus has leaned for repose,
I will not, I will not desert to its foes;
That soul, though all hell should endeavor to shake,
I'll never, no never, no never forsake.

When you pass through the waters, I will be with you; and through the rivers, they shall not overflow you.

—Isaiah 43:2

Great Is Thy Faithfulness

On **June 9, 1955**, Thomas O. Chisholm, the author of "Great Is Thy Faithfulness," wrote to William J. Reynolds, the noted church music historian, about his famous hymn. "There is no circumstantial background for 'Great Is Thy Faithfulness,'" wrote Chisholm. "I sent it, with a number of lyrics to Rev. W. M. Runyan and he used several, among them this one. This was in 1923, and I was then living in Vineland, New Jersey. It went rather slowly for several years, but was taken up by Dr. Houghton, then president of Moody Bible Institute, and began its wider usefulness there." It has since become one of the most loved hymns in Christendom.*

Great is Thy faithfulness, O God my Father;
There is no shadow of turning with Thee;
Thou changest not, Thy compassions, they fail not;
As Thou hast been, Thou forever wilt be.

Summer and winter and springtime and harvest,
Sun, moon and stars in their courses above
Join with all nature in manifold witness
To Thy great faithfulness, mercy and love.

Pardon for sin and a peace that endureth
Thine own dear presence to cheer and to guide;
Strength for today and bright hope for tomorrow,
Blessings all mine, with ten thousand beside!

Great is Thy faithfulness!
Great is Thy faithfulness!
Morning by morning new mercies I see.
All I have needed Thy hand hath provided;
Great is Thy faithfulness, Lord, unto me!

> *The LORD's mercies . . . are new every*
> *morning; great is Your faithfulness.*
>
> —Lamentations 3:22–23

---

* William J. Reynolds, *Companion to Baptist Hymnal* (Nashville: Broadman Press, 1976), 80.

Count Your Blessings

Mr. E. O. (Edwin Othello) Excell was a highly productive soloist, music director, composer, and publisher of hymns and gospel songs. He worked widely with the best-known evangelists of his day, including Sam Jones, Wilbur Chapman, and Gipsy Smith. He compiled about ninety songbooks and wrote the words or composed the music to about two thousand hymns. He was described as a big and robust man with a remarkable range of voice, and seemed happiest when leading mass choirs and audiences at large evangelistic rallies. He is best remembered today for the perky tune to the song "Count Your Blessings." Excell was assisting Gipsy Smith with a campaign in Louisville, Kentucky, when he became ill. He made it home to Chicago and died on **June 10, 1921**, at the age of sixty-nine.

When upon life's billows you are tempest tossed,
When you are discouraged, thinking all is lost,
Count your many blessings, name them one by one,
And it will surprise you what the Lord hath done.

Are you ever burdened with a load of care?
Does the cross seem heavy you are called to bear?
Count your many blessings, every doubt will fly,
And you will keep singing as the days go by.

So, amid the conflict whether great or small,
Do not be disheartened, God is over all;
Count your many blessings, angels will attend,
Help and comfort give you to your journey's end.

Count your blessings, name them one by one,
Count your blessings, see what God hath done!
Count your blessings, name them one by one,
And it will surprise you what the Lord hath done.

From the fullness of his grace we have all
received one blessing after another.

—John 1:16 NIV

The Benedicite

Among the heroes honored in England's famed Westminster Abbey is the Arctic explorer and devout Christian Sir John Franklin. On May 18, 1845, Franklin led Sunday services aboard his ships, and the following day he sailed down the River Thames and out to sea, hoping to complete discovery of the Northwest Passage. His two ships were spotted by a whaling vessel in July, but then they vanished off the face of the earth and were never seen again. Later excavations revealed that Franklin and his men were hemmed in by thick ice, and that Franklin died on **June 11, 1847**. His men abandoned their ships and tried to walk toward a Hudson Bay Company post, but they dropped dead as they walked. On Franklin's monument at Westminster Abbey are inscribed the words of an ancient hymn known as "The Benedicite." Here is a portion of the English version, as found in the Book of Common Prayer:

O ye Frost and Cold, bless ye the Lord;
Praise Him, and magnify Him forever.
O ye Ice and Snow, bless ye the Lord;
Praise Him, and magnify Him forever.
O ye Nights and Days, bless ye the Lord;
Praise Him, and magnify Him forever.
O ye Light and Darkness, bless ye the Lord;
Praise Him, and magnify Him forever. . . .
O all ye Beasts and Cattle, bless ye the Lord;
Praise Him, and magnify Him forever.
O ye Children of Men, bless ye the Lord;
Praise Him, and magnify Him forever.
O let Israel bless the Lord;
Praise Him and magnify Him forever. . . .
O ye Servants of the Lord, bless ye the Lord;
Praise Him, and magnify Him forever.

All Your works shall praise You, O LORD,
and Your saints shall bless You.

—Psalm 145:10

Trust and Obey

To be happy in Jesus, we must trust Him fully and obey Him totally. That's the message of this 1887 hymn by Presbyterian pastor John Sammis. Sammis, an Indiana businessman-turned-preacher, moved to Los Angeles in 1909 to teach at Bible Institute of Los Angeles (BIOLA). After a decade of fruitful ministry, he passed away there on **June 12, 1919**.

> When we walk with the Lord in the light of His Word,
> What a glory He sheds on our way!
> While we do His good will, He abides with us still,
> And with all who will trust and obey.
>
> Not a shadow can rise, not a cloud in the skies,
> But His smile quickly drives it away;
> Not a doubt or a fear, not a sigh or a tear,
> Can abide while we trust and obey.
>
> Not a burden we bear, not a sorrow we share,
> But our toil He doth richly repay;
> Not a grief or a loss, not a frown or a cross,
> But is blessed if we trust and obey.
>
> But we never can prove the delights of His love
> Until all on the altar we lay;
> For the favor He shows and the joy He bestows
> Are for them who will trust and obey.
>
> *Trust and obey, for there's no other way*
> *To be happy in Jesus, but to trust and obey.*

LORD, we show our trust in you by obeying your laws; our heart's desire is to glorify your name.

—Isaiah 26:8 NLT

O Happy Day

Perhaps you've heard "Oh Happy Day" in the movie *Sister Act 2* or in another of the many movies or TV shows that have featured it. As one of the most popular gospel songs of the 1970s, it's had a lot of airplay. It's based on the eighteenth-century hymn "O Happy Day" written by Philip Doddridge, which he based on Acts 8:35. The traditional music was composed in 1854 by Edward F. Rimbault, a London church organist who was born **June 13, 1816**. The newer version is more exciting, but I still love Rimbault's familiar notes that accompany the refrain: "Happy day, Happy day, when Jesus washed my sins away! / He taught me how to watch and pray, and live rejoicing every day."

> O happy day that fixed my choice
> On Thee, my Savior and my God!
> Well may this glowing heart rejoice,
> And tell its raptures all abroad.
>
> 'Tis done: the great transaction's done!
> I am the Lord's and He is mine;
> He drew me, and I followed on;
> Charmed to confess the voice divine.
>
> High heaven, that heard the solemn vow,
> That vow renewed shall daily hear,
> Till in life's latest hour I bow
> And bless in death a bond so dear.
>
> *Happy day, happy day, when Jesus washed my sins away!*
> *He taught me how to watch and pray, and live rejoicing every*
>   *day;*
> *Happy day, happy day, when Jesus washed my sins away!*

We had to celebrate this happy day. For your brother was dead and has come back to life! He was lost, but now he is found!

—Luke 15:32 NLT

What Child Is This?

The psalmist once confessed, "It is good for me that I have been afflicted, that I may learn Your statutes" (Ps. 119:71). William Chatterton Dix concurred with that testimony. He was born **June 14, 1837**, in Bristol, England, and grew up to become manager of Maritime Insurance Company in Glasgow. But as a young man, he was struck with a near-fatal illness and spent months in bed. A severe depression set in, but he emerged from it as a hymn writer. He's the author of two famous Christmas carols—"As with Gladness Men of Old" and "What Child Is This?"—which some scholars believe Dix wrote on the same day while on his sickbed.

What Child is this who, laid to rest
On Mary's lap is sleeping?
Whom angels greet with anthems sweet,
While shepherds watch are keeping?
This, this is Christ the King,
Whom shepherds guard and angels sing;
Haste, haste, to bring Him laud,
The Babe, the Son of Mary.

So bring Him incense, gold and myrrh,
Come peasant, king to own Him;
The King of kings salvation brings,
Let loving hearts enthrone Him.
Raise, raise a song on high,
The virgin sings her lullaby.
Joy, joy for Christ is born,
The Babe, the Son of Mary.

He will be great, and will be called the Son of the Highest; and the Lord God will give Him the throne of His father David. And He will reign over the house of Jacob forever.

—Luke 1:32–33

And Can It Be?

Charles Wesley's immortal hymn "And Can It Be" owes much of its power to the emphatic, exultant melody "Sagina," which was composed by Thomas Campbell, a wandering, well-known Scottish poet of the early 1800s. When Campbell fell ill in Boulogne, France, friends rushed to his deathbed. "Visits of angels from heaven," he said as they entered his room. For several days, they cared for him and read Scriptures and prayers. Finally one of them shared the gospel and asked, "Do you believe all this?" "Oh yes!" said Campbell with emphasis, "I do!" At 4:15 p.m., on Saturday, **June 15, 1844**, he passed away. His body was taken to London and buried in Westminster Abbey. "Sagina" is from *Bouquet*, Campbell's book of twenty-three hymn tunes.

And can it be that I should gain
An interest in the Savior's blood?
Died He for me, who caused His pain—
For me, who Him to death pursued?
Amazing love! How can it be,
That Thou, my God, shouldst die for me?
Amazing love! How can it be,
That Thou, my God, shouldst die for me?

Long my imprisoned spirit lay,
Fast bound in sin and nature's night;
Thine eye diffused a quickening ray—
I woke, the dungeon flamed with light;
My chains fell off, my heart was free,
I rose, went forth, and followed Thee.
My chains fell off, my heart was free,
I rose, went forth, and followed Thee.

*He brought them out of darkness and the shadow
of death, and broke their chains in pieces.*

—Psalm 107:14

Lead, Kindly Light

While John Henry Newman was traveling in Europe in 1833, he fell ill in the unbearably hot weather and developed Sicilian fever. Wanting to return to his native England, he booked passage on a boat carrying a load of oranges, but it became stranded by quiet winds, and for days Newman fretted and suffered. On **June 16, 1833**, while anchored in the straits of Bonifazio between Corsica and Sardinia, he penned this great hymn of guidance. It's a prayer for any of us who occasionally become stranded in life.

Lead, kindly Light, amid th'encircling gloom, lead Thou me on!
The night is dark, and I am far from home; lead Thou me on!
Keep Thou my feet; I do not ask to see
The distant scene; one step enough for me.

I was not ever thus, nor prayed that Thou shouldst lead me on;
I loved to choose and see my path; but now lead Thou me on!
I loved the garish day, and, spite of fears,
Pride ruled my will. Remember not past years!

So long Thy power hath blest me, sure it still will lead me on.
O'er moor and fen, o'er crag and torrent, till the night is gone,
And with the morn those angel faces smile, which I
Have loved long since, and lost awhile!

Meantime, along the narrow rugged path, Thyself hast trod,
Lead, Savior, lead me home in childlike faith, home to my God.
To rest forever after earthly strife
In the calm light of everlasting life.

Oh, send out Your light and Your truth! Let them lead me; let them bring me to Your holy hill.

—Psalm 43:3

One Day

Dr. J. Wilbur Chapman, a Presbyterian pastor and evangelist, was born **June 17, 1859,** and died on Christmas Day 1918. During a gospel service conducted by D. L. Moody, Chapman remained behind for counseling. Moody himself sat down beside him and, using John 5:24, led him to faith in Christ. Chapman later teamed up with musician Charles M. Alexander, and the two men became the first duo to travel completely around the globe in evangelistic campaigns.

In addition to "One Day," Chapman wrote the uplifting gospel song "Jesus, What a Friend for Sinners" (see January 14).

One day when heaven was filled with His praises,
One day when sin was as black as could be,
Jesus came forth to be born of a virgin,
Dwelt among men, my example is He!

One day they led Him up Calvary's mountain,
One day they nailed Him to die on the tree;
Suffering anguish, despised and rejected:
Bearing our sins, my Redeemer is He!

One day the trumpet will sound for His coming,
One day the skies with His glories will shine;
Wonderful day, my belovèd ones bringing;
Glorious Savior, this Jesus is mine!

Living, He loved me; dying, He saved me;
Buried, He carried my sins far away;
Rising, He justified freely forever;
One day He's coming—O glorious day!

Most assuredly, I say to you, he who hears My words and believes in Him who sent Me has everlasting life, and shall not come into judgment, but has passed from death into life.

—John 5:24

Beneath the Cross of Jesus

Psalm 34:5 says, "They looked to Him and were radiant." That perfectly describes Elizabeth Clephane, who was born into the home of a Scottish sheriff and his wife on **June 18, 1830**. Though her life was short (she died at age thirty-nine) and her health fragile, she was known locally as the Sunbeam. Her eyes took in every need, and she was often found ministering cheerfully to the sick, distressed, and needy. Her secret is found in the words of this hymn: "I ask no other sunshine than the sunshine of His face." Elizabeth wrote "Beneath the Cross of Jesus" about a year before her death, and it was published posthumously, as was her other poem that later became a famous gospel song, "The Ninety and Nine."

Beneath the cross of Jesus I fain would take my stand,
The shadow of a mighty rock within a weary land;
A home within the wilderness, a rest upon the way,
From the burning of the noontide heat, and the burden of the
     day.

Upon that cross of Jesus mine eye at times can see
The very dying form of One who suffered there for me;
And from my stricken heart with tears two wonders I confess—
The wonders of redeeming love and my unworthiness.

I take, O cross, thy shadow for my abiding place;
I ask no other sunshine than the sunshine of His face;
Content to let the world go by to know no gain nor loss,
My sinful self my only shame, my glory all the cross.

Now it was about the sixth hour, and there was darkness over all the earth until the ninth hour. Then the sun was darkened, and the veil of the temple was torn in two. And when Jesus had cried out with a loud voice, He said, "Father, 'into Your hands I commit My spirit.'"

—Luke 23:44–46

Servants of God, His Praise Proclaim

James Montgomery's story is worthy of a Dickens novel. After his birth in Scotland, his parents left him in school while they set off as missionaries to the West Indies, never to be heard from again. The lad ran away from school, and as a teenager he worked in a bakery for eighteen months, from January 1788 until **June 19, 1789**. He did little work, preferring to spend his time writing poetry—including this great hymn, which was based on Psalm 113. Later, he wandered into London and tried to sell his poems. Montgomery ended up as a journalist who was occasionally imprisoned because of his outspoken views. In the end, he became a zealous believer, a great advocate for Christian missions, and the author of four hundred hymns, including the Christmas carol "Angels from the Realms of Glory."

Servants of God, in joyful lays,
Sing ye the Lord Jehovah's praise;
His glorious name let all adore,
From age to age, forevermore.

Blest be that name, supremely blest,
From the sun's rising to its rest;
Above the heav'ns His pow'r is known,
Through all the earth His goodness shown.

Who is like God, so great, so high,
He bows Himself to view the sky;
And yet, with condescending grace,
Looks down upon the human race.

O then, aloud, in joyful lays,
Sing to the Lord Jehovah's praise;
His saving name let all adore,
From age to age, forevermore.

Praise the LORD! Praise, O servants of the LORD, praise the name of the LORD!

—Psalm 113:1

Savior, Like a Shepherd Lead Us

Sometimes the words of a hymn can express our prayers better than anything else. At critical times in my life when I've needed guidance, I've found myself quietly singing this hymn, and it's a favorite of mine. Sometimes when worried about my children, I've prayed it for them by changing the pronouns—"Savior, like a shepherd lead *them*, much *they* need Thy tender care." Little is known about the apparent author of these words, Dorothy Thrupp. She was born **June 20, 1779**, in London, and died in the same city in 1847. She compiled several hymnbooks for children. "Savior, Like a Shepherd Lead Us" appeared unsigned in her *Hymns for the Young*, published in 1836.

Savior, like a shepherd lead us, much we need Thy tender care;
In Thy pleasant pastures feed us, for our use Thy folds prepare.
Blessèd Jesus, blessèd Jesus! Thou hast bought us, Thine we are.
Blessèd Jesus, blessèd Jesus! Thou hast bought us, Thine we are.

We are Thine, Thou dost befriend us, be the guardian of our
way;
Keep Thy flock, from sin defend us, seek us when we go astray.
Blessèd Jesus, blessèd Jesus! Hear, O hear us when we pray.
Blessèd Jesus, blessèd Jesus! Hear, O hear us when we pray.

Thou hast promised to receive us, poor and sinful though we
be;
Thou hast mercy to relieve us, grace to cleanse and power to
free.
Blessèd Jesus, blessèd Jesus! We will early turn to Thee.
Blessèd Jesus, blessèd Jesus! We will early turn to Thee.

Early let us seek Thy favor, early let us do Thy will;
Blessèd Lord and only Savior, with Thy love our bosoms fill.
Blessèd Jesus, blessèd Jesus! Thou hast loved us, love us still.
Blessèd Jesus, blessèd Jesus! Thou hast loved us, love us still.

---

*I am the good shepherd; and I know My
sheep, and am known by My own.*

—John 10:14

Open My Eyes That I May See

On **June 21, 1897**, Clara Scott was returning home after a funeral service when a strap broke on her carriage. The horse bolted and the buggy careened down the street with accelerating speed. Clara was thrown from the carriage and killed, but she left behind this wonderful hymn. It's an interesting lesson on the mysterious ways of the Lord. None of us knows what may befall us from hour to hour. The Lord alone knows the length of our days. As long as He keeps us on earth, we need to have open eyes to study His Word, open ears to hear His voice, and open mouths to share His gospel. Let's consider this a hymn of rededication and aspiration to serve the Lord faithfully until He calls us home.

Open my eyes, that I may see
Glimpses of truth Thou hast for me;
Place in my hands the wonderful key
That shall unclasp and set me free.

Open my ears, that I may hear
Voices of truth Thou sendest clear;
And while the wave notes fall on my ear,
Everything false will disappear.

Open my mouth, and let me bear,
Gladly the warm truth everywhere;
Open my heart and let me prepare
Love with Thy children thus to share.

Silently now I wait for Thee,
Ready my God, Thy will to see,
Open my eyes, illumine me,
Spirit divine!

Open my eyes, that I may see wondrous things from Your law.

—Psalm 119:18

I Am Coming to the Cross

With regard to today's hymn, its author, William McDonald, wrote: "The hymn was written in 1870 in the city of Brooklyn, New York, while I was pastor in that city. I had felt the need of a hymn to aid seekers of heart purity while at the altar. I had desired something simple in expression, true to experience, and ending in the fullness of love. . . . As I was sitting in my study one day, the line of thought came rushing into my mind, and I began to write, and in a few minutes the hymn was on paper. It was first sung at a National Camp Meeting, being held in Hamilton, Mass., **June 22, 1870**. It has been translated into many languages and sung all around the globe."

I am coming to the cross;
I am poor and weak and blind;
I am counting all but dross;
I shall full salvation find.

Long my heart has sighed for Thee;
Long has evil reigned within;
Jesus sweetly speaks to me:
"I will cleanse you from all sin."

Here I give my all to Thee:
Friends and time and earthly store;
Soul and body Thine to be,
Wholly Thine forevermore.

I am trusting, Lord, in Thee.
Blessèd Lamb of Calvary;
Humbly at Thy cross I bow.
Save me, Jesus, save me now.

I . . . count all things loss for the excellence of the knowledge of Christ Jesus my Lord, for whom I have suffered the loss of all things, and count them as rubbish, that I may gain Christ.

—Philippians 3:8

Work for the Night Is Coming

The French mystic François Fénelon said, "Cheered by the presence of God, I will do at each moment, without anxiety, according to the strength which He shall give me, the work that His Providence assigns me. I will leave the rest without concern; it is not my affair. I ought to consider the duty to which I am called each day, as the work that God has given me to do." That was the attitude of Anna Walker Coghill, who was born on **June 23, 1836**, in Kiddermore, England. She wrote "Work for the Night Is Coming" when she was only eighteen. Later when it was set to music by the celebrated composer Lowell Mason, she complained loudly that he had altered some of her words to fit his music. Nevertheless, Anna spent the rest of her life living out her song—working for Jesus "through the morning hours," "through the sunny noon," and "every flying moment."

> Work, for the night is coming,
> Work through the morning hours;
> Work while the dew is sparkling,
> Work 'mid springing flowers;
> Work when the day grows brighter,
> Work in the glowing sun;
> Work, for the night is coming,
> When man's work is done.
>
> Work, for the night is coming,
> Work through the sunny noon;
> Fill brightest hours with labor,
> Rest comes sure and soon.
> Give every flying minute,
> Something to keep in store;
> Work, for the night is coming,
> When man works no more.

I must work the works of Him who sent Me while it is day; the night is coming when no one can work.

—John 9:4

Holy Bible, Book Divine

Originally written as a children's hymn, this song has been sung churchwide for two hundred years. Its author, John Burton, was an English Baptist layman who became involved in children's ministry and Sunday school work. He wrote many poems and hymns for children, and published several books with youngsters in mind. "Holy Bible, Book Divine" first appeared in the *Evangelical Magazine* in 1805, and Burton's son, born in 1808, later shared that his father taught him this hymn before he was even able to read. John Burton died on **June 24, 1822**.

> Holy Bible, Book divine,
> Precious treasure, thou art mine;
> Mine to tell me whence I came;
> Mine to teach me what I am.
>
> Mine to chide me when I rove;
> Mine to show a Savior's love;
> Mine thou art to guide and guard;
> Mine to punish or reward.
>
> Mine to comfort in distress;
> Suffering in this wilderness;
> Mine to show, by living faith,
> Man can triumph over death.
>
> Mine to tell of joys to come,
> And the rebel sinner's doom;
> O thou Holy Book divine,
> Precious treasure, thou art mine.

*All Scripture is given by inspiration of God,
and is profitable for doctrine, for reproof, for
correction, for instruction in righteousness.*

—2 Timothy 3:16

Jesus, the Very Thought of Thee

Sometimes the very mention of the name "Jesus" is enough to dispel the gloom and break out the sunshine, as this, one of our oldest hymns, tells us. It was written by Saint Bernard, who, on **June 25, 1115**, founded a monastery in the isolated Claire Vallee (Clairvaux) of the Champagne region of France. In teaching and writing, Bernard stressed the Word of God, the role of the Holy Spirit, and the importance of personal knowledge of God through Jesus Christ. He also wrote the hymn "O Sacred Head Now Wounded" (see March 13). Both hymns were translated into English in the mid-1800s, and both take us into the depths of the wonders of Jesus' love.

Jesus, the very thought of Thee
With sweetness fills the breast;
But sweeter far Thy face to see,
And in Thy presence rest.

Nor voice can sing, nor heart can frame,
Nor can the memory find
A sweeter sound than Thy blest name,
O Savior of mankind!

O hope of every contrite heart,
O joy of all the meek,
To those who fall, how kind Thou art!
How good to those who seek!

Jesus, our love and joy to Thee,
The virgin's holy Son,
All might and praise and glory be,
While endless ages run.

We have thought, O God, on Your lovingkindness,
in the midst of Your temple.

—Psalm 48:9

Waiting on the Eve of Labor

Even though it's obscure, I'm including this hymn because it's a great example of how any one of us can compose our own personal hymn or prayer on the eve of great occasions. It was written by Henry F. Colby, a young man in nineteenth-century Massachusetts, and was sung at the graduation of his class at Newton Theological Institution on **June 26, 1867**. The rhyme and rhythm of this poem make it easy to sing or recite, and its words are perfect for those beginning a new chapter in life or a new work for God. This hymn is included in *Baptist Hymn Writers and Their Hymns* by Henry S. Burrage, published in Portland, Maine, in 1888. I hope it will inspire you to write out an occasional prayer for God's aid at significant moments in your life.

Waiting on the eve of labor,
Knowing not the coming day,
Bowing at Thy throne, O Savior,
For a blessing, now, we pray.
Thou hast called us by Thy Spirit;
Thou hast brought us to this hour;
Vain will be our best endeavors,
If we lack that Spirit's power.

Stand beside us, gracious Savior;
All Thy promised aid impart;
Place Thine arm of strength around us;
Let us feel Thy beating heart.
Then, when days of toil are over,
When our latest sheaves are bound,
We will cast them all before Thee,
Joying most to see Thee crowned.

And Joshua said to the people, "Sanctify yourselves, for tomorrow the LORD will do wonders among you."

—Joshua 3:5

Shall We Gather at the River?

D. L. Moody and Ira Sankey were arguably the most famous preaching/singing duo in Christian history. They met at a YMCA convention in Indianapolis. Moody was impressed by Sankey's song-leading, and he sent the musician a note asking to meet him the next day on a particular street corner. When Sankey showed up, Moody stood on a soapbox and started preaching. After a crowd gathered, he asked Sankey to sing something while leading the group to a nearby auditorium. Sankey got the group going with "Shall We Gather at the River?" That was **June 27, 1870**, the beginning of a partnership that flooded the world with evangelism and spurred on a new genre of hymns, which we call gospel music.

> Shall we gather at the river,
> Where bright angel feet have trod,
> With its crystal tide forever
> Flowing by the throne of God?
>
> On the margin of the river,
> Washing up its silver spray,
> We will talk and worship ever,
> All the happy golden day.
>
> Soon we'll reach the silver river,
> Soon our pilgrimage will cease;
> Soon our happy hearts will quiver
> With the melody of peace.
>
> *Yes, we'll gather at the river,*
> *The beautiful, the beautiful river;*
> *Gather with the saints at the river*
> *That flows by the throne of God.*

And he showed me a pure river of water of life, clear as crystal, proceeding from the throne of God and of the Lamb.

—Revelation 22:1

My Faith Has Found a Resting Place

Today is the birthday of two great hymnists. Frederick W. Faber, the Roman Catholic author of "Faith of Our Fathers," was born on this day in 1814; and the evangelical poet Eliza Edmunds Hewitt was born on **June 28, 1851**. She became a schoolteacher but developed spinal problems likely due to an attack by an unruly student. For the rest of her life, Eliza suffered disability. That didn't stop the song in her heart, and we remember her for such hymns as "More About Jesus," "Singing I Go," "When We All Get to Heaven," "There Is Sunshine in My Soul Today," and "My Faith Has Found a Resting Place."

> My faith has found a resting place,
> Not in device or creed;
> I trust the ever-living One,
> His wounds for me shall plead.
>
> Enough for me that Jesus saves,
> This ends my fear and doubt;
> A sinful soul I come to Him,
> He'll never cast me out.
>
> My heart is leaning on the Word,
> The living Word of God,
> Salvation by my Savior's name,
> Salvation through His blood.
>
> *I need no other argument,*
> *I need no other plea,*
> *It is enough that Jesus died,*
> *And that He died for me.*

My people will dwell in a peaceful habitation, in secure dwellings, and in quiet resting places.

—Isaiah 32:18

Lord, It Belongs Not to My Care

On **June 29, 1685**, the great English Puritan Richard Baxter, author of the classic *Saints' Everlasting Rest,* was found guilty of unauthorized preaching. He was sentenced to be whipped, which thankfully was not carried out. He was also condemned to prison, and that part of his sentence was enforced. An early biographer said, "He continued in this imprisonment nearly two years, during which he enjoyed more quietness than he had done for many years before." Perhaps Baxter was sustained by his own hymn, which was published four years earlier. Though little known today, it is a deeply meaningful prayer of simple abiding trust in the Father's good will.

Lord, it belongs not to my care
Whether I die or live;
To love and serve Thee is my share,
And this Thy grace must give.

If life be long, I will be glad,
That I may long obey;
If short, yet why should I be sad
To welcome endless day?

Christ leads me through no darker rooms
Than He went through before;
He that unto God's kingdom comes
Must enter by this door.

My knowledge of that life is small,
The eye of faith is dim;
But 'tis enough that Christ knows all,
And I shall be with Him.

For to me, to live is Christ, and to die is gain.

—Philippians 1:21

More Love to Thee, O Christ

Elizabeth Prentiss was a colorful novelist in the 1800s. Her deep Christian faith withstood the tests of personal pressures and tragedies. During the summer of 1856, she vacationed at Ocean House, the family cottage on Cape Elizabeth, Maine. On **June 30, 1856**, she wrote in her journal, "I am finding this solitude and leisure very sweet and precious; God grant that it may bear the rich and abundant fruit it ought to do! Communion with Him is such a blessing, here at home in my own room, and out in the silent woods and on the wayside." According to her husband, George, it was probably at this time Elizabeth wrote "More Love to Thee," although she didn't show him the words for another thirteen years. He encouraged her to publish the words, and they were set to music by Howard Doane in 1870.

> More love to Thee, O Christ, more love to Thee!
> Hear Thou the prayer I make on bended knee.
> This is my earnest plea: More love, O Christ, to Thee;
> More love to Thee, more love to Thee!
>
> Once earthly joy I craved, sought peace and rest;
> Now Thee alone I seek, give what is best.
> This all my prayer shall be: More love, O Christ to Thee;
> More love to Thee, more love to Thee!
>
> Then shall my latest breath whisper Thy praise;
> This be the parting cry my heart shall raise;
> This still its prayer shall be: More love, O Christ to Thee;
> More love to Thee, more love to Thee!

. . . Jesus Christ, whom having not seen you love.

—1 Peter 1:7–8

Flung to the Heedless Winds

It may surprise you to know that for a thousand years the church of the Middle Ages discouraged congregational singing. Most music was performed by priests or choirs. It was Martin Luther who restored the gift of song to God's people and set the churches of Germany singing. Luther's first hymn, "A New Song Here Shall Be Begun," was written after two Augustinian monks, Heinrich Boes and Johann Esch, were burned at the stake in Brussels on **July 1, 1523**, the first to die for the Reformation. Luther, deeply moved, wrote a long hymn when he heard the news, on which the English hymn "Flung to the Heedless Winds" is based. He wrote only thirty-six other hymns, but he inspired other hymnists—so many that by the time of his death nearly one hundred hymnals had appeared. Luther's greatest hymn, of course, is "A Mighty Fortress," but that's a story for October 31.

> Flung to the heedless winds,
> Or on the waters cast,
> The martyrs' ashes, watched,
> Shall be gathered at last;
> And from that scattered dust,
> Around us and abroad,
> Shall spring a plenteous seed
> Of witness for God.
>
> The Father hath received
> Their latest living breath;
> And vain is Satan's boast
> Of victory in their death;
> Still, still, though dead, they speak,
> And trumpet-tongued proclaim,
> To many a wakening land,
> The one availing name.

If anyone desires to come after Me, let him deny himself, and take up his cross daily, and follow Me.

—Luke 9:23

I Surrender All

After William Borden, heir to the Borden fortune, graduated from high school in Chicago, he and a friend spent a year traveling the world. On **July 2, 1905**, he attended meetings in London being held by his own pastor, Dr. R. A. Torrey of Chicago. Dr. Torrey spoke on the subject of assurance of salvation, and Bill was deeply moved. After the sermon, a soloist sang "I Surrender All." With depth of feeling, Bill stood with several others and sang the chorus: "I surrender all; I surrender all. All to Thee, my blessed Savior, I surrender all." He was seventeen years old, but the die was cast. He returned home, gave away vast amounts of his fortune, and prepared for missionary service among the Muslims of China. Though he died of spinal meningitis in Egypt en route to China at age twenty-five, his story has influenced generations of young people for over one hundred years. His life slogan was: "No Reserve. No Retreat. No Regrets."

All to Jesus, I surrender;
All to Him I freely give;
I will ever love and trust Him,
In His presence daily live.

All to Jesus I surrender;
Humbly at His feet I bow,
Worldly pleasures all forsaken;
Take me, Jesus, take me now.

All to Jesus, I surrender;
Lord, I give myself to Thee;
Fill me with Thy love and power;
Let Thy blessing fall on me.

*I surrender all, I surrender all,
All to Thee, my blessed Savior,
I surrender all.*

All on the altar . . .

—Leviticus 1:9

He Lives

One day while conducting evangelistic meetings, Alfred Ackley was confronted by an angry Jewish student who said, "Why should I worship a dead Jew?" Ackley responded, "He lives, I tell you. He is not dead, but lives here and now. Jesus Christ is more alive today than ever before. I can prove it by my own experience, as well as the testimony of countless thousands." The young man eventually became a follower of Christ, and out of the experience, Alfred Ackley wrote this great hymn. Ackley passed away on **July 3, 1960**, in full expectation of the promise of Him who said, "Because I live, you will live also."

I serve a risen Savior; He's in the world today;
I know that He is living whatever men may say;
I see His hand of mercy; I hear His voice of cheer,
And just the time I need Him, He's always near.

Rejoice, rejoice, O Christian, Lift up your voice and sing.
Eternal hallelujahs to Jesus Christ the king!
The hope of all who seek Him, the help of all who find,
None other is so loving, so good and kind.

He lives, He lives, Christ Jesus lives today!
He walks with me and talks with me
Along life's narrow way.
He lives, He lives, salvation to impart!
You ask me how I know He lives?
He lives within my heart.

Do not be afraid, for I know that you seek Jesus who was crucified. He is not here; for He is risen, as He said. Come, see the place where the Lord lay. And go quickly and tell His disciples that He is risen from the dead.

—Matthew 28:5–7

America the Beautiful

"We hired a prairie wagon. Near the top we had to leave the wagon and go the rest of the way on mules. I was very tired. But when I saw the view, I felt great joy. All the wonder of America seemed displayed there, with a sea-like expanse. It was then and there . . . that the opening lines of the hymn floated into my mind." That's how Katherine Lee Bates described being atop Pike's Peak as she began composing "America the Beautiful," which was published by *The Congregationalist* on **July 4, 1895**. As we sing it today, we acknowledge that America's greatness is found in one simple fact: "God shed His grace on Thee."

> O beautiful for spacious skies,
> For amber waves of grain,
> For purple mountain majesties
> Above the fruited plain! . . .
>
> *America! America!*
> *God mend thine ev'ry flaw,*
> *Confirm thy soul in self-control,*
> *Thy liberty in law.*
>
> O beautiful for patriot dream
> That sees beyond the years
> Thine alabaster cities gleam
> Undimmed by human tears.
>
> *America! America!*
> *God shed His grace on thee,*
> *And crown thy good with brotherhood*
> *From sea to shining sea!*

If My people who are called by My name will humble themselves, and pray and seek My face, and turn from their wicked ways, then I will hear from heaven, and will forgive their sin and heal their land.

—2 Chronicles 7:14

Dear Savior, Hear Our Prayer

John Hewes, a prominent Boston printer who was born **July 5, 1803**, prided himself on being a descendant of one of the participants in the Boston Tea Party. He found an even greater heritage when he became a new creature in Christ in 1840. "Since his conversion," said his pastor, "he presented a blameless life and a warm interest in the church, its worship, its activities, and its prosperity. He was strong in his opposition to wrong and oppression, and an earnest advocate of the antislavery movement. He loved the great truths of the Gospel with increasing affection." Hewes became a prayer warrior, and he wrote some earnest hymns of prayer. The words of this one are especially meaningful to those who sometimes "sing their prayers."

> Dear Savior, hear our prayer,—
> We bow before Thy throne;
> O may we find acceptance there,
> And peace before unknown.
>
> Dear Savior, hear our prayer,—
> O turn not Thou away;
> For in temptation's fearful hour
> Thou art our only stay.
>
> Dear Savior, hear our prayer,—
> No other power but Thine
> Can fill our souls with heavenly joy,
> With rays of light divine.
>
> Dear Savior, hear our prayer,—
> On Thee alone we call;
> O keep our feet in wisdom's way
> That we may never fall.

Hear my prayer, O LORD, give ear to my supplications! In Your faithfulness answer me.

—Psalm 143:1

Glory Be to God the Father

I want to introduce you to a "new" hymn that you can sing at your church Sunday. It's not so new; the words by Horatius Bonar go back to 1866. And the tune, "Regent Square," was composed by the London organist Henry Smart, whose death on **July 6, 1879,** is commemorated on a broken tombstone in London's Hampstead Cemetery. You already know the exuberant melody from the Christmas carol "Angels from the Realms of Glory." Now see how wonderfully Bonar's high-spirited words of Trinitarian praise fit this tune and lift our hearts in praise.

Glory be to God the Father,
Glory be to God the Son,
Glory be to God the Spirit,
Great Jehovah, Three in One!
Glory, glory, glory, glory,
While eternal ages run!

Glory be to Him Who loved us,
Washed us from each spot and stain!
Glory be to Him Who bought us,
Made us kings with Him to reign!
Glory, glory, glory, glory,
To the Lamb that once was slain!

"Glory, blessing, praise eternal!"
Thus the choir of angels sings;
"Honor, riches, power, dominion!"
Thus its praise creation brings;
Glory, glory, glory, glory,
Glory to the King of kings!

Amen! Blessing and glory and wisdom, thanksgiving and honor and power and might, be to our God forever and ever. Amen.

—Revelation 7:12

Stand by Me

Today we're celebrating the birthday of the African-American Prince of Preachers and the Grandfather of Gospel Music. Charles Albert Tindley was born **July 7, 1851**, to a slave mother. After the Civil War, Charles moved to Philadelphia and became a church janitor while he did his best to put himself through school. A quarter century later, he was senior pastor of that same church, which had become a multiracial congregation of ten thousand. Tindley's hymns include "Nothing Between My Soul and My Savior," "Leave It There" ("If you trust and never doubt, He will surely bring you out. / Take your burden to the Lord and leave it there."), and this one:

> When the storms of life are raging,
> Stand by me;
> When the storms of life are raging,
> Stand by me;
> When the world is tossing me
> Like a ship upon the sea
> Thou who rulest wind and water,
> Stand by me.
>
> In the midst of tribulation,
> Stand by me;
> In the midst of tribulation,
> Stand by me;
> When the hosts of hell assail,
> And my strength begins to fail,
> Thou who never lost a battle,
> Stand by me (stand by me).

The LORD your God, He is the One who goes with you. He will not leave you nor forsake you.

—Deuteronomy 31:6

Praise to God, Immortal Praise

The popularity of this hymn is due, in large measure, to its re-soundingly happy melody—"Nuremberg"—which sounds like a happy march, a dance tune, a fanfare, and a children's song, all put together. The German composer Johann R. Ahle was born in Mühlhausen in 1625. As a young man, he moved to Erfurt to study theology; but he became better known there as an organist, though no record exists of his musical training. In 1650, Ahle returned to his hometown, married, and started playing the organ in church. He later became a member of the town council and then mayor. By the time Johann died on **July 8, 1673**, he left behind sixty organ pieces, a treatise on singing, a hymn-writing son who bore his name, and a profound legacy that mightily influenced the man who succeeded him as organist of the Mühlhausen church, J. S. Bach.

Praise to God, immortal praise,
For the love that crowns our days;
Bounteous Source of every joy,
Let Thy praise our tongues employ.

Flocks that whiten all the plain;
Yellow sheaves of ripened grain;
Clouds that drop their fattening dews,
Suns that temperate warmth diffuse.

These to Thee, my God, we owe,
Source whence all our blessings flow;
And for these my soul shall raise
Grateful vows and solemn praise.

I will sing to the LORD as long as I live; I will sing praise to my God while I have my being.

—Psalm 104:33

I Will Sing of My Redeemer

The words of this old gospel hymn were penned by Philip P. Bliss, who was born on **July 9, 1838**. The music was composed by James McGranahan, who died on **July 9, 1907**. But more than dates connected these men. McGranahan was a talented young soloist with a promising career in opera. He was a Christian, but his ambitions were for fame and fortune on the New York stage. Bliss was equally gifted, but he'd devoted his career to Christ. Bliss wrote McGranahan, challenging him to "reap for the Master!" As McGranahan read the letter and pondered its meaning, news arrived that Bliss, just thirty-eight years old, was dead—killed along with his wife in a tragic railroad accident in Ohio. McGranahan *did* devote his talents exclusively to God, and he composed the music for this hymn, which was found in Bliss's baggage following his death.

> I will sing of my Redeemer,
> And His wondrous love to me;
> On the cruel cross He suffered,
> From the curse to set me free.
>
> I will praise my dear Redeemer,
> His triumphant power I'll tell,
> How the victory He giveth
> Over sin, and death, and hell.
>
> I will sing of my Redeemer,
> And His heav'nly love to me;
> He from death to life hath brought me,
> Son of God with Him to be.
>
> *Sing, oh sing, of my Redeemer,*
> *With His blood, He purchased me.*
> *On the cross, He sealed my pardon,*
> *Paid the debt, and made me free.*

Jesus Christ, who gave Himself for us,
that He might redeem us . . .

—Titus 2:13–14

Tell It to Jesus

Edmund Simon Lorenz's parents were German missionaries to America, working among nineteenth-century German Americans in northern Ohio. Edmund himself grew up with a burden for the work, and as a young man he studied for the ministry and entered the pastorate. He worked himself into a breakdown; but while recovering he turned his attention to gospel music and went on to develop one of the largest American companies devoted to Christian music, the Lorenz Publishing Company. Edmund oversaw this ministry until a few days before his death on **July 10, 1942**, just three days shy of his eighty-eighth birthday. The words of "Tell It to Jesus" were originally penned by Edmund in German and translated into English by someone else. Edmund composed the tune.

Are you weary, are you heavy hearted?
Tell it to Jesus, tell it to Jesus.
Are you grieving over joys departed?
Tell it to Jesus alone.

Do the tears flow down your cheeks unbidden?
Tell it to Jesus, tell it to Jesus.
Have you sins that to men's eyes are hidden?
Tell it to Jesus alone.

Do you fear the gathering clouds of sorrow?
Tell it to Jesus, tell it to Jesus.
Are you anxious what shall be tomorrow?
Tell it to Jesus alone.

Tell it to Jesus, tell it to Jesus,
He is a Friend that's well known.
You've no other such a friend or brother,
Tell it to Jesus alone.

Be anxious for nothing, but in everything by
prayer and supplication, with thanksgiving,
let your requests be known to God.

—Philippians 4:6

Ivory Palaces

Henry Barraclough was the personal assistant to a member of Parliament, but he preferred the keys of his organ to the chambers of power. When the great evangelistic duo of Wilber Chapman and Charles Alexander came to England, Henry left politics behind and joined as the team musician. On **July 11, 1915**, Chapman and company came to Montreat, North Carolina, for meetings at the Presbyterian conference grounds. One night, Chapman preached from Psalm 45:8 on the ivory palaces of heaven. Afterward, Charles and Henry took a drive and stopped at a village store. There, in the front seat of the car, the young pianist jotted down the words to this hymn and began composing the music. It was sung the next morning at the conference service.

> My Lord has garments so wondrous fine,
> And myrrh their texture fills;
> Its fragrance reached to this heart of mine
> With joy my being thrills.
>
> His garments too were in cassia dipped,
> With healing in a touch;
> Each time my feet in some sin have slipped,
> He took me from its clutch.
>
> In garments glorious He will come,
> To open wide the door;
> And I shall enter my heav'nly home,
> To dwell forevermore.
>
> *Out of the ivory palaces,*
> *Into a world of woe,*
> *Only His great eternal love*
> *Made my Savior go.*

All Your garments are scented with myrrh and aloes and cassia,
out of the ivory palaces, by which they have made You glad.

—Psalm 45:8

Breathe on Me, Breath of God

This hymn of aspiration is a plea for the Holy Spirit's work in our lives. The words were written as a private prayer by Edwin Hatch, a brilliant Anglican clergyman and professor. The music was composed by Robert Jackson, a British organist. Jackson's father, Thomas, had been the organist at St. Peter's Church in Oldham for forty-eight years. In 1868, Robert took over his father's duties there and served for forty-six years. Between them, they served almost an entire century. Robert Jackson died on this day, **July 12, 1914**.

Breathe on me, breath of God,
Fill me with life anew,
That I may love what Thou dost love,
And do what Thou wouldst do.

Breathe on me, breath of God,
Until my heart is pure,
Until with Thee I will one will,
To do and to endure.

Breathe on me, breath of God,
Blend all my soul with Thine,
Until this earthly part of me
Glows with Thy fire divine.

Breathe on me, breath of God,
So shall I never die,
But live with Thee the perfect life
Of Thine eternity.

So Jesus said to them again, "Peace to you! As the Father has sent Me, I also send you." And when He had said this, He breathed on them, and said to them, "Receive the Holy Spirit."

—John 20:21–22

The Head That Once
Was Crowned with Thorns

Many hymns are devoted to our Lord's birth and life, or to His death and resurrection. Only a few celebrate His remarkable ascension into heaven and exaltation at the right hand of glory. He who descended through the womb of a virgin ascended in an equally remarkable way, rising from the Mount of Olives and disappearing into the clouds to the throne. Irish hymnist Thomas Kelly, who was born **July 13, 1769**, celebrated the ascension in his excellent hymn "The Head That Once Was Crowned with Thorns." Kelly himself had a hard time in ministry. He was a fervent evangelical in Ireland at a time when Ireland's established church didn't welcome such preaching. But he wouldn't be stilled, eventually becoming known as the Wesley of Ireland, preaching for souls and writing 760 hymns in the process.

> The head that once was crowned with thorns
> Is crowned with glory now;
> A royal diadem adorns
> The mighty victor's brow.
>
> The highest place that Heav'n affords
> Belongs to Him by right;
> The King of kings and Lord of lords,
> And Heaven's eternal Light.
>
> The joy of all who dwell above,
> The joy of all below,
> To whom He manifests His love,
> And grants His Name to know.

Now when He had spoken these things, while they watched, He was taken up, and a cloud received Him out of their sight.

—Acts 1:9

I Know Not How
That Bethlehem's Babe

Some hymns are profound in their simplicity. "I Know Not How That Bethlehem's Babe," for example, surveys the life of Christ, the mystery of our theology, and the implications of our salvation in three short stanzas that even children can learn. After all, its author, Harry Webb Farrington, was a famous lecturer who spoke to 2.5 million school children in assembly programs everywhere. Farrington was born in Nassau, the Bahamas, on **July 14, 1879**. He was orphaned in infancy but ended up a student athlete at Syracuse University. During World War I, he served as an ambulance driver in the French army and wrote a book of war poems. After the war, he entered the Methodist ministry and lectured widely. In July 1930, while vacationing with his wife in Ocean Grove, New Jersey, Farrington was leaning against the railing of a second-story porch when it gave way. He fell fifteen feet onto the concrete walk and died several months later of his injuries. He was only fifty, but he left behind this hymn, which can be sung to the tune "Jesus, the Very Thought of Thee."

> I know not how that Bethlehem's Babe
> Could in the Godhead be;
> I only know the manger Child
> Has brought God's life to me.
>
> I know not how that Calvary's cross
> A world from sin could free;
> I only know its matchless love
> Has brought God's love to me.
>
> I know not how that Joseph's tomb
> Could solve death's mystery;
> I only know a living Christ,
> Our immortality.

Great is the mystery of godliness: God was manifested in the flesh, justified in the Spirit, seen by angels, preached among the Gentiles, believed on in the world, received up in glory.

—1 Timothy 3:16

When Morning Gilds the Skies

This old hymn of praise comes from Germany and was translated by the Anglican-turned-Catholic scholar Edward Caswall when he was about forty years old. He was born **July 15, 1814**. Let's celebrate Caswall's birthday today by singing a few of its nearly thirty stanzas.

When morning gilds the skies my heart awaking cries:
May Jesus Christ be praised!
Alike at work and prayer, to Jesus I repair:
May Jesus Christ be praised!

When you begin the day, O never fail to say,
May Jesus Christ be praised!
And at your work rejoice, to sing with heart and voice,
May Jesus Christ be praised!

Does sadness fill my mind? A solace here I find,
May Jesus Christ be praised!
Or fades my earthly bliss? My comfort still is this,
May Jesus Christ be praised!

The night becomes as day when from the heart we say:
May Jesus Christ be praised!
The powers of darkness fear when this sweet chant they hear:
May Jesus Christ be praised!

Be this, while life is mine, my canticle divine:
May Jesus Christ be praised!
Sing this eternal song through all the ages long:
May Jesus Christ be praised!

Yes, I will sing aloud of Your mercy in the morning.

—Psalm 59:16

I Am His and He Is Mine

James Mountain, born **July 16, 1844**, was an Anglican pastor who collapsed under the strain of his work but found fresh fire through the ministry of D. L. Moody and Ira Sankey. He expressed his newfound fervor by composing the music to three great hymns of consecration: "Like a River Glorious," "Jesus, I Am Resting, Resting," and "I Am His and He Is Mine." All three can be found in his 1876 book, *Hymns of Consecration and Faith*. In 1904, James wrote another book, *My Baptism and What Led to It*. There he explained why he turned from the Anglican church and was baptized by immersion by Dr. F. B. Meyer, a decision that invited criticism. This composer of consecration hymns went on to found St. John's Free Church in Tunbridge Wells, from which pulpit he was an advocate for evangelical theology and a leader in the Victorious Christian Life (Keswick) Movement.

Loved with everlasting love, led by grace that love to know;
Gracious Spirit from above, Thou hast taught me it is so!
O this full and perfect peace! O this transport all divine!
In a love which cannot cease, I am His, and He is mine.

Heav'n above is softer blue, Earth around is sweeter green!
Something lives in every hue Christless eyes have never seen;
Birds with gladder songs o'erflow, flowers with deeper beauties shine,
Since I know, as now I know, I am His, and He is mine.

Things that once were wild alarms cannot now disturb my rest;
Closed in everlasting arms, pillowed on the loving breast.
O to lie forever here, doubt and care and self resign,
While He whispers in my ear, I am His, and He is mine.

My sheep hear My voice, and I know them, and they follow Me. And I will give them eternal life, and they shall never perish; neither shall anyone snatch them out of My hand.

—John 10:27–28

We're Marching to Zion

This is a red-letter day for the father of the English hymn, Isaac Watts. He was born **July 17, 1674**; he preached his first sermon on his twenty-fourth birthday, **July 17, 1698**; and a monument in his honor was erected in his hometown of Southampton, England, on **July 17, 1861**. The marble statue is eight feet high—three feet larger than life, for Watts was short and sickly. There's nothing short, however, about his influence. The Watts monument still stands in the center of Watts Park in Southampton, but his real memorial is in his hymns, including "Alas, and Did My Savior Bleed," "Joy to the World," "O God, Our Help in Ages Past," "When I Survey the Wondrous Cross," and "We're Marching to Zion."

Come, we that love the Lord,
And let our joys be known;
Join in a song with sweet accord,
Join in a song with sweet accord
And thus surround the throne,
And thus surround the throne.

Let those refuse to sing,
Who never knew our God;
But favorites of the heavenly King,
But favorites of the heavenly King
May speak their joys abroad,
May speak their joys abroad

Then let our songs abound,
And every tear be dry;
We're marching through Immanuel's ground,
We're marching through Immanuel's ground
To fairer worlds on high,
To fairer worlds on high.

We're marching to Zion,
Beautiful, beautiful Zion;
We're marching upward to Zion,
The beautiful city of God.

Let Israel rejoice in their Maker; let the children of Zion be joyful in their King.

—Psalm 149:2

He Is Gone, a Cloud of Light

Here's another of the handful of ascension songs in our hymn-books. It was written by Arthur Stanley, a church history professor whose personal warmth made him very popular with the students at Oxford. He later became Dean of Westminster Abbey where he was widely admired by royals and peasants alike, as preacher, pastor, writer, and friend. On Saturday, July 9, 1881, Stanley preached from the Beatitudes, then was taken ill and went to bed. During the night of **July 18, 1881**, he passed away peacefully and "was borne to his grave on the shoulders of an entire nation," as a biographer put it. Stanley's last words—"I am perfectly happy, perfectly satisfied; I have no misgivings"—reflect the hope he expressed in this hymn.

He is gone—a cloud of light
Has received Him from our sight;
High in Heav'n, where eye of men
Follows not, nor angels' ken;
Through the veils of time and space,
Passed into the holiest place;
All the toil, the sorrow done,
All the battle fought and won.

He is gone—but we once more
Shall behold Him as before;
In the heaven of heavens the same,
As on earth He went and came;
In the many mansions there,
Place for us He will prepare;
In that world unseen, unknown,
He and we shall yet be one.

Now it came to pass, while He blessed them, that He was parted from them and carried up into heaven. And they worshiped Him.

—Luke 24:51–52

The Lily of the Valley

The music of this happy hymn comes from William Shakespeare Hayes, who was born in Louisville, Kentucky, on **July 19, 1837**. Hayes grew up to become a composer of popular songs and minstrelsy. During the Civil War, he was imprisoned by Union forces for writing music sympathetic to the South. After his release, he took to the water, working on riverboats on the Ohio and Mississippi rivers. He finally settled down in Louisville where he became a successful journalist and newspaper columnist. Hayes never intended to write Christian music. He composed this melody in Louisville in 1871 to go with his song "The Little Old Log Cabin Down the Lane." Apparently it became a popular ditty in England. When Charles W. Fry, a Salvation Army musician, wrote the words "I have found a friend in Jesus" in June 1881 at a friend's house in Lincoln, England, he selected Hayes's melody as the hymn tune.

I have found a friend in Jesus, He's everything to me,
He's the fairest of ten thousand to my soul;
The Lily of the Valley, in Him alone I see
All I need to cleanse and make me fully whole.
In sorrow He's my comfort, in trouble He's my stay;
He tells me every care on Him to roll.

He will never, never leave me, nor yet forsake me here,
While I live by faith and do His blessèd will;
A wall of fire about me, I've nothing now to fear,
From His manna He my hungry soul shall fill.
Then sweeping up to glory to see His blessèd face,
Where the rivers of delight shall ever roll.

He's the Lily of the Valley, the Bright and Morning Star,
He's the fairest of ten thousand to my soul.

I am the rose of Sharon, and the lily of the valleys.

—Song of Solomon 2:1

The Spacious Firmament on High

The whole world knows that the first men walked on the moon on **July 20, 1969**. What isn't as well known is that they also observed Holy Communion there and partook of the Lord's Supper. Buzz Aldrin, an elder at Houston's Webster Presbyterian Church, had been given a bit of communion bread and a small vile of wine by his pastor. After the Lunar Lander set down on Tranquility Base, Aldrin opened the little plastic packages, poured some wine into a chalice, read John 15:5 from a card, and observed Communion. Every year since, on the Sunday closest to July 20, Webster Presbyterian Church has celebrated Lunar Communion Sunday, observing the Lord's Supper and singing great creation hymns like "The Spacious Firmament on High" by Joseph Addison, which opened a recent Lunar Communion service at the church.

> The spacious firmament on high,
> With all the blue ethereal sky,
> And spangled heavens, a shining frame
> Their great Original proclaim.
> Th'unwearied sun, from day to day,
> Does his Creator's powers display,
> And publishes to every land
> The work of an Almighty Hand.
>
> Soon as the evening shades prevail
> The moon takes up the wondrous tale,
> And nightly to the listening earth
> Repeats the story of her birth;
> While all the stars that round her burn
> And all the planets in their turn,
> Confirm the tidings as they roll,
> And spread the truth from pole to pole.

I am the vine, you are the branches. He who abides in Me, and I in him, bears much fruit; for without Me you can do nothing.

—John 15:5

Jesus Saves

Happy birthday to the author of "Jesus Saves"—Priscilla Owens, born **July 21, 1829**, in Baltimore, Maryland. Priscilla was a public school teacher in Baltimore who put forty-nine years into her career, devoting her spare time to her local Methodist Episcopal church. She wrote this hymn in 1882 for a missionary service for her Sunday school, and it was put to music by the celebrated William J. Kirkpatrick. Something about the exuberance of this hymn still motivates us to "give the winds a mighty voice: Jesus saves! Jesus saves!"

We have heard the joyful sound: Jesus saves! Jesus saves!
Spread the tidings all around: Jesus saves! Jesus saves!
Bear the news to every land, climb the steeps and cross the
    waves;
Onward! 'tis our Lord's command; Jesus saves! Jesus saves!

Waft it on the rolling tide: Jesus saves! Jesus saves!
Tell to sinners far and wide: Jesus saves! Jesus saves!
Sing, you islands of the sea; echo back, you ocean caves;
Earth shall keep her jubilee: Jesus saves! Jesus saves!

Sing above the battle strife: Jesus saves! Jesus saves!
By His death and endless life: Jesus saves! Jesus saves!
Shout it brightly through the gloom, when the heart for mercy
    craves;
Sing in triumph o'er the tomb: Jesus saves! Jesus saves!

Give the winds a mighty voice: Jesus saves! Jesus saves!
Let the nations now rejoice: Jesus saves! Jesus saves!
Shout salvation full and free, highest hills and deepest caves;
This our song of victory: Jesus saves! Jesus saves!

For the Son of Man has come to save that which was lost.

—Matthew 18:11

I Will Sing the Wondrous Story

The composer of the tune "Wondrous Story" was Peter Bilhorn, born **July 22, 1865**. Peter was a gifted musician who had a bright idea as he traveled around with various evangelists. He invented a folding pump organ that could travel easily, which led to his founding the Bilhorn Folding Organ Company in Chicago. The organs sold for about $150 each in 1916, and many models were produced. This letter from a missionary showed up in the Bilhorn catalogs:

> *Dear Brother Bilhorn: About 10 years ago I bought one of your folding organs to bring out to this swampy land. We have carried the organ on long itineraries on the Ubangi River; it has inspired our many services. The organ is a great attraction to the natives. We want to just let you know that your portable organ is a complete success here in the Equator in the Congo Swamps.*

I will sing the wondrous story
Of the Christ who died for me.
How He left His home in glory
For the cross of Calvary.

I was lost, but Jesus found me,
Found the sheep that went astray,
Threw His loving arms around me,
Drew me back into His way.

I was bruised, but Jesus healed me,
Faint was I from many a fall,
Sight was gone, and fears possessed me,
But He freed me from them all.

Yes, I'll sing the wondrous story
Of the Christ who died for me,
Sing it with the saints in glory,
Gathered by the crystal sea.

In due time Christ died for the ungodly. . . . Christ died for us.

—Romans 5:6, 8

Who Are These Arrayed in White?

Susanna Wesley was remarkable—the youngest of twenty-five children and the mother of nineteen more. Nine of her children died in infancy; but two who survived were named John Wesley and Charles Wesley, and they changed the world. As someone has said, Susanna never preached a sermon, wrote a book, pastored a church, or founded a movement, yet she's the mother of Methodism. After her husband's death, she lived with her children, principally with John. Returning from a trip in July of 1742, John wrote in his journal, "I found my Mother on the borders of eternity!" On the morning of **July 23, 1742**, Susanna awoke praising the Lord, and she praised Him all morning. She told her children, "As soon as I am released, sing a psalm of praise to God." She died about four o'clock in the afternoon, and they did as she asked. Three years later, with this memory still burning in his mind, Charles wrote this hymn.

Who are these arrayed in white,
Brighter than the noon-day sun?
Foremost of the sons of light;
Nearest the eternal throne?
These are they that bore the cross,
Nobly for their Master stood;
Sufferers in His righteous cause,
Followers of the dying God.

Out of great distress they came,
Washed their robes by faith below,
In the blood of yonder Lamb,
Blood that washes white as snow:
Therefore are they next the throne,
Serve their Maker day and night:
God resides among His own,
God doth in His saints delight.

Who are these arrayed in white robes . . . ? These are the ones who . . . washed their robes and made them white in the blood of the Lamb.

—Revelation 7:13–14

How Sweet the Name of Jesus Sounds

Here's John Newton's life in a thimble: Born **July 24, 1725**. Mother taught him the Bible but died when he was six. Boarding school. Sailed with father on six voyages. Vulgar. Captained slave ship. Pressed into naval service. Deserted at age eighteen. Ninety-six lashes before 350 sailors. Landed in Sierra Leone. Became the slave of a slave. Rescued by friend of his father. Nearly drowned in violent storm. Began to read Bible. Continued transporting slaves. Nearly died of fever. Nearly died of heatstroke. Found Christ. Married. Became surveyor in Liverpool. Became a preacher in Olney, England. Wrote hymns with William Cowper. Became influential pastor in London. Opposed slavery. Inspired Wilberforce. Wrote "Amazing Grace." Revered. Died December 21, 1807, leaving behind a heritage of hymns, including this one.

How sweet the name of Jesus sounds
In a believer's ear!
It soothes his sorrows, heals his wounds,
And drives away his fear.

Dear name! the rock on which I build,
My shield and hiding place,
My never-failing treasure, filled
With boundless stores of grace!

Jesus! my Shepherd, Husband, Friend,
O Prophet, Priest and King,
My Lord, my Life, my Way, my End,
Accept the praise I bring.

Weak is the effort of my heart,
And cold my warmest thought;
But when I see Thee as Thou art,
I'll praise Thee as I ought.

Whoever confesses that Jesus is the Son of God,
God abides in him, and he in God.

—1 John 4:15

Afflicted Saint, to Christ Draw Near

Here's just the promise from Scripture you need today—"As your days, so shall your strength be" (Deut. 33:25). It so impressed John Fawcett that he composed a hymn for his congregation to help them grasp its power and practicality. Fawcett, best known for "Blest Be the Tie That Binds," was prolific with many sermons, poems, tracts, books, and hymns to his credit. He so loved hymn singing that he once said, "If the Lord has given to man the ability to raise such melodious sounds and voices on earth, what delightful harmony will there be in heaven?" He found out on **July 25, 1817**, when he passed away in his seventy-seventh year. Over sixty years of his life had been devoted to the ministry of Christ.

> Afflicted saint, to Christ draw near—
> Thy Savior's gracious promise hear,
> His faithful Word declares to thee,
> That as thy days thy strength shall be.
>
> Let not thy heart despond and say,
> "How shall I stand the trying day?"
> He has engaged by firm decree,
> That as thy days thy strength shall be.
>
> Thy faith is weak, thy foes are strong,
> And if the conflict should be long,
> The Lord will make the tempter flee,
> For as thy days thy strength shall be.
>
> When called to bear thy weighty cross,
> Or sore affliction, pain, or loss,
> Or deep distress or poverty,
> Still as thy days thy strength shall be.

As your days, so shall your strength be.

—Deuteronomy 33:25

The Lord's My Shepherd

This is the best-loved musical rendition of Psalm 23. The quality of the translation in the Scottish Psalter is excellent, and the tune, "Crimond," suits the words perfectly. The melody was composed by Jessie Irvine, whose birthday we celebrate today (**July 26, 1836**). She was the daughter of the parish minister in the Scottish village of Crimond, where she composed the tune.

> The Lord's my Shepherd, I'll not want.
> He makes me down to lie
> In pastures green; He leadeth me
> The quiet waters by.
>
> My soul He doth restore again;
> And me to walk doth make
> Within the paths of righteousness,
> Even for His own Name's sake.
>
> Yea, though I walk in death's dark vale,
> Yet will I fear no ill;
> For Thou art with me; and Thy rod
> And staff my comfort still.
>
> My table Thou hast furnishèd
> In presence of my foes;
> My head Thou dost with oil anoint,
> And my cup overflows.
>
> Goodness and mercy all my life
> Shall surely follow me;
> And in God's house forevermore
> My dwelling place shall be.

The Lord is my shepherd; I shall not want.

—Psalm 23:1

Day by Day

Karolina Wilhelmina Sandell-Berg is known as the Fanny Crosby of Sweden. Lina's great tragedy in life occurred when she was twenty-six. While on holiday with her father, a beloved pastor, he fell from a boat on Lake Vättern and drowned before her eyes. Out of that experience came a flood of hymns and a lifetime of ministry. Lina died at age seventy-one on **July 27, 1903**, in Stockholm. Fifty years later, over ten thousand people in her hometown of Froderyd, Sweden, gathered to dedicate a bronze statue in her memory, and the cottage she lived in is now a national museum.

Day by day, and with each passing moment,
Strength I find, to meet my trials here;
Trusting in my Father's wise bestowment,
I've no cause for worry or for fear.
He whose heart is kind beyond all measure
Gives unto each day what He deems best—
Lovingly, its part of pain and pleasure,
Mingling toil with peace and rest.

Every day, the Lord Himself is near me
With a special mercy for each hour;
All my cares He fain would bear, and cheer me,
He whose name is Counselor and Power;
The protection of His child and treasure
Is a charge that on Himself He laid;
"As thy days, thy strength shall be in measure,"
This the pledge to me He made.

Therefore we do not lose heart. Even though our outward man is perishing, yet the inward man is being renewed day by day.

—2 Corinthians 4:16

Heaven

Annie Johnson Flint was born on Christmas Eve 1866 in a small New Jersey town, and her life was hard from the beginning. After her mother's early death, Annie was taken in by the Flint family, and she grew up to become a schoolteacher. Her professional life was cut short, however, by a crippling form of arthritis, and Annie was left an invalid with little income. Grasping a pen in gnarled fingers, she began writing poems and hymns, such as "He Giveth More Grace" and "What God Hath Promised." On **July 28, 1916**, her poem on heaven was read by Dr. James Gray at the funeral of Harry Monroe, the famous leader of the Old Lighthouse, the Pacific Garden Mission of Chicago.

'Tis not the golden streets,
'Tis not the pearly gates,
'Tis not the perfect rest
For weary hearts that waits,
'Tis not that we shall find
The joy earth has not given,
For which our souls have longed,
That makes it Heaven.

But 'tis because we know
Our Savior King is there
With all our loved and lost
In that blest land so fair;
That when to each of us
A place prepared is given,
His face and theirs we'll see,
That makes it Heaven.

God will wipe away every tear from their eyes; there shall be no more death, nor sorrow, nor crying. There shall be no more pain, for the former things have passed away.

—Revelation 21:4

The God of Abraham Praise

This is a Hebrew-sounding song with profound words and a haunting melody that somehow comforts the heart. Its author, Thomas Olivers, was a dissolute shoemaker who was saved under the preaching of evangelist George Whitefield. Olivers became a famous Methodist evangelist and wrote this hymn after attending a Jewish synagogue in London where he heard a soloist sing a plaintive Hebrew doxology from the early fifteenth century. Olivers, who is buried with John Wesley at City Road Church in London, wrote this hymn in about 1775. On **July 29, 1805**, as the great but lonely missionary Henry Martyn sailed for India, he comforted himself with this hymn, writing: "I was much engaged at intervals in learning the hymn, 'The God of Abraham praise. . . .' There was something peculiarly solemn and affecting to me in this hymn."

The God of Abraham praise, who reigns enthroned above;
Ancient of everlasting days, and God of love;
Jehovah, great I AM, by earth and heav'n confessed;
I bow and bless the sacred name, forever blest.

The God of Abraham praise, at whose supreme command
From earth I rise—and seek the joys at His right hand;
I all on earth forsake, its wisdom, fame, and power;
And Him my only portion make, my shield and tower.

The God of Abraham praise, whose all sufficient grace
Shall guide me all my happy days, in all my ways.
He calls a worm His friend, He calls Himself my God!
And He shall save me to the end, thro' Jesus' blood.

The God who reigns on high the great archangels sing,
And "Holy, holy, holy!" cry, "Almighty King!
Who was, and is, the same, and evermore shall be:
Jehovah—Father—great I AM, we worship Thee!"

I am the God of your fathers—the God of Abraham.

—Acts 7:32

Jesus, Name of Wondrous Love

William How was an indefatigable Anglican bishop, hymnist, and humanitarian. During the last year of his life, How suffered attacks of indigestion and palpitation. The hard travels, uncertain schedule, and heavy demands of his work had apparently taken their toll. This alarmed his friends, and they consulted his physician. But Dr. Lett told them the bishop would be miserable without his life's work. "Let him die in harness," he advised, and they did. On **July 30, 1897**, while at a conference, his friends found him passed out in a dead sleep on a sofa and took him to his lodgings. That evening How managed to write in his journal: "Very far from well. Could not stay in the conference . . . very poorly in the evening." He died "in harness" a few days later, leaving behind fifty hymns, including this one with its wonderful final verse.

Jesus! Name of wondrous love!
Name all other names above!
Unto which must every knee
Bow in deep humility.

Jesus! Name of priceless worth
To the fallen sons of earth,
For the promise that it gave—
"Jesus shall His people save."

Jesus! Only name that's given
Under all the mighty heaven,
Whereby man, to sin enslaved,
Bursts his fetters, and is saved.

Jesus! Name of wondrous love,
Human name of God above!
Pleading only this, we flee,
Helpless, O our God, to Thee.

For in Him dwells all the fullness of the Godhead bodily.

—Colossians 2:9

Fill Thou My Life

Recently I had the joy of spending a wonderful afternoon with Cliff Barrows as he shared stories from his years at Billy Graham's side, directing the crusades and leading excited choirs in stadiums around the world. Though older now, Cliff has lost none of his enthusiasm. His voice still has that trademark lilt, and his face radiates the happiness of the Lord. When I asked the secret of his exuberance, he told me, "The joy of the Lord is the strength of my life." Then he quoted from memory this hymn by the prince of Scottish hymn writers, Horatius Bonar, who died **July 31, 1889**. (It can be sung to the same tune as "I Sing the Mighty Power of God.")

Fill Thou my life, O Lord my God,
In every part with praise,
That my whole being may proclaim
Thy being and Thy ways. . . .

Fill every part of me with praise;
Let all my being speak
Of Thee and of Thy love, O Lord,
Poor though I be, and weak. . . .

So shall each fear, each fret, each care
Be turned into a song,
And every winding of the way
The echo shall prolong.

So shall no part of day or night
From sacredness be free;
But all my life, in every step
Be fellowship with Thee.

Let my mouth be filled with Your praise
and with Your glory all the day.

—Psalm 71:8

Sovereign Ruler of the Skies

John Ryland was born into a parsonage in England, was baptized by his father as a youth, and preached his first sermon at age eighteen. He labored alongside his dad and finally took over the work. Later in life, he established a wider ministry of preaching, writing, and composing hymns. From age twenty until his death, he wrote ninety-nine hymns, and they are all simple, devotional, practical, and personal. This one, "Sovereign Ruler of the Skies," was written on **August 1, 1777**, when Dr. Ryland was in his mid-twenties. It can be sung to the tune "Aletta" ("Holy Bible, Book Divine").

Sovereign Ruler of the skies!
Ever gracious, ever wise!
All my times are in Thy hand,
All events at Thy command.

He that formed me in the womb,
He shall guide me to the tomb;
All my times shall ever be
Ordered by His wise decree.

Times of sickness, times of health,
Times of poverty and wealth,
Times of trial and of grief,
Times of triumph and relief.

Thee at all times will I bless;
Having Thee I all possess;
How can I bereavèd be,
Since I cannot part with Thee.

*All the days ordained for me were written in
your book before one of them came to be.*

—Psalm 139:16 NIV

He the Pearly Gates Will Open

The author of this hymn was Fredrick A. Blom, a Swedish immigrant with a checkered story. He emigrated to America and pastored a church, but he fell into sin and was actually sent to prison. "He the Pearly Gates Will Open" was likely written behind bars as Blom struggled to regain his fellowship with the Lord (notice verses 2 and 3). Following his release, Blom returned to Sweden and labored for Christ until his death. His hymn was translated into English by Nathaniel Carlson, who died in Minneapolis on **August 2, 1957**. When the Billy Graham team was touring Scandinavia in the 1950s, they looked for Swedish hymns to sing, and this one became a hit. It was one of the few songs that Cliff Barrows and George Beverly Shea sang as a duet.

> Love divine, so great and wondrous,
> Deep and mighty, pure, sublime!
> Coming from the heart of Jesus,
> Just the same through tests of time.
>
> Like a dove when hunted, frightened,
> As a wounded fawn was I;
> Brokenhearted, yet He healed me,
> He will heed the sinner's cry.
>
> Love divine, so great and wondrous,
> All my sins He then forgave!
> I will sing His praise forever,
> For His blood, His power to save.
>
> *He the pearly gates will open,*
> *So that I may enter in;*
> *For He purchased my redemption*
> *And forgave me all my sin.*

The twelve gates were twelve pearls . . . and the street of the city was pure gold.

—Revelation 21:21

Someday He'll Make It Plain

Adam Geibel (September 15, 1855—**August 3, 1933**) was a blind German-American composer, best known for his tune "Stand Up, Stand Up for Jesus." He composed for Fanny Crosby and other hymnists around the turn of the twentieth century. This song, "Someday He'll Make It Plain," was deeply personal for Geibel. Word came that his son-in-law had been killed in a steel mill explosion, and Geibel was inconsolable. Tossing in bed, he seemed to hear a voice say, "Child, you do not understand it now, but someday you'll understand." Geibel cried out, "Yes, Lord, I believe. Help Thou mine unbelief." The next day, he wrote the music and jotted down ideas for the verses, which he sent to hymnist Lydia S. Leech who wrote the words.

I do not know why oft 'round me
My hopes all shattered seem to be;
God's perfect plan I cannot see,
But someday I'll understand.

I cannot tell the depth of love,
Which moves the Father's heart above;
My faith to test, my love to prove,
But someday I'll understand.

Tho' trials come thro' passing days,
My life will still be filled with praise;
For God will lead thro' darkened ways,
But someday I'll understand.

Someday He'll make it plain to me,
Someday when I His face shall see;
Someday from tears I shall be free,
For someday I shall understand.

Jesus answered and said to him, "What I am doing you do not understand now, but you will know after this."

—John 13:7

O for a Thousand Tongues to Sing

The inimitable evangelist Rodney Smith suffered a heart attack and died aboard the *Queen Mary* on **August 4, 1947**, leaving behind a fascinating autobiography of his childhood and life. Gipsy Smith, as he was known, was raised in a gypsy wagon in England. In his memoirs, he tells of being awakened once around 4 a.m. by a knock on the wagon door. It was the police. Gipsy's dad, Cornelius, was arrested for camping near town. Cornelius was a new Christian, and as he was led away in handcuffs, he began preaching to the officers. Arriving in jail, he began singing "O for a Thousand Tongues to Sing," emphasizing the verse, "He breaks the power of cancelled sin and sets the prisoner free." The other prisoners were touched, and the jailer's wife was converted. News spread across town, and when Cornelius was released, he conducted evangelistic services in a nearby meadow, which resulted in many conversions. It's no wonder Cornelius's son became a world-class evangelist who circled the globe with the message, "His blood can make the foulest clean, His blood availed for me."

O for a thousand tongues to sing
My great Redeemer's praise,
The glories of my God and King,
The triumphs of His grace!

Jesus! The name that charms our fears,
That bids our sorrows cease;
'Tis music in the sinner's ears,
'Tis life, and health, and peace.

He breaks the power of canceled sin,
He sets the prisoner free;
His blood can make the foulest clean,
His blood availed for me.

At midnight, Paul and Silas were . . . singing hymns
to God, and the prisoners were listening to them.

—Acts 16:25

When the Day of Toil Is Done

On **August 5, 1876**, Mary Slessor sailed from Liverpool for Calabar (modern Nigeria). There she poured herself into missionary service, healing the sick, teaching the literate, resolving disputes, saving lives, and preaching Christ—constantly risking herself for the work. "Had I not felt my Savior close beside me," she said, "I would have lost my reason." When she passed away in 1915, the native peoples were grief-stricken. They felt they'd lost their mother, the White Queen of Calabar, as she was known. Villagers wailed as her body was borne to the little cemetery where a simple service was conducted. There they composed themselves enough to sing this old hymn—no doubt one they had learned from her—as her body was laid to rest.

> When the day of toil is done,
> When the race of life is run,
> Father, grant Thy wearied one
> Rest forevermore.
>
> When the strife of sin is stilled,
> When the foe within is killed,
> Be Thy gracious Word fulfilled:
> Peace forevermore.
>
> When the darkness melts away
> At the breaking of the day,
> Bid us hail the cheering ray:
> Light forevermore.
>
> When the heart by sorrow tried,
> Feels at length its throbs subside,
> Bring us, where all tears are dried,
> Joy forevermore.

Blessed are the dead who die in the Lord. . . . That they may rest from their labors, and their works follow them.

—Revelation 14:13

Rejoice, Ye Pure in Heart

Edward Hayes Plumptre, born in London on **August 6, 1821**, graduated from Oxford University and became a noted Anglican theologian, professor, preacher, author, and composer of hymns. He was forty-four years old when he wrote this stately anthem. The occasion was a choral festival at Peterborough Cathedral in May 1865, and Plumptre was inspired by Psalm 20:5: "We will rejoice in your salvation, and in the name of our God we will set up our banners!" I love this hymn for its pure exuberance. It's almost impossible to sing without truly rejoicing!

Rejoice ye pure in heart;
Rejoice, give thanks, and sing;
Your glorious banner wave on high,
The cross of Christ your King.
Rejoice, rejoice, rejoice,
Give thanks and sing.

Bright youth and snow crowned age,
Strong men and maidens meek,
Raise high your free, exultant song,
God's wondrous praises speak.
Rejoice, rejoice, rejoice,
Give thanks and sing.

With all the angel choirs,
With all the saints of earth,
Pour out the strains of joy and bliss,
True rapture, noblest mirth.
Rejoice, rejoice, rejoice,
Give thanks and sing.

Rejoice in the LORD, O you righteous! For praise from the upright is beautiful. Praise the LORD . . . make melody to Him. . . . Sing to Him a new song.

—Psalm 33:1–3

Come, Holy Spirit, Come

Benjamin Beddome was born into a preacher's home in 1717. He grew up with a love for medicine and was apprenticed to a surgeon and pharmacist. But that changed on **August 7, 1737**, when he heard a sermon at his father's church from Luke 15:7 on the joy in heaven when a sinner is converted. He gave his life to Christ and headed into the ministry. For over fifty years, Beddome pastored a Baptist church in the idyllic riverside town of Bourton-on-the-Water, in the eastern part of Gloucestershire, England. There he wrote a hymn for each of his sermons, to be sung at the close of each Sunday's service. He lived to a ripe old age and was seen writing a hymn only a few hours before his death. His hymns were generally known for their simplicity and brevity, as we see in this poignant prayer, which can be sung to the tune of "Blest Be the Tie That Binds" or "Breathe on Me, Breath of God."

Come, Holy Spirit, come,
With energy divine,
And on this poor, benighted soul
With beams of mercy shine.

O melt this frozen heart;
This stubborn will subdue;
Each evil passion overcome,
And form me all anew!

The profit will be mine,
But Thine shall be the praise;
And unto Thee will I devote
The remnant of my days.

And when they had prayed, the place where they were assembled together was shaken; and they were all filled with the Holy Spirit, and they spoke the word of God with boldness.

—Acts 4:31

Jesus Calls Us

When we read the story of Jesus calling His first disciples, we must always remember that His words were aimed at us too. His summons rings across the ages and into our own hearts. That impression came so deeply upon Mrs. Cecil F. Alexander as she read Matthew 4:18–20 that she wrote the words to this hymn, "Jesus Calls Us." William H. Jude composed the tune, which is called "Galilee." He was an organist in England who became highly popular as a lecturer, and he traveled widely giving recitals and sermons. He also edited a number of hymnbooks. He died **August 8, 1922**.

Jesus calls us o'er the tumult
Of our life's wild, restless, sea;
Day by day His sweet voice soundeth,
Saying, "Christian, follow Me!"

Jesus calls us from the worship
Of the vain world's golden store,
From each idol that would keep us,
Saying, "Christian, love Me more!"

In our joys and in our sorrows,
Days of toil and hours of ease,
Still He calls, in cares and pleasures,
"Christian, love Me more than these!"

Jesus calls us! By Thy mercies,
Savior may we hear Thy call,
Give our hearts to Thine obedience,
Serve and love Thee best of all.

He said to them, "Follow Me, and I will make you fishers of men." They immediately left their nets and followed Him.

—Matthew 4:19–20

When All Thy Mercies, O My God

Today is the publication anniversary of this hymn, which was first printed in *The Spectator*, a London magazine, on Saturday, **August 9, 1712.** The author was a British politician named Joseph Addison, who wrote hymns on the side. Addison had been in a terrible shipwreck off the coast of Genoa and had been rescued by God's providential care. In gratitude, he wrote a poem of thirteen original verses, which became the basis for this popular hymn. It was accompanied in *The Spectator* by an article Addison wrote on thanksgiving, which began with the words, "There is not a more pleasing exercise of the mind than gratitude."

When all Thy mercies, O my God,
My rising soul surveys,
Transported with the view, I'm lost
In wonder, love and praise.

Ten thousand thousand precious gifts
My daily thanks employ;
Nor is the last a cheerful heart
That tastes those gifts with joy.

When worn with sickness, oft hast Thou
With health renewed my face;
And, when in sins and sorrows sunk,
Revived my soul with grace.

Through all eternity to Thee
A joyful song I'll raise;
For, oh, eternity's too short
To utter all Thy praise!

Oh, give thanks to the Lord of lords! For
His mercy endures forever.

—Psalm 136:3

Teach Me Thy Way, O Lord

Today's opening paragraph is brief, for I want to include all four stanzas of this great hymn of prayer and aspiration. Both words and music were written by Benjamin M. Ramsey, a British composer and music teacher in the Bournemouth area of England. His birthday is today—**August 10, 1849**. The hymn is worth not only singing, but memorizing.

Teach me Thy way, O Lord, teach me Thy way!
Thy guiding grace afford, teach me Thy way!
Help me to walk aright, more by faith, less by sight;
Lead me with heav'nly light, teach me Thy way!

When I am sad at heart, teach me Thy way!
When earthly joys depart, teach me Thy way!
In hours of loneliness, in times of dire distress,
In failure or success, teach me Thy way!

When doubts and fears arise, teach me Thy way!
When storms o'erspread the skies, teach me Thy way!
Shine through the cloud and rain, through sorrow, toil and pain;
Make Thou my pathway plain, teach me Thy way!

Long as my life shall last, teach me Thy way!
Where'er my lot be cast, teach me Thy way!
Until the race is run, until the journey's done,
Until the crown is won, teach me Thy way!

Teach me Your way, O Lord, and lead me in a smooth path.

—Psalm 27:11

Teach me Your way, O Lord; I will walk in Your truth.

—Psalm 86:11

On Jordan's Stormy Banks

Samuel Stennett, the author of this hymn, was the son of the pastor of Little Wild Street Church in London. As a young man, Samuel became his dad's assistant at the church and eventually took over the pastorate when his dad retired. Samuel's sermons, as well as his hymns, were greatly appreciated. A wealthy philanthropist named John Howard visited the church whenever he was in London. On **August 11, 1786**, he sent Samuel a note, saying, "With unabated pleasure I have attended your ministry; no man ever entered more into my religious sentiments, or more happily expressed them. It was some little disappointment when any one occupied your pulpit. Oh, sir, how many Sabbaths I ardently long to spend in Little Wild Street."

On Jordan's stormy banks I stand,
And cast a wishful eye
To Canaan's fair and happy land,
Where my possessions lie.

O'er all those wide extended plains
Shines one eternal day;
There God the Son forever reigns,
And scatters night away.

No chilling winds or poisonous breath
Can reach that healthful shore;
Sickness and sorrow, pain and death,
Are felt and feared no more.

I am bound for the promised land,
I am bound for the promised land;
Oh who will come and go with me?
I am bound for the promised land.

There is a river whose streams shall make glad the city of God.

—Psalm 46:4

The Lord Is My Shepherd

August 12, 1838, is the birthday of a British musical prodigy, Sir Joseph Barnby. He sang in accomplished choirs at age seven and was leading them at age twelve. Following in his father's footsteps, Joseph became a gifted organist and a renowned composer who helped form the London Musical Society. I appreciate him because he wrote the music to two of my favorite hymns for opening and closing the day: "When Morning Gilds the Skies" and "Now the Day Is Over." His tune "Good Shepherd" was written for this rendition of the Twenty-third Psalm by journalist and hymnist James Montgomery.

The Lord is my Shepherd, no want shall I know;
I feed in green pastures, safe folded I rest;
He leadeth my soul where the still waters flow,
Restores me when wand'ring, redeems when oppressed.

Through valley and shadow of death though I stray,
Since Thou art my Guardian, no evil I fear;
Thy rod shall defend me, Thy staff be my stay;
No harm can befall, with my Comforter near.

In midst of affliction my table is spread;
With blessings unmeasured my cup runneth o'er;
With perfume and oil Thou anointest my head;
O what shall I ask of Thy providence more?

Let goodness and mercy, my bountiful God,
Still follow my steps till I meet Thee above;
I seek, by the path which my forefathers trod,
Through land of their sojourn, Thy Kingdom of love.

You anoint my head with oil; my cup runs over.

—Psalm 23:5

I Love to Tell the Story

The composer of this hymn tune was William Fischer, who died on **August 13, 1912.** The *New York Times* carried his obituary, which read as follows: "WILLIAM G. FISCHER DEAD. William Gustavus Fischer, noted throughout the world as the composer of sacred music, died at his home here last night, after a short illness, aged 77 years. During the original Moody and Sankey revival services in this city he acted as the leader of a chorus of more than 1,000 voices. From 1858 to 1868 he was Professor of Music at Girard College. Among his most famous compositions were 'I Love to Tell the Story' and 'Whiter Than Snow.' " While Katherine Hankey wrote the verses to this hymn, Fischer composed the music and wrote the refrain, which says, "I love to tell the story! 'Twill be my theme in glory, to tell the old, old story of Jesus and His love."

I love to tell the story of unseen things above,
Of Jesus and His glory, of Jesus and His love.
I love to tell the story, because I know 'tis true;
It satisfies my longings as nothing else can do.

I love to tell the story; more wonderful it seems
Than all the golden fancies of all our golden dreams.
I love to tell the story, it did so much for me;
And that is just the reason I tell it now to thee.

I love to tell the story; 'tis pleasant to repeat
What seems, each time I tell it, more wonderfully sweet.
I love to tell the story, for some have never heard
The message of salvation from God's own holy Word.

I love to tell the story, for those who know it best
Seem hungering and thirsting to hear it like the rest.
And when, in scenes of glory, I sing the new, new song,
'Twill be the old, old story that I have loved so long.

Woe is me if I do not preach the gospel!
—1 Corinthians 9:16

The Church's One Foundation

Samuel Sebastian Wesley, grandson of the great Charles Wesley, was born **August 14, 1810**, and grew up with two great loves in his life—music and fishing. He became a marvelous organist and composer for the Church of England, but it's said that he would accept or turn down positions based on fishing prospects in the area. On one occasion, as Wesley traveled to a church for a concert, he passed a river known for its fine fishing—and he never made it to the service! Though he was eccentric, Wesley's music filled the greatest churches and cathedrals of his day. Perhaps his most moving score is "Aurelia," the tune for two of our hymns: "Another Year Is Dawning" by Frances Havergal, and "The Church's One Foundation" by Samuel Stone.

> The Church's one foundation
> Is Jesus Christ her Lord,
> She is His new creation
> By water and the Word.
> From heaven He came and sought her
> To be His holy bride;
> With His own blood He bought her
> And for her life He died.
>
> Elect from every nation,
> Yet one o'er all the earth;
> Her charter of salvation,
> One Lord, one faith, one birth;
> One holy name she blesses,
> Partakes one holy food,
> And to one hope she presses,
> With every grace endued.

To Him be glory in the church by Christ Jesus to all generations, forever and ever. Amen.

—Ephesians 3:21

Jesus, Lover of My Soul

Charles Finney was a six-foot-three, drunken lawyer who, after a dramatic conversion, became one of the most powerful evangelists in US history. He's called the Father of American Revivalism, and under his piercing sermons thousands came to Christ. On Sunday, **August 15, 1875**, the eighty-three-year-old Finney, weary after a lifetime of exhausting ministry, was strolling with his wife when they heard the opening of a worship service from a nearby church. The strains of Wesley's great hymn "Jesus, Lover of My Soul" wafted through the air, and Finney paused in the gathering shadows and joined the singing. Later that night he was stricken with an apparent heart attack, and by morning he was singing with the choirs of heaven.

Jesus, lover of my soul, let me to Thy bosom fly,
While the nearer waters roll, while the tempest still is high.
Hide me, O my Savior, hide, till the storm of life is past;
Safe into the haven guide; O receive my soul at last.

Other refuge have I none, hangs my helpless soul on Thee;
Leave, ah! leave me not alone, still support and comfort me.
All my trust on Thee is stayed, all my help from Thee I bring;
Cover my defenseless head with the shadow of Thy wing.

Thou, O Christ, art all I want, more than all in Thee I find;
Raise the fallen, cheer the faint, heal the sick, and lead the blind.
Just and holy is Thy name, I am all unrighteousness;
False and full of sin I am; Thou art full of truth and grace.

Plenteous grace with Thee is found, grace to cover all my sin;
Let the healing streams abound; make and keep me pure
    within.
Thou of life the fountain art, freely let me take of Thee;
Spring Thou up within my heart; rise to all eternity.

Who shall separate us from the love of Christ?

—Romans 8:35

O Jesus Christ, Grow Thou in Me

This beautiful Swiss hymn was penned by Johann Heinrich Lavater, the twelfth child of a Zürich doctor. Johann possessed a gifted mind, and he eventually became a leading pastor in his native city. Unfortunately, Zürich became caught up in the trauma of the French Revolution, and in April 1779, invading French troops deported some of the city's leading citizens. Johann protested this action from his pulpit, and as a result he, too, was seized and banished. He returned to Zürich on **August 16, 1799**, but five weeks later was shot by a drunken French officer. He never recovered from his wounds, dying nearly two years later, but he left behind a deeply meaningful body of hymnology, including this musical prayer for spiritual growth.

O Jesus Christ, grow Thou in me,
And all things else recede!
My heart be daily nearer Thee,
From sin be daily freed.

More of Thy glory let me see,
Thou Holy, Wise and True!
I would Thy living image be,
In joy and sorrow, too.

Fill me with gladness from above,
Hold me by strength divine;
Lord, make the glow of Thy great love
Through my whole being shine.

Make this poor self grow less and less,
Be Thou my life and aim;
O make me daily through Thy grace,
More meet to bear Thy name!

Grow up in all things into Him who is the head—Christ.

—Ephesians 4:15

God of Our Fathers

Daniel Roberts, a small-town Episcopalian pastor in Vermont, wrote this patriotic hymn for the United States Centennial on July 4, 1876. It was originally sung without fanfare to a ponderous melody called the "Russian Hymn." Then an accomplished New York organist, George Warren, got hold of the words. Feeling they deserved something regal and majestic, he wrote a dramatic tune, "National Hymn," with trumpet calls at the beginning of each stanza. Today is the composer's birthday: George Warren was born **August 17, 1828**, in Albany, New York.

God of our fathers, whose almighty hand
Leads forth in beauty all the starry band
Of shining worlds in splendor through the skies
Our grateful songs before Thy throne arise.

Thy love divine hath led us in the past,
In this free land by Thee our lot is cast,
Be Thou our Ruler, Guardian, Guide and Stay,
Thy Word our law, Thy paths our chosen way.

From war's alarms, from deadly pestilence,
Be Thy strong arm our ever sure defense;
Thy true religion in our hearts increase,
Thy bounteous goodness nourish us in peace.

Refresh Thy people on their toilsome way,
Lead us from night to never ending day;
Fill all our lives with love and grace divine,
And glory, laud, and praise be ever Thine.

Blessed be the LORD God of our fathers.
—Ezra 7:27

I Know That My Redeemer Lives

Behind this hymn stands a grandfather's love for a prodigal. It was written by Samuel Medley, who, as a wild-living seventeen-year-old, ran off to sea with the Royal Navy. Being severely wounded in a sea battle off Cape Lagos on **August 18, 1759**, the lad was transported back to England and carried to the home of his grandfather, a deacon in the Baptist church. There, under the old man's care, Samuel gave his life fully to Christ and subsequently became a Baptist pastor. His poems were primarily written for his sermons, and his best-known hymn is "Awake, My Soul, in Joyful Lays." The following hymn is my favorite Medley hymn, and it can be sung to the tune of "Duke Street" ("Jesus Shall Reign Where'er the Sun").

I know that my Redeemer lives;
What comfort this sweet sentence gives!
He lives, He lives, who once was dead;
He lives, my ever living Head.

He lives to bless me with His love,
He lives to plead for me above.
He lives my hungry soul to feed,
He lives to help in time of need.

He lives triumphant from the grave,
He lives eternally to save,
He lives all glorious in the sky,
He lives exalted there on high.

He lives, all glory to His name!
He lives, my Jesus, still the same.
Oh, the sweet joy this sentence gives,
I know that my Redeemer lives!

He is also able to save to the uttermost those
who come to God through Him, since He always
lives to make intercession for them.

—Hebrews 7:25

I Would Be True

For a hundred years, this hymn has been hailed as a clarion call for young people. It was written by Howard A. Walter, born **August 19, 1883**, in Connecticut. As a young man, Walter went to Japan to teach English as a second language. He wrote these words to give his mother a statement of his life's creed. In 1909, he showed it to a Methodist friend, who immediately started whistling a tune for the words, thus giving birth to the hymn. Several years later, Walter enlisted with the YMCA and traveled to India to work with students. Though only in his thirties, he died there suddenly during the 1918 flu epidemic. His death catapulted this song to global popularity, for it was seen that these words provide an authentic, livable creed for a life of service.

> I would be true, for there are those who trust me;
> I would be pure, for there are those who care;
> I would be strong, for there is much to suffer;
> I would be brave, for there is much to dare;
> I would be brave, for there is much to dare.
>
> I would be friend of all—the foe, the friendless;
> I would be giving, and forget the gift;
> I would be humble, for I know my weakness;
> I would look up, and laugh, and love and lift.
> I would look up, and laugh, and love and lift.
>
> I would be faithful through each passing moment;
> I would be constantly in touch with God;
> I would be strong to follow where He leads me;
> I would have faith to keep the path Christ trod;
> I would have faith to keep the path Christ trod.

Do not be conformed to this world, but be transformed by the renewing of your mind, that you may prove what is that good and acceptable and perfect will of God.

—Romans 12:2

Spirit of God, Descend Upon My Heart

During my college days, when I was fresh and flush in newfound faith, I cherished singing this hymn in chapel services and have loved it ever since. Its original title was "Holiness Desired," and it was written by George Croly, an Irishman who spent most of his life ministering in London. He was a man of restless energy and a prolific writer. As an Anglican pastor, he served in a small church until 1835, when he was asked to reopen a church that had been closed for a hundred years. It was in the heart of the London slums, but Croly's powerful preaching attracted large crowds. At age seventy-four, he prepared a fresh hymnal for the church, and he included this hymn he'd written. The music is by Frederick C. Atkinson—the organist and chorister at the majestic Norwich Cathedral—whose birthday was **August 20, 1841**.

Spirit of God, descend upon my heart;
Wean it from earth; through all its pulses move;
Stoop to my weakness, mighty as Thou art;
And make me love Thee as I ought to love.

I ask no dream, no prophet ecstasies,
No sudden rending of the veil of clay,
No angel visitant, no opening skies;
But take the dimness of my soul away.

Teach me to feel that Thou art always nigh;
Teach me the struggles of the soul to bear.
To check the rising doubt, the rebel sigh,
Teach me the patience of unanswered prayer.

Teach me to love Thee as Thine angels love,
One holy passion filling all my frame;
The kindling of the heaven descended Dove,
My heart an altar, and Thy love the flame.

Do not be drunk with wine, in which is
dissipation; but be filled with the Spirit.

—Ephesians 5:18

His Eye Is on the Sparrow

Today is a great day to sing twin hymns about God's care—"His Eye Is on the Sparrow" and the song that begins with the reassuring words, "Be not dismayed whate'er betide, God will take care of you." Both were penned by Civilla D. Martin, a Nova Scotia native, who was born **August 21, 1869**. In the springtime of 1905, as Civilla and her husband were traveling in upstate New York, they met a couple named Doolittle. The husband was confined to a wheelchair, and his wife had been bedridden for years. When asked how he remained bright and cheerful, Mr. Doolittle replied, "His eye is on the sparrow, and I know He watches me." Inspired by that simple phrase, Civilla had soon written the words of this popular hymn.

Why should I feel discouraged, why should the shadows come,
Why should my heart be lonely, and long for heaven and home,
When Jesus is my portion? My constant friend is He:
His eye is on the sparrow, and I know He watches me;
His eye is on the sparrow, and I know He watches me.

"Let not your heart be troubled," His tender word I hear,
And resting on His goodness, I lose my doubts and fears;
Though by the path He leadeth, but one step I may see;
His eye is on the sparrow, and I know He watches me;
His eye is on the sparrow, and I know He watches me.

Whenever I am tempted, whenever clouds arise,
When songs give place to sighing, when hope within me dies,
I draw the closer to Him, from care He sets me free;
His eye is on the sparrow, and I know He watches me;
His eye is on the sparrow, and I know He watches me.

I sing because I'm happy, I sing because I'm free,
For His eye is on the sparrow, and I know He watches me.

Do not fear therefore; you are of more value than many sparrows.

—Matthew 10:31

To God Be the Glory

I live in Nashville, Tennessee, home of Vanderbilt University and its football stadium, Dudley Field. In the early 1950s, Billy Graham wanted to hold an evangelistic crusade in this venue, but the stadium was unlighted; all football games were played during the day. After much prayer and consideration, crusade organizers donated money for stadium lights in exchange for free rent, and the meetings opened on **August 22, 1954**. It was here that music director Cliff Barrows introduced an obscure hymn he had recently found in London. It was an old Fanny Crosby song, originally published in 1875, which had never "caught on." Well, it caught on in Nashville and has been sung around the world ever since.

To God be the glory, great things He has done;
So loved He the world that He gave us His Son,
Who yielded His life an atonement for sin,
And opened the life gate that all may go in.

O perfect redemption, the purchase of blood,
To every believer the promise of God;
The vilest offender who truly believes,
That moment from Jesus a pardon receives.

Great things He has taught us, great things He has done,
And great our rejoicing through Jesus the Son;
But purer, and higher, and greater will be
Our wonder, our transport, when Jesus we see.

Praise the Lord, praise the Lord, let the earth hear His voice!
Praise the Lord, praise the Lord, let the people rejoice!
O come to the Father, through Jesus the Son,
And give Him the glory, great things He has done.

To Him be the glory and the dominion forever and ever. Amen.

—1 Peter 5:11

Standing on the Promises

Russell Kelso Carter, who passed away on **August 23, 1928**, is one of the most interesting characters in American hymnody. He was born into a devout family in Baltimore in 1849, and he gave his life to Christ at age fifteen during a prayer meeting at his military academy, where he was a gifted student athlete. He later became a professor of chemistry, mathematics, and engineering; then he moved to California to raise sheep, perhaps because of problems with his health and marriage. Entering the ministry, he became an advocate for the holiness and healing movement. He was also a prolific writer. Later in life he took up the study of medicine and even became a practicing physician in Baltimore. He's best remembered, however, for writing both the words and music to "Standing on the Promises."

> Standing on the promises of Christ my King,
> Through eternal ages let His praises ring,
> Glory in the highest, I will shout and sing,
> Standing on the promises of God.
>
> Standing on the promises that cannot fail,
> When the howling storms of doubt and fear assail,
> By the living Word of God I shall prevail,
> Standing on the promises of God.
>
> Standing on the promises I cannot fall,
> Listening every moment to the Spirit's call,
> Resting in my Savior as my all in all,
> Standing on the promises of God.
>
> *Standing, standing,*
> *Standing on the promises of God my Savior;*
> *Standing, standing,*
> *I'm standing on the promises of God.*

He has given us his very great and precious promises.

—2 Peter 1:4 NIV

Lead On, O King Eternal

Ernest Warburton Shurtleff began writing columns for newspapers and magazines at age fourteen. Later he published a book of poems he'd written as a teenager. At Andover Theological Seminary, he wrote "Lead On, O King Eternal" for his own 1888 graduating class. Ernest married his Texas sweetheart, Helen, and for several years the couple pastored churches in California, Massachusetts, Minnesota, and Frankfurt, Germany. In 1906, the Lord led them to Paris to provide spiritual and moral support to expatriate American students on the Left Bank. Ernest's workload increased to the breaking point during World War I until, on **August 24, 1917**, he collapsed at the dinner table and died from heart failure brought on by overwork. He was fifty-five.

Lead on, O King eternal,
The day of march has come;
Henceforth in fields of conquest
Thy tents shall be our home.
Through days of preparation
Thy grace has made us strong;
And now, O King eternal,
We lift our battle song.

Lead on, O King eternal,
We follow, not with fears,
For gladness breaks like morning
Where'er Thy face appears.
Thy cross is lifted over us,
We journey in its light;
The crown awaits the conquest;
Lead on, O God of might.

I will lead them in paths they have not known. I will make darkness light before them, and crooked places straight. These things I will do for them, and not forsake them.

—Isaiah 42:16

The Old Account Was Settled

As He died on Calvary's cross, our Lord spoke three words that ring through the ages: "It is finished!" (John 19:30). The Greek word used in this verse is *telelestai*. Modern archaeologists have found ancient papyri receipts for taxes with that same word written across them, and in today's language it means "paid in full." Our debt has been paid, the account has been settled, our sins are forgiven, and we are heirs of God through the blood of Jesus. That's the message of this lively and picturesque old Southern hymn by the Methodist preacher Frank Graham (March 1, 1859—**August 25, 1931**).

> There was a time on earth, when in the book of Heav'n
> An old account was standing for sins yet unforgiv'n;
> My name was at the top, and many things below,
> I went unto the Keeper, and settled long ago.
>
> The old account was large, and growing every day,
> For I was always sinning, and never tried to pay;
> But when I looked ahead, and saw such pain and woe,
> I said that I would settle, I settled long ago.
>
> O sinner, trust the Lord, be cleansed of all your sin,
> For thus He hath provided for you to enter in;
> And then if you should live a hundred years below,
> Up there you'll not regret it, you settled long ago.
>
> *Long ago (down on my knees), long ago (I settled it all),*
> *Yes, the old account was settled long ago (Hallelujah!);*
> *And the record's clear today, for He washed my sins away,*
> *When the old account was settled long ago.*

He said, "It is finished!" And bowing His
head, He gave up His spirit.

—John 19:30

O Word of God Incarnate

This hymn, inspired by Psalm 119:105, tells us God's Word is a lamp, a light, a banner, a beacon, a chart, a compass; it is truth unchanging. The words were written by William How, the beloved bishop of Wakefield (see July 30). The melody, titled "Munich," was originally from a 1693 German hymnal. The tune was rediscovered and rewritten by the great German composer Felix Mendelssohn. He used it for the chorale "Cast Thy Burden on the Lord" in his oratorio *Elijah*, which was first performed in England on **August 26, 1846**, shortly before Mendelssohn's death. It was subsequently adapted for this hymn.

O Word of God incarnate, O Wisdom from on high,
O Truth unchanged, unchanging, O Light of our dark sky:
We praise You for the radiance that from the hallowed page,
A Lantern to our footsteps, shines on from age to age.

The Church from You, our Savior, received the Gift divine,
And still that Light is lifted o'er all the earth to shine.
It is the sacred Vessel where gems of truth are stored;
It is the heav'n-drawn Picture of Christ, the living Word.

The Scripture is a banner before God's host unfurled;
It is a shining Beacon above the darkling world.
It is the Chart and Compass that o'er life's surging tide,
Mid mists and rocks and quicksands, to You, O Christ, will
    guide.

O make your Church, dear Savior, a lamp of purest gold,
To bear before the nations Your true light as of old.
O teach your wandering pilgrims by this their path to trace,
Till, clouds and darkness ended, they see You face to face.

Your word is a lamp to my feet and a light to my path.

—Psalm 119:105

Come to the Savior Now

We can do more for Christ than we think. Consider how many roles John Murch Wigner fulfilled during his life. He was the son of an English preacher who helped his dad establish a Baptist church in London. He was the husband of Ellen Turnbull, whom he married on **August 27, 1878**. He was the father of twelve children, and a grandfather whose legacy lasts to this day. He was a civil servant for the British government and a senior officer in the East India Company. He was a Bible teacher who traveled across the United Kingdom with a homemade scale model of the tabernacle, giving lessons and lectures. He was a personal evangelist who led many people to faith in Christ. And he was a hymnist whose passion for souls is reflected in this hymn of invitation and appeal, "Come to the Savior Now."

Come to the Savior now,
He gently calleth thee;
In true repentance bow,
Before Him bend the knee;
He waiteth to bestow
Salvation, peace, and love,
True joy on earth below,
A home in Heav'n above.

Come to the Savior, all,
Whate'er your burdens be;
Hear now His loving call,
"Cast all your care on Me."
Come, and for ev'ry grief
In Jesus you will find
A sure and safe relief,
A loving Friend and kind.

So teach us to number our days, that we
may gain a heart of wisdom.

—Psalm 90:12

The Ninety and Nine

One day in 1874, evangelist D. L. Moody was in Scotland, preaching on the subject of the Good Shepherd. As he finished his sermon, he turned to his musician, Ira Sankey, and asked for an appropriate solo. For an instant, Sankey froze; then he remembered a poem he'd cut from a newspaper a couple of days before. Placing the clipping on the organ, Sankey struck the key of A-flat and made up a melody for the poem as he sang. Note by note, the tune came to him, and somehow he remembered the melody for the subsequent verses. And thus a great hymn was born—"The Ninety and Nine."

Happy birthday, Ira Sankey! He was born **August 28, 1849**, in Edinburg, Pennsylvania.

There were ninety and nine that safely lay
In the shelter of the fold.
But one was out on the hills away,
Far off from the gates of gold.
Away on the mountains wild and bare.
Away from the tender Shepherd's care.

But none of the ransomed ever knew
How deep were the waters crossed;
Nor how dark was the night the Lord passed through
Ere He found His sheep that was lost.
Out in the desert He heard its cry,
Sick and helpless and ready to die.

And all through the mountains, thunder riven
And up from the rocky steep,
There arose a glad cry to the gate of Heaven,
"Rejoice! I have found My sheep!"
And the angels echoed around the throne,
"Rejoice, for the Lord brings back His own!"

Rejoice with me, for I have found my sheep which was lost!

—Luke 15:6

Immortal, Invisible, God Only Wise

"Immortal, Invisible, God Only Wise" is such a great hymn because it combines sturdy Scottish words with a strong Welsh melody. The lyrics are by Walter Smith of Edinburgh, and they lift up the glorious attributes of almighty God. The melody comes from a Welsh folk song that was crafted into a hymn tune by John Roberts, a pastor in Wales who was ordained into the ministry on **August 29, 1865**. Roberts was a multigifted man—an accomplished musician who conducted music festivals across Wales, a teacher, a writer, an editor, a journalist, a lecturer, a poet, and a preacher. His tune perfectly matches Smith's words extolling our immortal, invisible God—the most blessed, most glorious Ancient of Days.

Immortal, invisible, God only wise,
In light inaccessible hid from our eyes,
Most blessèd, most glorious, the Ancient of Days,
Almighty, victorious, Thy great name we praise.

To all, life Thou givest, to both great and small;
In all life Thou livest, the true life of all;
We blossom and flourish as leaves on the tree,
And wither and perish—but naught changeth Thee.

Great Father of glory, pure Father of light,
Thine angels adore Thee, all veiling their sight;
But of all Thy rich graces this grace, Lord, impart,
Take the veil from our faces, the vile from our heart.

All laud we would render; O help us to see
'Tis only the splendor of light hideth Thee,
And so let Thy glory, Almighty, impart,
Through Christ in His story, Thy Christ to the heart.

Now to the King eternal, immortal, invisible, to God who alone is wise, be honor and glory forever and ever. Amen.

—1 Timothy 1:17

We've a Story to Tell to the Nations

For thirty years, I've been telling my church in Nashville that our gospel cannot be contained within the walls of our church, the boundaries of our town, or the borders of our nation. It's a message for all the earth, and any congregation that doesn't have missions in its DNA is missing some molecules. We need more hymns to trumpet this theme, but here's a great missionary song combining energetic words with determined music. Both text and tune were composed by H. Ernest Nichol, who was born December 10, 1862, in the Yorkshire region of England, and died in the same part of the country on **August 30, 1926**. In writing what he called "Sunday school songs," Nichol often rearranged the letters of his name and published under the pseudonym Colin Sterne.

> We've a story to tell to the nations,
> That shall turn their hearts to the right,
> A story of truth and mercy,
> A story of peace and light,
> A story of peace and light.
>
> We've a message to give to the nations,
> That the Lord who reigns up above
> Has sent us His Son to save us,
> And show us that God is love,
> And show us that God is love.
>
> We've a Savior to show to the nations,
> Who the path of sorrow has trod,
> That all of the world's great peoples
> Might come to the truth of God,
> Might come to the truth of God.
>
> *For the darkness shall turn to dawning,*
> *And the dawning to noonday bright;*
> *And Christ's great kingdom shall come on earth,*
> *The kingdom of love and light.*

Declare His glory among the nations,
His wonders among all peoples.

—Psalm 96:3

Jesus Loves Me

I once spent several days at the United States Military Academy at West Point researching the lives of Anna and Susan Warner for a book about this hymn. The financial panic of 1837 had destroyed their family's financial empire, forcing them into a ramshackle house on Constitution Island. There the sisters began writing novels to help pay bills; and in one of the novels, Anna crafted the words of this children's hymn. Cadets arriving at West Point soon learned that the famous authors and hymnists lived just across the Hudson. Using a simple strategy of lemonade, cookies, and Bible study, Anna and Susan mentored a generation of these young men. Today their graves are side by side in the military cemetery at West Point.

Happy birthday, Anna Warner, author of "Jesus Loves Me"—**August 31, 1827**.

Jesus loves me! This I know,
For the Bible tells me so.
Little ones to Him belong;
They are weak, but He is strong.

Jesus loves me! This I know,
As He loved so long ago,
Taking children on His knee,
Saying, "Let them come to Me."

Jesus loves me! He who died
Heaven's gate to open wide;
He will wash away my sin,
Let His little child come in.

Yes, Jesus loves me!
Yes, Jesus loves me!
Yes, Jesus loves me!
The Bible tells me so.

Christ also has loved us and given Himself for us.

—Ephesians 5:2

Take Time to Be Holy

George Stebbins was a farmer for his first twenty-three years, then he decided to move to Chicago and sow the seed of the gospel. He was soon recruited by D. L. Moody and Ira Sankey to assist them in their evangelistic campaigns. On **September 1, 1876**, Stebbins began this new chapter in his life by organizing a choir of a thousand voices for an upcoming series of meetings. In the years that followed, his unceasing passion for souls led him to compose the music to some of our greatest hymns of invitation, including "Have Thine Own Way," "Jesus, I Come," "Saved by Grace," and "Ye Must Be Born Again." In 1890, Stebbins composed the melody for this hymn exhorting new converts to take time for the Lord in their everyday lives. The words, written by William Longstaff, are based on the biblical command to be holy as God is holy.

Take time to be holy, speak oft with thy Lord;
Abide in Him always, and feed on His Word.
Make friends of God's children, help those who are weak,
Forgetting in nothing His blessing to seek.

Take time to be holy, the world rushes on;
Spend much time in secret, with Jesus alone.
By looking to Jesus, like Him thou shalt be;
Thy friends in thy conduct His likeness shall see.

Take time to be holy, let Him be thy Guide;
And run not before Him, whatever betide.
In joy or in sorrow, still follow the Lord,
And, looking to Jesus, still trust in His Word.

Take time to be holy, be calm in thy soul,
Each thought and each motive beneath His control.
Thus led by His Spirit to fountains of love,
Thou soon shalt be fitted for service above.

You shall be holy, for I the Lord your God am holy.

—Leviticus 19:2

Take the Name of Jesus with You

Lydia Baxter, born **September 2, 1809**, in Petersburgh, New York, was converted by a Baptist home missionary. After her marriage some years later, she moved to New York City, where her home on West Forty-ninth Street became a center of Christian activity. Unfortunately, Lydia was stricken by a disability and was seldom able to leave her home (though on one occasion she managed to visit a church where children were singing one of her hymns). A friend once asked Lydia how she could be so radiant despite her infirmity. "I have a very special armor," she said. "I have the name of Jesus. When the tempter tries to make me blue or despondent, I mention the name of Jesus, and He can't get through to me anymore."

Take the name of Jesus with you,
Child of sorrow and of woe,
It will joy and comfort give you;
Take it then, where'er you go.

Take the name of Jesus ever,
As a shield from every snare;
If temptations round you gather,
Breathe that holy name in prayer.

O the precious name of Jesus!
How it thrills our souls with joy,
When His loving arms receive us,
And His songs our tongues employ!

Precious name, O how sweet!
Hope of earth and joy of heav'n.
Precious name, O how sweet!
Hope of earth and joy of heav'n.

Therefore, to you who believe, He is precious.

—1 Peter 2:7

Jesus, My Savior, Let Me Be

When we decide to follow Christ, the Holy Spirit goes to work in us, gradually and progressively forming our personalities to be like Jesus. We're to be authentic reproductions of Christ, walking around on this earth as replicas of His deportment and demeanor, and as examples of His conduct and character. Here's a practical hymn to speed the process. It was penned by the early Baptist leader in Britain, Benjamin Beddome, who was determined to serve the Lord until the very hour of his death. When he was too feeble to stand in the pulpit, he had himself carried to his church where he preached sitting down. On **September 3, 1795**, he was in the process of writing another hymn within an hour of his death at age seventy-eight. Try it to the tunes for "When I Survey the Wondrous Cross," "Lord, Speak to Me," "Just As I Am"—or make up your own melody!

Jesus, my Savior, let me be
More perfectly conformed to Thee;
Implant each grace, each sin dethrone,
And form my temper like Thine own.

My foe, when hungry, let me feed,
Share in his grief, supply his need;
The haughty frown may I not fear,
But with a lowly meekness bear.

Let the envenomed heart and tongue,
The hand outstretched to do me wrong,
Excite no feeling in my breast,
But such as Jesus once expressed.

To others let me always give
What I from others would receive;
Good deeds for evil ones return,
Nor when provoked, with anger burn.

Follow my example, as I follow the example of Christ.

—1 Corinthians 11:1 NIV

Abide with Me

"It's better to wear out than to rust out," said Rev. Henry Lyte, a beloved pastor in the fishing village of Lower Brixham, Devonshire, England. He labored there for twenty-three years, preaching, writing, and composing hymns. His lungs began to fail when he was in his early fifties; on **September 4, 1847**, he entered the pulpit with difficulty and preached his final sermon, planning to leave the next day for a therapeutic trip to warmer coasts. That afternoon as he walked and prayed, this hymn came to him. En route to Italy, he sent a polished copy to his wife, then he checked into a hotel in Nice where he died. His last words were, "Peace! Joy!"

Abide with me; fast falls the eventide;
The darkness deepens; Lord with me abide.
When other helpers fail and comforts flee,
Help of the helpless, O abide with me.

Swift to its close ebbs out life's little day;
Earth's joys grow dim; its glories pass away;
Change and decay in all around I see;
O Thou who changest not, abide with me.

I need Thy presence every passing hour.
What but Thy grace can foil the tempter's power?
Who, like Thyself, my guide and stay can be?
Through cloud and sunshine, Lord, abide with me.

Hold Thou Thy cross before my closing eyes;
Shine through the gloom and point me to the skies.
Heaven's morning breaks, and earth's vain shadows flee;
In life, in death, O Lord, abide with me.

*If you abide in Me, and My words abide in you, you will
ask what you desire, and it shall be done for you.*

—John 15:7

Faith Is the Victory

It's a wonder John Yates survived. Once when his family was traveling, a storm hit their ship and young John was thrown across the deck, breaking his leg. On election day in 1844, he fell from a high set of steps in a hotel, fracturing his skull. At sixteen, he was acting in a play and fell on an open knife, piercing his lungs. Other tragedies later befell him. His wife and two sons all died the same week from diphtheria. Yet Yates pressed on, pastoring a Free Will Baptist church in New York State and writing popular ballads and poems. He passed away on **September 5, 1900**, and this marker rests over his grave: "In Memory of the Poet-Preacher Rev. John H. Yates . . . Faith is the Victory, Oh, Glorious Victory, That Overcomes the World."

Encamped along the hills of light,
Ye Christian soldiers, rise.
And press the battle ere the night
Shall veil the glowing skies.
Against the foe in vales below
Let all our strength be hurled.
Faith is the victory, we know,
That overcomes the world.

His banner over us is love,
Our sword the Word of God.
We tread the road the saints above
With shouts of triumph trod.
By faith, they like a whirlwind's breath,
Swept on o'er every field.
The faith by which they conquered death
Is still our shining shield.

Faith is the victory! Faith is the victory!
O glorious victory, that overcomes the world.

And this is the victory that has overcome the world—our faith.

—1 John 5:4

Make Me a Blessing

We are blessed by God to bless others, comforted to comfort, encouraged to encourage, enriched to enrich, and saved to share our message with someone else. The author of this gospel song, Ira B. Wilson, was born into a musical family in Iowa on **September 6, 1880**. He moved to Chicago at age twenty-two to attend Moody Bible Institute. After graduation, he worked on the staff of the First Presbyterian Church at Oshkosh, Wisconsin, before going to work for the Lorenz Publishing Company. The polka-like melody for this song was composed by George Shuler, who, according to some accounts, had been Wilson's roommate at Moody.

> Out in the highways and byways of life,
> Many are weary and sad
> Carry the sunshine where darkness is rife,
> Making the sorrowing glad.
>
> Tell the sweet story of Christ and His love;
> Tell of His pow'r to forgive.
> Others will trust Him if only you prove
> True ev'ry moment you live.
>
> Give as 'twas given to you in your need;
> Love as the Master loved you;
> Be to the helpless a helper indeed;
> Unto your mission be true.
>
> *Make me a blessing, make me a blessing,*
> *Out of my life may Jesus shine;*
> *Make me a blessing, O Savior, I pray,*
> *Make me a blessing to someone today.*

I will bless you . . . and you shall be a blessing.

—Genesis 12:2

Have Faith in God

B. B. McKinney was a tall, silver-haired Southern song leader who wrote the words and music of 149 gospel hymns, including this one. Much of his life was spent teaching sacred music, leading music in revivals and conferences, and establishing the music ministries that shaped the Southern Baptist Convention. He was warm, friendly, outgoing, and full of the love of Jesus. His personality was as humble as his melodies were singable. His life was cut short at age sixty-six when, on **September 7, 1952**, he was killed in a fatal car wreck while returning from a music conference. Among his hymns is this challenge to trust God through thick and thin.

Have faith in God when your pathway is lonely.
He sees and knows all the way you have trod;
Never alone are the least of His children;
Have faith in God, have faith in God.

Have faith in God when your prayers are unanswered,
Your earnest plea He will never forget;
Wait on the Lord, trust His word and be patient,
Have faith in God. He'll answer yet.

Have faith in God in your pain and your sorrow,
His heart is touched with your grief and despair;
Cast all your cares and your burdens upon Him,
And leave them there, oh, leave them there.

Have faith in God though all else fall about you;
Have faith in God, He provides for His own:
He cannot fail though all kingdoms shall perish.
He rules. He reigns upon His throne.

Have faith in God, He's on His throne,
Have faith in God, He watches over His own;
He cannot fail, He must prevail,
Have faith in God, Have faith in God.

So Jesus answered and said to them, "Have faith in God."

—Mark 11:22

He Giveth More Grace

Only God's "more grace" can take a disabled adult who had been orphaned in childhood and turn that person into the Poet of Helpfulness, with a legacy that outlives her earthly span. When Annie Johnson Flint passed away on **September 8, 1932**, her obituary in the *New York Times* gave testimony to the sufficiency of God's grace. The headline read "Annie J. Flint Dead; Widely Known Poet. Bedridden for Thirty Years, She Wrote Verse." The article itself said: "Miss Annie Johnson Flint, writer of religious poetry and widely known as the 'poet of helpfulness,' died last night in a sanitarium here. She was 70 years old. Bedridden for thirty years suffering from arthritis, Miss Flint first wrote poetry as gifts to friends, but later her poems became widely known and many were set to music. She also wrote a book of prose, 'Out of Doors.' She was born in Vineland, N.J., and adopted the name of her foster parents. Her own parents died when she was 6."

He giveth more grace as our burdens grow greater,
He sendeth more strength as our labors increase;
To added afflictions He addeth His mercy,
To multiplied trials he multiplies peace.

When we have exhausted our store of endurance,
When our strength has failed ere the day is half done,
When we reach the end of our hoarded resources
Our Father's full giving is only begun.

His love has no limits, His grace has no measure,
His power no boundary known unto men;
For out of His infinite riches in Jesus
He giveth, and giveth, and giveth again.

But He gives more grace. Therefore He says: "God resists the proud, but gives grace to the humble."

—James 4:6

Let the World Their Virtue Boast

Charles Wesley was attending a Methodist conference in Bristol, England, in 1783, when he suddenly fell ill and thought he was dying. He was given three doses of opium, which stopped his seizure but left him "like a mere log." As friends gathered around, he spoke what he thought were his last words, quoting his own hymn: "I the chief of sinners am, but Jesus died for me." Wesley recovered, but many years later, on **September 9, 1828**, his daughter Sarah, age sixty-nine, lay on her deathbed in the same city. A friend who visited her found her almost too weak to talk, but bending near he heard her quoting her father's same lines: "I the chief of sinners am, but Jesus died for me."

Let the world their virtue boast,
Their works of righteousness,
I, a wretch undone and lost,
Am freely saved by grace;
Other title I disclaim;
This, only this, is all my plea:
I the chief of sinners am,
But Jesus died for me.

Jesus, Thou for me hast died,
And Thou in me wilt live;
I shall feel Thy death applied,
I shall Thy life receive;
Yet, when melted in the flame
Of love, this shall be all my plea:
I the chief of sinners am,
But Jesus died for me.

Christ Jesus came into the world to save sinners, of whom I am chief.

—1 Timothy 1:15

What a Friend We Have in Jesus

Joseph Scriven was born **September 10, 1819**, in Ireland, the son of a military captain and a minister's daughter. As a young man, he tried to tread in his father's footsteps, enrolling in military school; but his health failed, and Joseph ended up a schoolteacher in Canada. His hopes of marriage were dashed twice—once when his fiancée drowned on the eve of their wedding, and later when another fiancée died suddenly from pneumonia. As Scriven's own health failed, he grew depressed; and when his body was found in a small pond, no one knew if his death was accidental or suicidal. His famous hymn, however, lives on. Joseph wrote it as a gift of encouragement for his ailing mother back in Ireland when he found he didn't have enough money to return home to comfort her in person. He called it "Pray Without Ceasing."

What a Friend we have in Jesus, all our sins and griefs to bear!
What a privilege to carry everything to God in prayer!
O what peace we often forfeit, O what needless pain we bear,
All because we do not carry everything to God in prayer.

Have we trials and temptations? Is there trouble anywhere?
We should never be discouraged; take it to the Lord in prayer.
Can we find a friend so faithful who will all our sorrows share?
Jesus knows our every weakness; take it to the Lord in prayer.

Are we weak and heavy laden, cumbered with a load of care?
Precious Savior, still our refuge, take it to the Lord in prayer.
Do your friends despise, forsake you? Take it to the Lord in
    prayer!
In His arms He'll take and shield you; you will find a solace
    there.

Blessed Savior, Thou hast promised Thou wilt all our burdens
    bear;
May we ever, Lord, be bringing all to Thee in earnest prayer.
Soon in glory bright unclouded there will be no need for prayer;
Rapture, praise and endless worship will be our sweet portion
    there.

Pray without ceasing.

—1 Thessalonians 5:17

Once It Was the Blessing

At age twenty-one, Albert Benjamin (A. B.) Simpson delivered his maiden sermon at Knox Presbyterian Church in Hamilton, Ontario, on **September 11, 1865**. The next day he was ordained by the laying on of hands; and that evening he caught a train for Toronto, where he was married the following day. His life never slowed down. He went on to found the Christian and Missionary Alliance and is remembered today as a remarkable missionary statesman and devotional hymnist. This unusual hymn (sometimes titled "Himself") reflects Simpson's theme that it is not the benefits of our faith that are so precious to us—it is the Lord Jesus Himself; and it's not what we do for Him, but what He Himself does through us that makes the difference.

> Once it was the blessing, now it is the Lord;
> Once it was the feeling, now it is His Word;
> Once His gift I wanted, now, the Giver own;
> Once I sought for healing, now Himself alone.
>
> Once 'twas painful trying, now 'tis perfect trust;
> Once a half salvation, now the uttermost;
> Once 'twas ceaseless holding, now He holds me fast;
> Once 'twas constant drifting, now my anchor's cast.
>
> Once 'twas busy planning, now 'tis trustful prayer;
> Once 'twas anxious caring, now He has the care;
> Once 'twas what I wanted, now what Jesus says;
> Once 'twas constant asking, now 'tis ceaseless praise.
>
> *All in all forever, Jesus will I sing;*
> *Everything in Jesus, and Jesus everything.*

When they had lifted up their eyes, they saw no one but Jesus only.

—Matthew 17:8

Blessèd Savior, Thee I Love

Four generations of Duffields helped mold the spiritual life of America. The first George Duffield was such an effective Colonial chaplain during the Revolutionary War that the British put a price on his head. His grandson, George Duffield II, continued his grandfather's ministry until he literally died in the pulpit while preaching in Detroit in 1868. His last words were, "You will have to excuse me; my head reels." George Duffield III, born **September 12, 1818**, also preached, but was better known for his hymns "Stand Up, Stand Up for Jesus" and "Blessèd Savior." His son, Samuel Duffield, became a powerful preacher as well. George and Samuel worked side by side during their final years, dying within fourteen months of one another.

Blessèd Savior, Thee I love,
All my other joys above;
All my hopes in Thee abide,
Thou my Hope, and naught betide;
Ever let my glory be,
Only, only, only Thee.

Once again beside the cross,
All my gain I count but loss;
Earthly pleasures fade away,
Clouds they are that hide my day;
Hence, vain shadows! let me see
Jesus, crucified for me.

Blessèd Savior, Thine am I,
Thine to live, and Thine to die;
Height or depth, or creature power,
Ne'er shall hide my Savior more;
Ever shall my glory be,
Only, only, only Thee.

Lord, You know all things; You know that I love You.

—John 21:17

Sweet Hour of Prayer

"Sweet Hour of Prayer" first appeared in the *New York Observer* on **September 13, 1845**, along with a note by a British minister who claimed it had been written by a blind preacher named W. W. Walford of Warwickshire, England. But no record has ever been found of such a man, and his identity is a mystery. Whoever it was, the author understood the power of spending a conscious hour in the presence of God in Bible study and prayer: "In seasons of distress and grief, / My soul has often found relief / And oft escaped the tempter's snare / By thy return, sweet hour of prayer!"

Sweet hour of prayer! sweet hour of prayer!
That calls me from a world of care,
And bids me at my Father's throne
Make all my wants and wishes known.
In seasons of distress and grief,
My soul has often found relief
And oft escaped the tempter's snare
By thy return, sweet hour of prayer!

Sweet hour of prayer! sweet hour of prayer!
Thy wings shall my petition bear
To Him whose truth and faithfulness
Engage the waiting soul to bless.
And since He bids me seek His face,
Believe His Word and trust His grace,
I'll cast on Him my every care,
And wait for thee, sweet hour of prayer!

Could you not watch one hour? Watch and pray, lest you enter into temptation.

—Mark 14:37–38

Nearer, My God, to Thee

President William McKinley was enjoying himself at the Temple of Music in Buffalo, New York, when a man approached him with a pistol hidden under a handkerchief and fired two bullets into his body. As McKinley collapsed, he whispered to an aide, "My wife . . . be careful how you tell her." For several days, the nation prayed for the president's recovery; but in the early hours of **September 14, 1901**, he was heard faintly singing his favorite hymn, "Nearer, My God, to Thee." He died shortly after, and on the day of his funeral this hymn rose up from churches all across America. It was said that the president's fondness for this hymn floated over the nation like a cloud and profoundly touched the popular heart.

Nearer, my God, to Thee, nearer to Thee!
E'en though it be a cross that raiseth me,
Still all my song shall be, nearer, my God, to Thee.
Nearer, my God, to Thee, nearer to Thee!

Though like the wanderer, the sun gone down,
Darkness be over me, my rest a stone.
Yet in my dreams I'd be nearer, my God, to Thee.
Nearer, my God, to Thee, nearer to Thee!

There let the way appear, steps unto Heav'n;
All that Thou sendest me, in mercy given;
Angels to beckon me nearer, my God, to Thee.
Nearer, my God, to Thee, nearer to Thee!

There in my Father's home, safe and at rest,
There in my Savior's love, perfectly blest;
Age after age to be, nearer my God to Thee.
Nearer, my God, to Thee, nearer to Thee!

But it is good for me to draw near to God; I have put my trust in the Lord God, that I may declare all Your works.

—Psalm 73:28

I Stand Amazed in the Presence

With a name like Gabriel, we'd expect some music—and that's what we got. Even as a child, Charles H. Gabriel was drawn to music. He taught himself to play the organ as a boy, and he began leading singing schools as a teenager. As an adult, he led music, wrote music, sang music, and published music—lots of it. When he died in Los Angeles on **September 15, 1932**, he left behind thirty-five books of gospel songs, eight Sunday school songbooks, seven songbooks for men, six for women, ten for children, nineteen collections of anthems, and twenty-three cantatas. It's no wonder I grew up in a church that sang Gabriel's songs nearly every Sunday. This was one of our favorites:

I stand amazed in the presence
Of Jesus the Nazarene,
And wonder how He could love me,
A sinner, condemned, unclean.

For me it was in the garden
He prayed: "Not My will, but Thine."
He had no tears for His own griefs,
But sweat drops of blood for mine.

When with the ransomed in glory
His face I at last shall see,
'Twill be my joy through the ages
To sing of His love for me.

O how marvelous! O how wonderful!
And my song shall ever be:
O how marvelous! O how wonderful!
Is my Savior's love for me!

The men were amazed and asked, "What kind of man
is this? Even the winds and the waves obey him!"

—Matthew 8:27 NIV

Little Is Much When God Is in It

I believe in the bigness of little things. It's great to launch a vast enterprise for Christ if God leads; but in the long run, more good may be done by a simple word of witness to a child in Sunday school or the passing out of a tract. There are concentric, ever-expanding ripples to small deeds done faithfully for Him. One day years ago, a woman encouraged a shy Canadian teen to sing his first solo. He later became "America's Beloved Gospel Singer"— George Beverly Shea. That woman, Kittie Louise Suffield, born **September 16, 1884**, is the author of this song.

> In the harvest field now ripened
> There's a work for all to do;
> Hark! the voice of God is calling
> To the harvest calling you.
>
> Does the place you're called to labor
> Seem too small and little known?
> It is great if God is in it,
> And He'll not forget His own.
>
> Are you laid aside from service,
> Body worn from toil and care?
> You can still be in the battle,
> In the sacred place of prayer.
>
> When the conflict here is ended
> And our race on earth is run,
> He will say, if we are faithful,
> "Welcome home, My child—well done!"
>
> *Little is much when God is in it! Labor not for wealth or fame.*
> *There's a crown—and you can win it, if you go in Jesus' name.*

For who has despised the day of small things?

—Zechariah 4:10

Day by Day

I'm in a dilemma today—which of Josiah Conder's hymns to use! It's not his most majestic piece, but I've chosen "Day by Day" because its quaint lesson is so powerful. Conder was born **September 17, 1789.** After being blinded in one eye at age five by an inoculation for smallpox, he was treated by the new medical practice of electrical shocking to prevent blindness in his other eye. It must have worked, because he recovered and went on to become a powerful writer, hymnist, journalist, abolitionist, and layman in the Congregational Church of England. Notice how the phrases in this hymn carry a punch, such as this line in the last stanza: "Oh, to live exempt from care / By the energy of prayer"!

Day by day the manna fell;
O to learn this lesson well!
Still by constant mercy fed,
Give me, Lord, my daily bread.

"Day by day," the promise reads,
Daily strength for daily needs;
Cast foreboding fears away;
Take the manna of today.

Lord! my times are in Thy hand;
All my sanguine hopes have planned,
To Thy wisdom I resign,
And would make Thy purpose mine.

Oh, to live exempt from care
By the energy of prayer:
Strong in faith, with mind subdued,
Yet elate with gratitude!

He . . . fed you with manna which you did not know nor did your fathers know, that He might make you know that man shall not live by bread alone; but man lives by every word that proceeds from the mouth of the LORD.

—Deuteronomy 8:3

Only Trust Him

When D. L. Moody crisscrossed the British Isles in a highly publicized evangelistic campaign in 1873, everyone wanted copies of the songs Ira Sankey was introducing to the crowds. Publishers were reluctant to invest in a new hymnal, so Moody put up his life savings to guarantee the project. On **September 18, 1873**, the first advertisement appeared for this small new hymnal called *Sacred Songs and Solos*. It became a publishing phenomenon, selling over eighty million copies within fifty years, and changing the sound of sacred music in England and America for the next hundred years. Included was this old favorite by John Stockton, "Only Trust Him," which Sankey had discovered in his scrapbook en route to England.

September 18

Come, every soul by sin oppressed;
There's mercy with the Lord,
And He will surely give you rest
By trusting in His Word.

For Jesus shed His precious blood
Rich blessings to bestow;
Plunge now into the crimson flood
That washes white as snow.

Come, then, and join this holy band,
And on to glory go
To dwell in that celestial land
Where joys immortal flow.

Only trust Him, only trust Him,
Only trust Him now;
He will save you, He will save you,
He will save you now.

The LORD is good, a stronghold in the day of trouble;
and He knows those who trust in Him.

—Nahum 1:7

Master, the Tempest Is Raging

This hymn by Mary Ann Baker was published in 1874 and sprang into national consciousness when Present James A. Garfield was shot by an assassin shortly after his inauguration. For two months, as Garfield's life hung in the balance, "Master, the Tempest Is Raging" was sung in churches, schools, and family circles across the nation. When the president died on **September 19, 1881**, it was sung at many events in his memory. Years later, when President John F. Kennedy addressed the eleventh annual Presidential Prayer Breakfast, he said, "Perhaps the wisest thing that was said in the Bible was the words, 'Peace, be still.'" I vividly recall the choir of my childhood church singing this hymn, which occupied a two-page spread in our hymnal. The dramatic words of the chorus have stayed with me all my life. *No waters can swallow the ship where lies / The Master of ocean, and earth, and skies. . . .*

Master, the tempest is raging!
The billows are tossing high!
The sky is o'ershadow with blackness,
No shelter or help is nigh;
Carest Thou not that we perish?
How canst Thou lie asleep,
When each moment so madly is threatening
A grave in the angry deep?

The winds and the waves shall obey Thy will, Peace, be still!
Whether the wrath of the storm tossed sea,
Or demons or men, or whatever it be
No waters can swallow the ship where lies
The Master of ocean, and earth, and skies;
They all shall sweetly obey Thy will,
Peace, be still! Peace, be still!
They all shall sweetly obey Thy will,
Peace, peace, be still!

Then He arose and rebuked the wind, and
said to the sea, "Peace, be still!"

—Mark 4:39

O to Be Like Thee

September 20, 1921, marked the death of William Kirkpatrick, a humble carpenter with musical aspirations. His violin and cello opened doors of opportunity, and by the end of his life, the erstwhile carpenter had become a world-famous composer of gospel tunes, including this hymn by Thomas Chisholm (of "Great Is Thy Faithfulness" fame). It's wonderful when we find another person whom we want to emulate; we all need to have good mentors and models. But nothing compares to developing the attitudes, personality traits, wisdom, and usefulness of Jesus Christ Himself as the Holy Spirit "makes us more and more like him as we are changed into his glorious image" (2 Cor. 3:18 NLT). Oh, to be like Him!

O to be like Thee! Blessèd Redeemer,
This is my constant longing and prayer;
Gladly I'll forfeit all of earth's treasures,
Jesus, Thy perfect likeness to wear.

O to be like Thee! Full of compassion,
Loving, forgiving, tender and kind,
Helping the helpless, cheering the fainting,
Seeking the wandering sinner to find.

O to be like Thee! Lowly in spirit,
Holy and harmless, patient and brave;
Meekly enduring cruel reproaches,
Willing to suffer others to save.

O to be like Thee! O to be like Thee,
Blessèd Redeemer, pure as Thou art;
Come in Thy sweetness, come in Thy fullness;
Stamp Thine own image deep on my heart.

We all, with unveiled face, beholding as in a mirror the glory of the Lord, are being transformed into the same image from glory to glory, just as by the Spirit of the Lord.

—2 Corinthians 3:18

Eternal Depth of Love Divine

Count Nicolaus Ludwig von Zinzendorf wrote hymns all his life, about two thousand in all. The Moravian village of Herrnhut, sheltered from persecution on his estate, became a place of singing. On one occasion, as the Moravians sent out their first pair of missionaries, they sang far into the night and it was later reported that perhaps as many as a hundred hymns were used. Zinzendorf wrote this hymn, "Eternal Depth of Love Divine," to honor the birthday of his friend, Count Henkel of Oderberg, on **September 21, 1726.** Thirteen years later, it was translated into English by John Wesley.

> Eternal depth of love divine,
> In Jesus, God with us, displayed;
> How bright Thy beaming glories shine!
> How wide Thy healing streams are spread!
>
> With whom dost Thou delight to dwell?
> Sinners, a vile and thankless race:
> O God, what tongue aright can tell
> How vast Thy love, how great Thy grace!
>
> The dictates of Thy sovereign will
> With joy our grateful hearts receive:
> All Thy delight in us fulfill;
> Lo! all we are to Thee we give.
>
> Still, Lord, Thy saving health display,
> And arm our souls with heav'nly zeal;
> So fearless shall we urge our way
> Through all the powers of earth and hell.

The Son is the radiance of God's glory and the exact representation of his being, sustaining all things by his powerful word.

—Hebrews 1:3 NIV

The Hour of Prayer

Charlotte Elliott died **September 22, 1871**, at the age of eighty-two. She's best known for her famous hymn "Just As I Am," but she published other songs from her sickbed, including this one about prayer. It's a reminder that the best part of the day is our quiet time. Our daily devotions keep us going from "blush of morn to evening star," hushing doubts, banishing fears, and renewing our strength.

My God, is any hour so sweet
From blush of morn to evening star,
As that which calls me to Thy feet—
The hour of prayer?

Blest is that tranquil hour of morn,
And blest that hour of solemn eve,
When, on the wings of prayer upborne,
The world I leave.

Then is my strength by Thee renewed;
Then are my sins by Thee forgiv'n;
Then dost Thou cheer my solitude
With hopes of Heav'n.

Hushed is each doubt, gone ev'ry fear;
My spirit seems in Heav'n to stay;
And e'en the penitential tear
Is wiped away.

Lord, till I reach yon blissful shore,
No privilege so dear shall be
As thus my inmost soul to pour
In prayer to Thee.

Rejoicing in hope, patient in tribulation,
continuing steadfastly in prayer.

—Romans 12:12

I Can Hear My Savior Calling

The probing, repetitive words of this simple hymn are attributed to Ernest W. Blandy, about whom nothing is known. The music, which fits the words perfectly and makes this one of our great hymns of invitation, was composed by pastor and evangelist John Samuel Norris (December 4, 1844–**September 23, 1907**). Norris was born on the Isle of Wight but emigrated to Canada with his family. In 1868, he was ordained into the Methodist ministry, and ten years later became a Congregationalist. Norris pastored several churches in Canada and the United States, but his most lasting legacy is the tune for this hymn. Only heaven knows how many people have given their lives fully to Jesus during the singing of this simple song.

I can hear my Savior calling,
I can hear my Savior calling,
I can hear my Savior calling,
"Take thy cross and follow, follow Me."

I'll go with Him through the garden,
I'll go with Him through the garden,
I'll go with Him through the garden,
I'll go with Him, with Him all the way.

He will give me grace and glory,
He will give me grace and glory,
He will give me grace and glory,
And go with me, with me all the way.

Where He leads me I will follow,
Where He leads me I will follow,
Where He leads me I will follow;
I'll go with Him, with Him, all the way.

Whoever desires to come after Me, let him deny
himself, and take up his cross, and follow Me.

—Mark 8:34

Come, Ye Sinners, Poor and Needy

In Magnolia Cemetery, Spartanburg, South Carolina, a timeworn historical marker stands in recognition of a musician who died on this day, **September 24, 1875**. It reads: "GRAVE OF WILLIAM WALKER. William 'Singin' Billy' Walker (1809–75) was the author of *Southern Harmony*, a collection of religious music employing shaped musical notes to aid those who could not read standard musical notation. He later published the more elaborate *Christian Harmony* and taught singing schools throughout the middle, southern, and western states." William Walker was the creative composer who gave us the tunes to some of our most deeply felt Southern hymns, including "What Wondrous Love Is This," "Jesus Calls Us O'er the Tumult," and "Come, Ye Sinners, Poor and Needy."

Come, ye sinners, poor and needy,
Weak and wounded, sick and sore;
Jesus ready stands to save you,
Full of pity, love and power.

Come, ye thirsty, come, and welcome,
God's free bounty glorify;
True belief and true repentance,
Every grace that brings you nigh.

Come, ye weary, heavy laden,
Lost and ruined by the fall;
If you tarry till you're better,
You will never come at all.

I will arise and go to Jesus,
He will embrace me in His arms;
In the arms of my dear Savior,
O there are ten thousand charms.

I will arise and go to my father, and will
say to him, "Father, I have sinned."

—Luke 15:18

Near to the Heart of God

One day in 1901, Cleland Boyd McAfee, the much-loved pastor of Chicago's First Presbyterian Church, was shaken by the news that his two beloved nieces had died from diphtheria. He penned the words and music of this hymn, and on the day of the double funeral, he sang it outside his brother's quarantined house. The following Sunday, the First Presbyterian choir sang this song as a Communion hymn. Today is McAfee's birthday, **September 25, 1866**.

There is a place of quiet rest,
Near to the heart of God.
A place where sin cannot molest,
Near to the heart of God.

There is a place of comfort sweet,
Near to the heart of God.
A place where we our Savior meet,
Near to the heart of God.

There is a place of full release,
Near to the heart of God.
A place where all is joy and peace,
Near to the heart of God.

O Jesus, blest Redeemer,
Sent from the heart of God,
Hold us who wait before Thee
Near to the heart of God.

He tends his flock like a shepherd: He gathers the
lambs in his arms and carries them close to his
heart; he gently leads those that have young.

—Isaiah 40:11 NIV

Faith of Our Fathers

Our hymns and heritage are important, because history gives us roots and routes—a sense of who we are and where we're going. "Faith of Our Fathers" was written by Frederick W. Faber in memory of English Catholics who died for their faith during the reign of Henry VIII. It vaulted into worldwide popularity when sung at the funeral of President Franklin Roosevelt. Faber was an Anglican-turned-Catholic who ministered in London until 1863, when it became apparent his health was failing from Bright's disease. His legs became covered with open wounds and his stamina collapsed. When told death was near, he exclaimed, "God be praised!" He was only forty-nine when he passed away on **September 26, 1863**.

Faith of our fathers, living still,
In spite of dungeon, fire and sword;
O how our hearts beat high with joy
Whene'er we hear that glorious Word!

Faith of our fathers, we will strive
To win all nations unto Thee;
And through the truth that comes from God,
We all shall then be truly free.

Faith of our fathers, we will love
Both friend and foe in all our strife;
And preach Thee, too, as love knows how
By kindly words and virtuous life.

Faith of our fathers, holy faith!
We will be true to Thee till death.

Then we cried out to the LORD God of our
fathers, and the LORD heard our voice.

—Deuteronomy 26:7

There Is Joy in Serving Jesus

The work of the kingdom is sometimes wearying and occasionally frustrating; but we can't do it out of fear, fatigue, or failure. It's inappropriate to serve Christ with drudgery or discouragement. We must serve Him with joy! The two Ackley brothers, Alfred and Benton, left a wonderful heritage of joyful gospel songs. Alfred, a Presbyterian pastor, wrote about a thousand hymns and hymn tunes, including the Easter favorite "I Serve a Risen Savior." Benton D. Ackley, born **September 27, 1872**, was the pianist for the Billy Sunday campaigns and later served as composer and compiler for the Rodeheaver Publishing Company. He wrote more than three thousand hymn tunes. He also teamed up with Dr. Oswald J. Smith, and the first hymn they wrote together was "There Is Joy in Serving Jesus," Smith writing the words and Ackley the music.

There is joy in serving Jesus
As I journey on my way
Joy that fills my heart with praises
Every hour and every day

There is joy in serving Jesus
Joy; that triumphs over pain
Fills my heart with heaven's music
Till I join the glad refrain

There is joy in serving Jesus
Joy amid the darkest night
For I've learned the wondrous secret
And I'm walking in the light

There is joy, joy, joy in serving Jesus
Joy that throbs within my heart
Every moment, every hour as I draw upon His power
There is joy, joy, joy that never shall depart

Tell of his works with songs of joy.

—Psalm 107:22 NIV

In Thy Great Name, O Lord, We Come

If you visit the cemetery in Bristol, England, containing the grave of the author of this hymn, you'll read this quaint epitaph: "Here lie interred the mortal remains of the Rev. Joseph Hoskins, the lively, active, and successful minister of the Church of Christ assembling in Castle-Green, in this City: Who (by the blessing of God on his labors), in the course of ten years that he presided over the Church as a faithful pastor, raised it, from a low and languid estate, to a truly respectable and flourishing condition. . . . The soundness of his doctrine . . . and that amazing gift in prayer, which God had blessed him, raised him to the highest pitch of admiration. . . . He died on the **28th of September, 1788**, aged 43 years."

In Thy great Name, O Lord, we come,
To worship at Thy feet;
Oh, pour Thy Holy Spirit down
On all that now shall meet.

We come to hear Jehovah speak,
To hear the Savior's voice;
Thy face and favor, Lord, we seek,
Now make our hearts rejoice.

Teach us to pray, and praise, and hear,
And understand Thy Word;
To feel Thy blissful presence near,
And trust our living Lord.

Here let Thy power and grace be felt,
Thy love and mercy known;
Our icy hearts, dear Jesus, melt,
And break this flinty stone.

I was in the Spirit on the Lord's Day.

—Revelation 1:10

Jerusalem, My Happy Home

Dr. R. F. Littledale, an Anglican cleric in London, sat at his desk on **September 29, 1866,** and completed the preface to a volume of hymns compiled by his late friend J. M. Neale titled *The Invalid's Hymn-Book: Being a Selection of Hymns Appropriate to the Sick-Room.* "That [these hymns]," wrote Littledale, "have proved singularly acceptable and soothing at sick and dying beds, whatever the rank or age of the suffering might be, is known to the experience of very many of those whose duties call them amidst such scenes." Included in this volume was "Jerusalem, My Happy Home," a versified rendition of Revelation 21–22. The original version of this hymn dates from the late 1500s.

> Jerusalem, my happy home,
> When shall I come to thee?
> When shall my sorrows have an end?
> Thy joys when shall I see?
>
> O happy harbor of the saints!
> O sweet and pleasant soil!
> In thee no sorrow may be found,
> No grief, no care, no toil.
>
> Thy walls are made of precious stones,
> Thy bulwarks diamonds square;
> Thy gates are of right orient pearl;
> Exceeding rich and rare;
>
> Aye, my sweet home, Jerusalem,
> Would God I were in thee:
> Would God my woes were at an end,
> Thy joys that I might see.

The construction of its wall was of jasper; and the city was pure gold, like clear glass.

—Revelation 21:18

Why Do We Mourn
Departing Friends?

There was never a preacher like George Whitefield, the British evangelist who brought revival to pre-Revolutionary America. He preached his last sermon at a friend's home in Newburyport, Massachusetts, while holding a candle on the landing of the stairs. When the candle burned out, he went upstairs to bed and had his evening devotions using his Bible and a copy of Watts's hymns. Whitefield passed away as the sun came up the next morning, Sunday, **September 30, 1770**. On Tuesday, amid throngs of weeping people, he was buried beneath the pulpit of the local church as his friends sang Watts's famous hymn "Why Do We Mourn Departing Friends?" (It can be sung to the tune of "God Moves in a Mysterious Way.")

Why do we mourn departing friends,
Or shake at death's alarms?
'Tis but the voice that Jesus sends
To call them to His arms.

Why should we tremble to convey
Their bodies to the tomb?
There the dear flesh of Jesus lay,
And left a long perfume.

Thence He arose, ascending high,
And showed our feet the way;
Up to the Lord our flesh shall fly,
At the great rising day.

Then let the last loud trumpet sound,
And bid our kindred rise;
Awake, ye nations under ground;
Ye saints, ascend the skies.

A little while longer and the world will see Me no more, but you will see Me. Because I live, you will live also.

—John 14:19

Faith Is a Living Power from Heaven

A man once said to me, "Faith is believing in something despite the evidence." No, it isn't. Faith is placing logical trust in something that gives evidence of being true and trustworthy. And nothing is more dependable than the promises of Scripture! Whenever we face a difficulty of any kind, there's invariably a promise in the Bible just for our need. As we find and focus on that promise, we discover the Lord is faithful and our faith grows accordingly. Here's a great hymn on the subject. It was penned by a leading sixteenth-century Bohemian Brethren hymnist named Petrus Herbert. Today marks the date of his death, **October 1, 1571.**

Faith is a living power from Heaven
That grasps the promise God hath given,
A trust that cannot be o'erthrown,
Fixed heartily on Christ alone.

Faith finds in Christ whate'er we need
To save or strengthen us indeed,
Receives the grace that He sends down,
And makes us share His cross and crown.

Faith in the conscience worketh peace,
And bids the mourner's weeping cease;
Faith feels the Spirit's kindling breath,
In love and hope that conquer death.

And from His fullness grant each soul
The rightful faith's true end and goal,
The blessedness no foes destroy,
Eternal love and light and joy.

Yet he did not waver through unbelief regarding the promise of God, but was strengthened in his faith and gave glory to God, being fully persuaded that God had power to do what he had promised.

—Romans 4:20–21 NIV

Lord Jesus, Think on Me

Allen William Chatfield was born **October 2, 1808**. He attended the university in his hometown of Cambridge and then devoted his life to being a simple Anglican vicar. In his spare time, he found and translated ancient hymns. Here's an example of a Greek hymn by Synesius of Cyrene, dating from the fifth century. Chatfield rendered it into English, and it appeared in his 1876 hymnal, *Songs and Hymns of Earliest Greek Christian Poets*. What a hymn for personal devotions!

> Lord Jesus, think on me
> And purge away my sin;
> From earthborn passions set me free
> And make me pure within.
>
> Lord Jesus, think on me,
> With many a care oppressed;
> Let me Thy loving servant be
> And taste Thy promised rest.
>
> Lord Jesus, think on me
> Amid the battle's strife;
> In all my pain and misery
> Be Thou my Health and Life.
>
> Lord Jesus, think on me
> That I may sing above
> To Father, Spirit, and to Thee
> The strains of praise and love.

How precious also are Your thoughts to me, O God!
How great is the sum of them! If I should count them,
they would be more in number than the sand.

—Psalm 139:17–18

Children of the Heavenly Father

Birthday greetings to the Fanny Crosby of Sweden—Karolina Wilhelmina Sandell-Berg, known affectionately as "Lina." She was born into a pastor's family on **October 3, 1832**, and was very close to her father. When Lina was twenty-six, she and her dad were traveling by boat. He fell overboard and drowned before her eyes. Perhaps this tragedy helps explain the unusual level of comfort afforded by her hymns, such as "Day by Day" (see July 27) and "Children of the Heavenly Father," with its tender portrayal of our relationship with our Father in heaven.

Children of the heav'nly Father
Safely in His bosom gather;
Nestling bird nor star in Heaven
Such a refuge e'er was given.

God His own doth tend and nourish;
In His holy courts they flourish;
From all evil things He spares them;
In His mighty arms He bears them.

Neither life nor death shall ever
From the Lord His children sever;
Unto them His grace He showeth,
And their sorrows all He knoweth.

Though He giveth or He taketh,
God His children ne'er forsaketh;
His the loving purpose solely
To preserve them pure and holy.

Neither death nor life, nor angels nor principalities nor powers, nor things present nor things to come, nor height nor depth, nor any other created thing, shall be able to separate us from the love of God which is in Christ Jesus our Lord.

—Romans 8:38–39

All for Jesus

When the author of this hymn, Mary D. James, passed away on **October 4, 1883**, the Christian world lost a tireless worker in the kingdom. *The Christian Advocate* paid tribute to her in its next issue: "Her life during the great part of her more than seventy years was hid with Christ in God. Spirituality was her normal state. . . . Who that ever saw her can forget her pale face, her speaking eyes, her winning smile . . . ? Her presence was a benediction to all whom she met." Just before she died, Mary told the friend who was to preach her funeral, "Please don't exalt me, but exalt Christ. I am of no account; let Christ be all in all."

All for Jesus, all for Jesus!
All my being's ransomed powers:
All my thoughts and words and doings,
All my days and all my hours.

Let my hands perform His bidding,
Let my feet run in His ways;
Let my eyes see Jesus only,
Let my lips speak forth His praise.

Since my eyes were fixed on Jesus,
I've lost sight of all beside;
So enchained my spirit's vision,
Looking at the Crucified.

All for Jesus! All for Jesus!
All my days and all my hours;
All for Jesus! All for Jesus!
All my days and all my hours.

So when they had brought their boats to land,
they forsook all and followed Him.

—Luke 5:11

Swing Low, Sweet Chariot

Fisk University in Nashville was established after the Civil War to provide training for newly liberated African Americans who wanted to gain an education. The school's treasurer, George Leonard White, a devout Christian, put together a singing group that came to be known as the Jubilee Singers. One of White's finest singers, Ella Sheppard, brought him this song, "Swing Low, Sweet Chariot," claiming her mother had written it in slavery. On the evening of **October 5, 1871**, White and his singers gathered for prayer, and the next morning they took off from the Nashville train station, hoping that a string of concerts would raise much-needed funds for the school. No one dreamed they were about to introduce the world to a new genre of Christian music—the Negro spiritual.

I looked over Jordan and what did I see
Coming for to carry me home
A band of angels coming after me
Coming for to carry me home

Sometimes I'm up and sometimes I'm down
Coming for to carry me home
But still my soul feels heavenly bound
Coming for to carry me home

The brightest day that I can say
Coming for to carry me home
When Jesus washed my sins away
Coming for to carry me home

Swing low, sweet chariot
Coming for to carry me home
Swing low, sweet chariot
Coming for to carry me home

Suddenly a chariot of fire appeared . . . and
Elijah went up by a whirlwind into heaven.

—2 Kings 2:11

Saved by Grace

This is a red-letter day for two of the greatest composers of the gospel song era. William Bradbury was born **October 6, 1816**. He's the musician who gave us tunes such as "Just As I Am" and "Jesus Loves Me." And **October 6, 1945**, marks the death of George Stebbins, the great composer who gave us the tunes to "Have Thine Own Way" and this beloved Fanny Crosby hymn, "Saved by Grace." Fanny Crosby once said of George Stebbins, "If ever there was a man of high honor and culture of character, it is Mr. Stebbins. He has filled up every nook of my life with his goodness." This Crosby/Stebbins hymn is a classic, reminding us that when we close our eyes on earth, we'll open them within the palace of the King, and we shall see Him face-to-face.

Some day the silver cord will break,
And I no more as now shall sing;
But oh, the joy when I shall wake
Within the palace of the King!

Some day my earthly house will fall.
I cannot tell how soon 'twill be;
But this I know—my All in All
Has now a place in Heav'n for me.

Some day, when fades the golden sun
Beneath the rosy tinted west,
My blessèd Lord will say, "Well done!"
And I shall enter into rest.

And I shall see Him face to face,
And tell the story—Saved by grace;
And I shall see Him face to face,
And tell the story—Saved by grace.

By grace you have been saved.
—Ephesians 2:5

For the Beauty of the Earth

Folliot S. Pierpoint was born **October 7, 1835**, in Bath, England. He graduated from Cambridge in 1857 and became a professor of the classics. According to some accounts, when Pierpoint was twenty-nine, he returned to his home in Bath during the springtime, perhaps suffering fatigue. During a walk along the Avon River he was reassured of God's love by the beauty of creation, and out of that experience came this hymn for Holy Communion in the Anglican church. Pierpoint's actual closing line has been altered in modern hymnals. What he originally wrote was, "Christ, our God, to Thee we raise / This our sacrifice of praise."

For the beauty of the earth
For the glory of the skies,
For the love which from our birth
Over and around us lies.
Lord of all to Thee we raise
This our hymn of grateful praise.

For the beauty of each hour,
Of the day and of the night,
Hill and vale, and tree and flower,
Sun and moon, and stars of light.
Lord of all to Thee we raise
This our hymn of grateful praise.

For Thy Church, that evermore
Lifteth holy hands above,
Offering up on every shore
Her pure sacrifice of love.
Lord of all to Thee we raise
This our hymn of grateful praise.

*By Him let us continually offer the sacrifice of praise to God,
that is, the fruit of our lips, giving thanks to His name.*

—Hebrews 13:15

From Every Stormy Wind That Blows

Every detail of the Old Testament tabernacle was an object lesson predating and predicting the coming Messiah. At the heart of the tabernacle, within the Holy of Holies, was the ark of the covenant and its covering, the mercy seat. Once a year the high priest sprinkled the blood of a lamb on the mercy seat, thus making atonement for the people. The mercy seat represents the place where God meets us with forgiveness and fellowships with us on the basis of the blood of the Lamb. That's the imagery behind this hymn by Hugh Stowell, who died at age sixty-six on **October 8, 1865**. Stowell was an energetic minister who only slowed down after an attack of diphtheria in September of that year. Those at his deathbed reported, "Almost every word was prayer. . . . The morning of his death the only articulate words that we could catch . . . were 'Amen! Amen!'"

From every stormy wind that blows,
From every swelling tide of woes,
There is a calm, a sure retreat;
'Tis found beneath the mercy seat.

There is a place where Jesus sheds
The oil of gladness on our heads;
A place than all besides more sweet;
It is the blood-bought mercy seat.

There, there, on eagles' wings we soar,
And time and sense seem all no more;
And heaven comes down, our souls to greet,
And glory crowns the mercy seat.

You shall put the mercy seat on top of the ark. . . .
And there I will meet with you, and I will speak
with you from above the mercy seat.

—Exodus 25:21–22

He Abides

The Bible tells us to rejoice in the Lord always, and hymnist Herbert Buffum embodied that command in his personality. Converted to Christ at age eighteen, Buffum entered the ministry and became a Pentecostal evangelist and one of the most prolific hymn writers of all time, having ten thousand songs to his credit (about a thousand were actually published). *Ripley's Believe It or Not* claimed he once composed twelve songs in an hour. Some of his songs became Sunday school hits when I was a child, such as "Isn't He Wonderful?" and "Let's Talk about Jesus." Buffum's "I'm Going Higher" is still a choice Southern Gospel song about heaven. When he died on **October 9, 1939**, the *Los Angeles Times* called Herbert Buffum "The King of Gospel Song Writers."

I'm rejoicing night and day
As I walk the narrow way,
For the hand of God in all my life I see.
And the reason of my bliss,
Yes, the secret all is this:
That the Comforter abides with me.

He is with me everywhere,
And He knows my ev'ry care;
I'm as happy as a bird and just as free.
For the Spirit has control;
Jesus satisfies my soul,
Since the Comforter abides with me.

He abides, He abides.
Hallelujah, He abides with me!
I'm rejoicing night and day
As I walk the narrow way,
For the Comforter abides with me.

I will pray the Father, and He will give you another Helper,
that He may abide with you forever—the Spirit of truth.

—John 14:16–17

He Is Able to Deliver Thee

Want to study the "grandest theme through the ages rung"? Look up the "ables" of God, such as: "God is *able* to make all grace abound toward you" (2 Cor. 9:8). "He is *able* to keep what [we] have committed to Him until that Day" (2 Tim. 1:12). "He is *able* to save completely those who come to God through him" (Heb. 7:25 NIV). "He is *able* even to subdue all things to Himself" (Phil. 3:21). "[He] is *able* to keep you from stumbling, and to present you faultless before the presence of His glory" (Jude 24). And there are so many more. What a Bible study! And all of them are summarized in this joyful gospel song by William Ogden, who was born on this date, **October 10, 1841**.

'Tis the grandest theme through the ages rung;
'Tis the grandest theme for a mortal tongue;
'Tis the grandest theme that the world e'er sung,
"Our God is able to deliver thee."

'Tis the grandest theme in the earth or main;
'Tis the grandest theme for a mortal strain;
'Tis the grandest theme, tell the world again,
"Our God is able to deliver thee."

'Tis the grandest theme, let the tidings roll,
To the guilty heart, to the sinful soul;
Look to God in faith, He will make thee whole,
"Our God is able to deliver thee."

He is able to deliver thee,
He is able to deliver thee;
Though by sin oppressed, go to Him for rest;
"Our God is able to deliver thee."

For in that He Himself has suffered, being tempted,
He is able to aid those who are tempted.

—Hebrews 2:18

God Be with You Till We Meet Again

William G. Tomer had been teaching singing schools for ten years when, on **October 11, 1862**, he enlisted in the Union Army and became an aide to General William Sherman. After the war, he found a job in the Treasury Department in Washington, D.C., and also began serving as music director at Grace Methodist Episcopal Church. Down the street, Rev. Jeremiah Rankin pastored the First Congregational Church. Rankin, wanting a fresh song to close his Sunday night services, wrote the words to this hymn and asked Tomer to write the melody. It became the most famous closing hymn in America for the next hundred years.

God be with you till we meet again;
By His counsels guide, uphold you,
With His sheep securely fold you;
God be with you till we meet again.

God be with you till we meet again;
'Neath His wings protecting hide you;
Daily manna still provide you;
God be with you till we meet again.

God be with you till we meet again;
With the oil of joy anoint you;
Sacred ministries appoint you;
God be with you till we meet again.

Till we meet, till we meet,
Till we meet at Jesus' feet;
Till we meet, till we meet,
God be with you till we meet again.

May the LORD watch between you and me
when we are absent one from another.

—Genesis 31:49

My Faith Looks Up to Thee

On **October 12, 1882**, the *New York Times* carried a happy article about the golden wedding anniversary of the Rev. and Mrs. Ray Palmer, which had been celebrated the night before at their home on Mount Pleasant Avenue in Newark, New Jersey. Several dignitaries spoke, and their son, Rev. Charles Ray Palmer, presented them with "a scrap-book beautifully bound in Russian leather, and containing 120 letters from friends." The article concluded, "Dr. Palmer will be 74 years old next month, and is a graduate of Yale College, being a member of the Class of '30. In that year [1830] he wrote the hymn, 'My Faith Looks Up to Thee.'"

> My faith looks up to Thee,
> Thou Lamb of Calvary, Savior divine!
> Now hear me while I pray, take all my guilt away,
> O let me from this day be wholly Thine!
>
> May Thy rich grace impart
> Strength to my fainting heart, my zeal inspire!
> As Thou hast died for me, O may my love to Thee,
> Pure, warm, and changeless be, a living fire!
>
> While life's dark maze I tread,
> And griefs around me spread, be Thou my Guide;
> Bid darkness turn to day, wipe sorrow's tears away,
> Nor let me ever stray from Thee aside.
>
> When ends life's transient dream,
> When death's cold sullen stream over me roll;
> Blest Savior, then in love, fear and distrust remove;
> O bear me safe above, a ransomed soul!

Now when these things begin to happen, look up and lift up your heads, because your redemption draws near.

—Luke 21:28

Bringing in the Sheaves

When I grow discouraged in ministry, I remind myself of God's promises in 1 Corinthians 15:58; 1 Chronicles 28:20; Galatians 6:9; and Psalm 126:6. That last verse is the inspiration for this hymn by Knowles Shaw, who was born **October 13, 1834**. When Knowles was about twelve, his dying father gave him his cherished violin and told him to live for the Lord. The boy grew up to become a "singing evangelist" who led eleven thousand souls to Christ. His singing brought in the crowds and his preaching converted them. In 1878, while traveling by rail across Texas, he told a friend he never became discouraged, for he loved his work and had confidence in the gospel's power. Moments later, the train careened off the tracks and Shaw was killed in the wreck.

Sowing in the morning, sowing seeds of kindness,
Sowing in the noontide and the dewy eve;
Waiting for the harvest, and the time of reaping,
We shall come rejoicing, bringing in the sheaves.

Sowing in the sunshine, sowing in the shadows,
Fearing neither clouds nor winter's chilling breeze;
By and by the harvest, and the labor ended,
We shall come rejoicing, bringing in the sheaves.

Going forth with weeping, sowing for the Master,
Though the loss sustained our spirit often grieves;
When our weeping's over, He will bid us welcome,
We shall come rejoicing, bringing in the sheaves.

Bringing in the sheaves, bringing in the sheaves,
We shall come rejoicing, bringing in the sheaves,
Bringing in the sheaves, bringing in the sheaves,
We shall come rejoicing, bringing in the sheaves,

He who continually goes forth weeping, bearing seed for sowing, shall doubtless come again with rejoicing, bringing his sheaves with him.

—Psalm 126:6

Whiter Than Snow

In one of the hymnals on my bookshelf, there's a section titled "Hymns of Aspiration." These are songs expressing our desire for a deeper faith, a purer life, and a stronger walk with God. "Whiter Than Snow," by James Nicholson, is such a hymn. It asks the Lord to work within us to "break down every idol, cast out every foe" so that our lives may be "whiter than snow." The tune was composed by William Gustavus Fischer, who was born **October 14, 1835**, to German immigrants in Baltimore. He began singing in church as a child. As a young man he moved to Philadelphia where he remained the rest of his life, writing and teaching music, and leading choirs and choral societies for the gospel.

Lord Jesus, I long to be perfectly whole;
I want Thee forever to live in my soul.
Break down every idol, cast out every foe;
Now wash me, and I shall be whiter than snow.

Lord Jesus, let nothing unholy remain,
Apply Thine own blood and extract ev'ry stain;
To get this blest cleansing, I all things forego—
Now wash me, and I shall be whiter than snow.

Lord Jesus, look down from Thy throne in the skies,
And help me to make a complete sacrifice.
I give up myself, and whatever I know,
Now wash me, and I shall be whiter than snow.

Whiter than snow, yes, whiter than snow.
Now wash me, and I shall be whiter than snow.

"Come now, and let us reason together," says the LORD, "though your sins are like scarlet, they shall be as white as snow; though they are red like crimson, they shall be as wool."

—Isaiah 1:18

All Hail the Power of Jesus' Name

As the Methodist evangelist and hymnist Charles Wesley preached his way across England, he had the joy of personally leading a remarkable young man to faith in Christ. On Tuesday, October 7, 1746, Wesley wrote in his journal: "I prayed with Edward Perronet, just on the point of receiving faith." By Friday, Edward was totally given to Christ, and Wesley wrote, "I set out for Newcastle with my young companion and friend, Edward Perronet, whose heart the Lord hath given me." The following Wednesday, **October 15, 1746**, Wesley's lodgings were invaded by a hostile group threatening violence. Wesley took such incidents in stride, but he kept an eye cast in the direction of his new convert. "Edward Perronet I was a little concerned for," he wrote that evening in his journal, "lest such rough treatment at his first setting out should daunt him; but he abounded in valor." It was such formative experiences that later led Edward Perronet to write this immortal hymn.

> All hail the power of Jesus' name! Let angels prostrate fall;
> Bring forth the royal diadem, and crown Him Lord of all.
> Bring forth the royal diadem, and crown Him Lord of all.
>
> Let highborn seraphs tune the lyre, and as they tune it, fall
> Before His face who tunes their choir, and crown Him Lord of all.
> Before His face who tunes their choir, and crown Him Lord of all.
>
> Ye chosen seed of Israel's race, ye ransomed from the fall,
> Hail Him who saves you by His grace, and crown Him Lord of all.
> Hail Him who saves you by His grace, and crown Him Lord of all.
>
> Let every tribe and every tongue before Him prostrate fall
> And shout in universal song the crownèd Lord of all.
> And shout in universal song the crownèd Lord of all.
>
> O that, with yonder sacred throng, we at His feet may fall,
> Join in the everlasting song, and crown Him Lord of all.
> Join in the everlasting song, and crown Him Lord of all.

He is Lord of all.

—Acts 10:36

O Blessèd Home Where Man and Wife

Marriage was ordained by God at the beginning of history as the foundation of home life and social order, and it must remain so until the end of time. This rare marriage hymn was written by the Norwegian Lutheran pastor Magnus B. Landstad, who compiled a new hymnal that was authorized for use in Norway on **October 16, 1869.** "O Blessèd Home" was translated into English in 1908. Though seldom sung in American churches, its closing stanza offers a powerful prayer for holiness and happiness in our homes today. What a great hymn to sing or quote at weddings!

O blessèd home where man and wife
Together lead a godly life
By deeds their faith confessing!
There many a happy day is spent,
There Jesus gladly will consent
To tarry with His blessing.

If they have given Him their heart,
The place of honor set apart
For Him each night and morrow,
Then He the storms of life will calm,
Will bring for every wound a balm,
And change to joy their sorrow.

O Lord, we come before Thy face;
In every home bestow Thy grace
On children, father, mother,
Relieve their wants, their burdens ease,
Let them together dwell in peace
And love to one another.

Therefore a man shall leave his father and mother and be joined to his wife, and they shall become one flesh.

—Genesis 2:24

The Battle Hymn of the Republic

Julia Ward Howe, author of this patriotic hymn, was irrepressible. When she was ninety, she wrote a friend about the "good work which I have yet to do. . . . My crabbed hand shows how time abridges my working powers, but I march to the brave music still." Shortly afterward, Brown University conferred on her an honorary doctorate, and she went to Providence, Rhode Island, to receive it. "The band played the air of my 'Battle Hymn,' and applause followed me as I went back to my seat. So there!" Then she traveled to Smith College for a similar honor as the crowd sang her "Battle Hymn." It was the last time she heard it. Returning home, she took to bed saying, "God will help me. I am so tired!" She passed away Monday morning, **October 17, 1910**, at age ninety-one.

> Mine eyes have seen the glory of the coming of the Lord;
> He is trampling out the vintage where the grapes of wrath are
>   stored;
> He hath loosed the fateful lightning of His terrible swift sword;
> His truth is marching on.
> *Glory! Glory! Hallelujah! Glory! Glory! Hallelujah!*
> *Glory! Glory! Hallelujah! His truth is marching on.*
>
> In the beauty of the lilies Christ was born across the sea,
> With a glory in His bosom that transfigures you and me:
> As He died to make men holy, let us live to make men free;
> While God is marching on.
> *Glory! Glory! Hallelujah! Glory! Glory! Hallelujah!*
> *Glory! Glory! Hallelujah! While God is marching on.*
>
> He is coming like the glory of the morning on the wave,
> He is wisdom to the mighty, He is honor to the brave;
> So the world shall be His footstool, and the soul of wrong His
>   slave,
> Our God is marching on.
> *Glory! Glory! Hallelujah! Glory! Glory! Hallelujah!*
> *Glory! Glory! Hallelujah! Our God is marching on.*

Fear God and give glory to Him, for the
hour of His judgment has come.

—Revelation 14:7

Hark, the Voice of Jesus Calling

On **October 18, 1868**, Rev. Daniel March was asked to preach from Isaiah 6:8 at a rally in Philadelphia. As he looked over the program, he disliked one of the songs. In great haste, he composed the words to this hymn on the spot, and it was sung from the manuscript. What an encouragement for those of us who feel we have modest gifts or small ministries.

Hark, the voice of Jesus calling,
"Who will go and work today?
Fields are ripe and harvests waiting,
Who will bear the sheaves away?"

If you cannot cross the ocean,
And the distant lands explore,
You can find the lost around you,
You can help them at your door.

If you cannot speak like angels,
If you cannot preach like Paul,
You can tell the love of Jesus,
You can say He died for all.

Let none hear you idly saying,
"There is nothing I can do."
While the lost of earth are dying,
And the Master calls for you;

Take the task He gives you gladly;
Let His work your pleasure be;
Answer quickly when He calls you,
"Here am I, send me, send me."

Then I said, "Here am I! Send me."

—Isaiah 6:8

Under His Wings

Rev. W. O. Cushing was hard at work in his New York church when, still in his forties, he suffered a paralysis that affected his voice. "O Lord, give me something to do for Thee," he prayed. He started writing hymns, and soon his silenced voice was replaced with thousands of other voices singing "Down in the Valley," "Ring the Bells of Heaven," "When He Cometh," and others of his three hundred hymns. When Cushing was seventy-three, Ira Sankey sent him a message, asking for "something new to help me in my Gospel work." After reading "Hide me under the shadow of Your wings" in Psalm 17:8, Cushing penned this famous hymn, which Sankey set to music. Today is the anniversary of Cushing's death on **October 19, 1902**.

Under His wings I am safely abiding,
Though the night deepens and tempests are wild,
Still I can trust Him; I know He will keep me,
He has redeemed me, and I am His child.

Under His wings, what a refuge in sorrow!
How the heart yearningly turns to His rest!
Often when earth has no balm for my healing,
There I find comfort, and there I am blessed.

Under His wings, oh, what precious enjoyment!
There will I hide till life's trials are o'er;
Sheltered, protected, no evil can harm me,
Resting in Jesus, I'm safe evermore.

Under His wings, under His wings,
Who from His love can sever?
Under His wings my soul shall abide,
Safely abide forever.

He shall cover you with His feathers, and
under His wings you shall take refuge.

—Psalm 91:4

Christ the Lord Is Risen Today

On **October 20, 1779**, John Wesley completed the preface to a Methodist milestone, one of history's definitive hymnals: *A Collection of Hymns for the Use of the People Called Methodists*. Hymn #716 in the collection was "Christ the Lord Is Risen Today" by Charles Wesley. The famous "alleluias" hadn't yet been added to each line, but it was only a matter of time. After all, when we hear the news "Christ the Lord Is Risen Today," what else can we say but "Alleluia!"? I once read of a man who was asked to conduct a funeral. This man was a journalist, not a pastor; he'd never officiated a funeral before. Wanting to do it as Christ would, he read through the New Testament to find an example of how Jesus conducted a funeral. To his amazement, he found that Jesus never conducted a funeral at all. All Jesus dealt with were resurrections. Jesus, of course, *is* Himself the resurrection. Because He lives, we will live also!

> Christ, the Lord, is risen today, Alleluia!
> Sons of men and angels say, Alleluia!
> Raise your joys and triumphs high, Alleluia!
> Sing, ye heavens, and earth, reply, Alleluia!
>
> Love's redeeming work is done, Alleluia!
> Fought the fight, the battle won, Alleluia!
> Death in vain forbids Him rise, Alleluia!
> Christ hath opened paradise, Alleluia!
>
> Lives again our glorious King, Alleluia!
> Where, O death, is now thy sting? Alleluia!
> Once He died our souls to save, Alleluia!
> Where thy victory, O grave? Alleluia!
>
> Soar we now where Christ hath led, Alleluia!
> Following our exalted Head, Alleluia!
> Made like Him, like Him we rise, Alleluia!
> Ours the cross, the grave, the skies, Alleluia!

But now Christ is risen from the dead, and has become the firstfruits of those who have fallen asleep.

—1 Corinthians 15:20

Let Us Love and Sing and Wonder

In a letter dated **October 21, 1775**, Rev. John Newton wrote to a fellow preacher whose sermons lacked the clear call of the gospel. "We are not agreed in our views," Newton said kindly. He told the man that moralistic preaching was not sufficient; our sermons need the blood of Jesus. "Ah! My dear sir, when we are brought to estimate our disobedience by comparing it with such a sense of the majesty, holiness, and authority of God . . . we shall be convinced that nothing but the blood of the Son of God can atone for the smallest instance of disobedience. . . . There is but one mode of preaching which the Holy Spirit owns to the producing of [conversions]. . . . It is to seek forgiveness by the blood of Jesus." This great theme also dominated Newton's hymns, including this one.

> Let us love and sing and wonder,
> Let us praise the Savior's name!
> He has hushed the law's loud thunder,
> He has quenched Mount Sinai's flame.
> He has washed us with His blood,
> He has brought us nigh to God.
>
> Let us love the Lord who bought us,
> Pitied us when enemies,
> Called us by His grace, and taught us,
> Gave us ears and gave us eyes:
> He has washed us with His blood,
> He presents our souls to God.
>
> Let us praise, and join the chorus
> Of the saints enthroned on high;
> Here they trusted Him before us,
> Now their praises fill the sky:
> "Thou hast washed us with Your blood;
> Thou art worthy, Lamb of God!"

The blood of Jesus Christ His Son cleanses us from all sin.

—1 John 1:7

Love Divine, All Loves Excelling

When Americans worship in Great Britain, they're often surprised that familiar hymns are sung to different tunes than in the States. Wesley's "Love Divine, All Loves Excelling" is often sung in England to the lovely melody "Blaenwern," by William P. Rowlands, who died **October 22, 1937**. Cliff Barrows relates how this tune helped him in London in 1961. At the last minute he was unnerved to discover he had to fill in for Billy Graham, who was sick. Westminster's Central Hall was packed with British clergymen. Suddenly the grand organ burst into "Blaenwern," and the cathedral burst into "Love Divine." As so often happens, the richness of song strengthened God's servant, and Barrows spoke with confidence and power.

Love divine, all loves excelling,
Joy of heaven to earth come down;
Fix in us thy humble dwelling;
All thy faithful mercies crown!
Jesus, Thou art all compassion,
Pure unbounded love Thou art;
Visit us with Thy salvation;
Enter every trembling heart.

Breathe, O breathe Thy loving Spirit,
Into every troubled breast!
Let us all in Thee inherit;
Let us find that second rest.
Take away our bent to sinning;
Alpha and Omega be;
End of faith, as its Beginning,
Set our hearts at liberty.

For God so loved the world that He gave His only begotten Son, that whoever believes in Him should not perish but have everlasting life.

—John 3:16

Speak, Lord, in the Stillness

Jesus once told us to find a quiet room of the house and retire there for regular private prayer (Matt. 6:6), and He Himself arose early in the morning for a time of communion with the Father before the day began (Mark 1:35). Our daily "quiet time" is the key to Christian serenity and sanctity. As we open our Bibles and our prayer notebooks in His presence, we can pray with Samuel, who said, "Speak, LORD, for your servant is listening" (1 Sam. 3:9 NIV). This simple hymn is such a prayer. Sometimes called "The Quiet Hour," it was written by missionary-poet May Grimes nearly a hundred years ago, and set to the beautiful melody "Quietude" by Harold Green, who was born into a minister's home on this day, **October 23, 1930**. Both Grimes and Green were British missionaries serving in Pondoland, South Africa.

Speak, Lord, in the stillness
While I wait on Thee;
Hushed my heart to listen,
In expectancy.

Speak, O blessèd Master,
In this quiet hour,
Let me see Thy face, Lord,
Feel Thy touch of power.

For the words Thou speakest,
"They are life" indeed;
Living Bread from Heaven,
Now my spirit feed!

Fill me with the knowledge
Of Thy glorious will;
All Thine own good pleasure
In my life fulfill.

*If your law had not been my delight, I would
have perished in my affliction.*

—Psalm 119:92 NIV

Rejoice and Be Glad

As part of their global evangelistic efforts, evangelist D. L. Moody and musician Ira Sankey opened a crusade at the Brooklyn Rink on Sunday, **October 24, 1875**. The *New York Times* reported the streets thronged with thousands of people heading to the Rink hours in advance of the 9 a.m. service. All the streetcars ran one way from the ferries. The building was packed. Thousands were unable to get in. When Sankey shouted, "Please rise and sing heartily," the audience turned to #24 in their songbooks and sang Bonar's hymn "Rejoice and Be Glad" (to the tune of "Revive Us Again"). The building shook with the thousands of voices, and the *Times* reporter, deeply moved, printed the words to the entire hymn in the newspaper story the next day.

Rejoice and be glad!
The Redeemer has come!
Go look on His cradle,
His cross, and His tomb.

Rejoice and be glad!
For the Lamb that was slain
O'er death is triumphant,
And liveth again.

Rejoice and be glad!
For He cometh again;
He cometh to glory,
The Lamb that was slain.

Sound His praises, tell the story,
Of Him who was slain;
Sound His praises, tell with gladness,
He cometh again.

This is the day the LORD has made; we
will rejoice and be glad in it.

—Psalm 118:24

The Great Archangel's Trump

There's some confusion about the background of this hymn by Charles Wesley. Its original name is either "After Deliverance from Death by the Fall of a *House*," or "After Deliverance from Death by the Fall of a *Horse*." Wesley experienced both. On March 14, 1744, as he was speaking in Leeds, England, the building collapsed, severely injuring many people. Four years later, on **October 25, 1748**, Wesley wrote in his journal, "I rode to Paulton, where my horse cast me to the ground with such violence as if I had been shot out of an engine. I lay breathless for some time. They sat me on the horse and led me to Bristol, got a surgeon to dress my arm and hand, which were much bruised, and my foot was crushed." Perhaps Wesley was thinking of both incidents when he penned this hymn, which was published in 1749.

> The great archangel's trump shall sound,
> While twice ten thousand thunders roar
> Tear up the graves, and cleave the ground,
> And make the greedy sea restore.
>
> The greedy sea shall yield her dead,
> The earth no more her slain conceal;
> Sinners shall lift their guilty head,
> And shrink to see a yawning hell.
>
> But we, who now our Lord confess,
> And faithful to the end endure,
> Shall stand in Jesus' righteousness,
> Stand, as the Rock of ages, sure.
>
> By faith we now transcend the skies,
> And on that ruined world look down;
> By love above all height we rise,
> And share the everlasting throne.

Even so, Lord God Almighty, true and righteous are Your judgments.

—Revelation 16:7

All Things Praise Thee

As I've prepared the manuscript for this book, the greatest lesson I've rediscovered is the psychological and spiritual power of praise. God has built praise into the fabric of the universe, from the bird's song and the cricket's chirp to the mysterious hum of the universe that our astronomers detect. If all creation is built for praise, should we not praise Him too? George Conder wrote this hymn on the subject, and Henry Smart wrote its tune. Smart, best known for the melody of "Angels from the Realms of Glory," is a prominent composer in Christian hymnology. Today is the anniversary of his birth on **October 26, 1813**.

OCTOBER 26

All things praise Thee, Lord most high,
Heav'n and earth and sea and sky,
All were for Thy glory made,
That Thy greatness thus displayed
Should all worship bring to Thee;
All things praise Thee—Lord, may we!

All things praise Thee—night to night
Sings in silent hymns of light;
All things praise Thee—day to day
Chants Thy power in burning ray;
Time and space are praising Thee,
All things praise Thee—Lord, may we!

All things praise Thee—high and low,
Rain and dew and sparkling snow,
Crimson sunset, fleecy cloud,
Rippling stream, and tempest loud;
Summer, winter, all to Thee
Glory render—Lord, may we!

Let everything that has breath praise the LORD. Praise the LORD!

—Psalm 150:6

My Maker, Be Thou Nigh

Our omnipresent God is constantly with us, everywhere, all the time, in every place, day and night. True spirituality is learning to enjoy a constant awareness of His presence. That's the message contained in this hymn by Johann Rambach, the son of a Lutheran cabinetmaker from Halle, Germany. While working for his dad one day, Johann dislocated his ankle. His recovery gave him time to think, and he decided to go back to school. On **October 27, 1712**, Johann entered the University of Halle as a medical student. His attention was soon diverted to the Scriptures, and he eventually became a renowned Pietistic professor of theology. His beautiful Trinitarian hymn was published in 1735.

My Maker, be Thou nigh
The light of life to give
And guide me with Thine eye
While here on earth I live.
To Thee my heart I tender
And all my powers surrender;
Make it my one endeavor
To love and serve Thee ever.
Upon Thy promise I rely;
My Maker, be Thou nigh.

O Holy Trinity!
To whom I all things owe,
Thine image graciously
Within my heart bestow.
Choose me, though weak and lowly,
To be Thy temple holy
Where praise shall rise unending
For grace so condescending.
O heav'nly bliss, Thine own to be,
O Holy Trinity!

In Your presence is fullness of joy.

—Psalm 16:11

Someday We'll Understand

"Not now, but in the coming years . . . we'll understand." This hymn by Maxwell Cornelius was a favorite of Horace Tracy Pitkin, who was born **October 28, 1869**. While a student at Yale, Horace was influenced by the student volunteer movement to offer himself as a missionary to China. Once there, he proved a brilliant worker and gifted musician. His friends later recalled how he gathered them on summer Sunday evenings on the veranda at Pei-tai-ho, overlooking the sea. Sitting at a little organ, he would lead them in singing "Someday We'll Understand." It was strangely prophetic. In July 1900, Horace was captured and beheaded during the Boxer Rebellion in China, leaving behind a wife and infant son.

Someday we'll understand; till then we'll "trust in God through all the days."

Not now, but in the coming years,
It may be in the better land,
We'll read the meaning of our tears,
And there, some time, we'll understand.

We'll catch the broken thread again,
And finish what we here began;
Heav'n will the mysteries explain,
And then, ah then, we'll understand.

God knows the way, He holds the key,
He guides us with unerring hand;
Some time with tearless eyes we'll see;
Yes, there, up there, we'll understand.

Then trust in God through all the days;
Fear not, for He doth hold thy hand;
Though dark thy way, still sing and praise,
Some time, some time we'll understand.

We know that all things work together
for good to those who love God.

—Romans 8:28

Thy Word Have I Hid in My Heart

If you want to know one single habit that accelerates the transformation process of creating within us a Christian personality, it is Scripture memory. What verse or verses are you hiding in your heart this week? Ernest Orlando Sellers, born **October 29, 1869**, in Hastings, Michigan, wrote this hymn as an encouragement to memorize Scripture. Sellers was a city official in Hastings when he met Jesus as his Savior. He resigned from civic life, attended Moody Bible Institute, and became a traveling musician before settling down in Louisiana to head up the worship ministries at New Orleans Baptist Theological Seminary, where he stayed until his retirement in 1945. He wrote "Thy Word Have I Hid in My Heart" in 1908.

Thy Word is a lamp to my feet,
A light to my path alway,
To guide and to save me from sin,
And show me the heav'nly way.

Forever, O Lord, is Thy Word
Established and fixed on high;
Thy faithfulness unto all men
Abideth forever nigh.

At morning, at noon, and at night
I ever will give Thee praise;
For Thou art my portion, O Lord, .
And shall be through all my days!

Thy Word have I hid in my heart,
That I might not sin against Thee;
That I might not sin, that I might not sin,
Thy Word have I hid in my heart.

Your word I have hidden in my heart, that
I might not sin against You.

—Psalm 119:11

Desponding Soul, O Cease Thy Woe

The next time you see the majestic dome rising above the United States Capitol in Washington, D.C., you can thank hymnist Thomas U. Walter (September 4, 1804–**October 30, 1887**). Dr. Walter, a Philadelphia architect, undertook the project of expanding the Capitol in 1850, and he's the one who designed the grand dome. Today he is remembered as the Dean of American Architecture. But the most important thing about Dr. Walter was his personal commitment to Jesus Christ. He attended Baptist churches wherever he lived, and gladly served as Sunday school superintendent, deacon, and hymnist. Here is one of his hymns:

Desponding soul, O cease thy woe;
Dry up thy tears, to Jesus go,
In faith's appointed way;
Let not thy unbelieving fears
Still hold thee back—thy Savior hears—
From him no longer stray.

No works of thine can e'er impart
A balm to heal thy wounded heart,
Or solid comfort give;
Turn, turn to Him who freely gave
His precious blood thy soul to save;
E'en now He bids them live.

Helpless and lost, to Jesus fly!
His power and love are ever nigh
To those who seek His face;
Thy deepest guilt on Him was laid,
He bore thy sins, thy ransom paid;
O haste to share His grace.

Why are you cast down, O my soul? And why are you disquieted within me? Hope in God, for I shall yet praise Him for the help of His countenance.

—Psalm 42:5

A Mighty Fortress

Today is Reformation Day, marking the moment on **October 31, 1517**, when Martin Luther nailed his Ninety-five Theses to the cathedral door in the little university town of Wittenberg, Germany. It was a turning point in history. Luther's great Reformation hymn "Ein' feste Burg ist unser Gott" ("A Mighty Fortress Is Our God"), inspired by Psalm 46, was likely written during the time of the Diet of Speyer, where the Reformers were first called Protestants.

> A mighty fortress is our God, a bulwark never failing;
> Our helper He, amid the flood of mortal ills prevailing:
> For still our ancient foe doth seek to work us woe;
> His craft and power are great, and, armed with cruel hate,
> On earth is not his equal.
>
> Did we in our own strength confide, our striving would be
>   losing;
> Were not the right Man on our side, the Man of God's own
>   choosing:
> Dost ask who that may be? Christ Jesus, it is He;
> Lord Sabaoth, His name, from age to age the same,
> And He must win the battle.
>
> And though this world, with devils filled, should threaten to
>   undo us,
> We will not fear, for God hath willed His truth to triumph
>   through us:
> The Prince of Darkness grim, we tremble not for him;
> His rage we can endure, for lo, his doom is sure,
> One little word shall fell him.
>
> That word above all earthly powers, no thanks to them, abideth;
> The Spirit and the gifts are ours through Him who with us
>   sideth:
> Let goods and kindred go, this mortal life also;
> The body they may kill: God's truth abideth still,
> His kingdom is forever.

God is our refuge and strength, a very present help in trouble.

—Psalm 46:1

Eternal Father, Strong to Save

Psalm 121 is called the Traveler's Psalm because of its assurance of God's watchcare over our pathways: "The Lord shall preserve your going out and your coming in from this time forth, and even forevermore" (v. 8). In the same way, "Eternal Father, Strong to Save" is sometimes called the Traveler's Hymn, and it's known in American history as the Navy Hymn. It was written in 1860 by William Whiting, who was born on this day, **November 1, 1825**. Its solemn strains were heard at the funerals of Franklin Roosevelt in 1945 and John F. Kennedy in 1963.

> Eternal Father, strong to save,
> Whose arm hath bound the restless wave,
> Who bids the mighty ocean deep
> Its own appointed limits keep:
> Oh, hear us when we cry to Thee
> For those in peril on the sea!
>
> O Christ! Whose voice the waters heard
> And hushed their raging at Thy Word,
> Who walkèd on the foaming deep,
> And calm amidst its rage didst sleep:
> Oh, hear us when we cry to Thee,
> For those in peril on the sea!
>
> O Trinity of love and power!
> Our family shield in danger's hour;
> From rock and tempest, fire and foe,
> Protect us wheresoe'er we go;
> Thus evermore shall rise to Thee
> Glad hymns of praise from land and sea.

The Lord shall preserve you from all evil;
He shall preserve your soul.

—Psalm 121:7

Beautiful Words of Jesus

This hymn by the inimitable Christian poet Eliza Hewitt owes much of its appeal to the happy-sounding, carnival-like tune composed by Isaac Meredith, who came by his love of music naturally. His parents were both musicians, and Isaac started playing and singing in childhood. After his conversion as a teenager, he felt a definite call to the ministry of music. He sang each Sunday in the county jail, and as a young man he traveled the evangelistic circuit as a soloist, singing "with rare power" at rallies and services. He also became a noted music publisher and is credited with having composed over one thousand songs before his death on **November 2, 1962**, in Orlando.

Beautiful words of Jesus,
Spoken so long ago,
Yet, as we sing them over,
Dearer to us they grow,
Calling the heavy laden,
Calling to hearts oppressed,
"Come unto Me, ye weary;
Come, I will give you rest."

Beautiful words of Jesus,
Cheering us day by day;
Throwing a gleam of sunshine
Over a cloudy way;
Casting on Him the burden
We are too weak to bear;
He will give grace sufficient;
He will regard our prayer.

Hear the call of His voice, so sweet; bring your load to the
*   Savior's feet;*
Lean your heart on His loving breast; come, O come, and He will
*   give you rest.*

> *Come to Me, all you who labor and are heavy*
> *laden, and I will give you rest.*
>
> —Matthew 11:28

Lord, I Am Thine

Samuel Davies, the "Apostle of Virginia," was born **November 3, 1723**. He's a hero of Colonial Christian history, a leader of the Great Awakening, and a Presbyterian leader who advanced freedom of religion and ministered to slaves. Davies insisted on the right of slaves to share in church services, and he established a school for them. Though Colonial Presbyterians were slow to accept hymn singing, Davies was amazed at how quickly the slaves in his church fell in love with the songs of Isaac Watts. This motivated him to write hymns of his own, and he became one of America's first hymnists. At the beginning of 1761, Davies seems to have had a premonition of death, for he preached on the subject "This year thou shalt die." Five weeks later, he passed away of pneumonia at the age of thirty-seven.

Lord, I am Thine, entirely Thine,
Purchased and saved by blood divine;
With full consent Thine I would be,
And own Thy sovereign right in me.

Grant one poor sinner more a place
Among the children of Thy grace—
A wretched sinner, lost to God,
But ransomed by Immanuel's blood.

Thine would I live, Thine would I die,
Be Thine through all eternity;
The vow is past beyond repeal,
And now I set the solemn seal.

Here, at that cross where flows the blood
That bought my guilty soul for God,
Thee my new Master now I call,
And consecrate to Thee my all.

O Lord, truly I am Your servant; I am Your servant.

—Psalm 116:16

Does Jesus Care?

In a fit of despondency, the psalmist once bemoaned, "No one cares for my soul" (Ps. 142:4). But in the next verse he turned his gloom into a prayer, declaring to God, "You are my refuge." The word *care* occurs eighty-two times in the Bible, which frequently reminds us that when "the days are weary, the long nights dreary," our Savior cares. Frank Graeff wrote "Does Jesus Care?" in 1901, and it was set to music by the noted conductor and composer, Dr. J. Lincoln Hall (born **November 4, 1866**), who later called it his most inspired piece of music. The form of the hymn is unusual. Each stanza asks questions about God's care for us in various situations, and the chorus resounds with the bolstering answer: "Oh yes, He cares, I know He cares!"

> Does Jesus care when my heart is pained
> Too deeply for mirth or song,
> As the burdens press, and the cares distress
> And the way grows weary and long?
>
> Does Jesus care when I've tried and failed
> To resist some temptation strong;
> When for my deep grief there is no relief,
> Though my tears flow all the night long?
>
> Does Jesus care when I've said "good-bye"
> To the dearest on earth to me,
> And my sad heart aches till it nearly breaks,
> Is it aught to Him? Does He see?
>
> *Oh yes, He cares, I know He cares,*
> *His heart is touched with my grief;*
> *When the days are weary, the long nights dreary,*
> *I know my Savior cares.*

. . . casting all your care upon Him, for He cares for you.

—1 Peter 5:7

God Is Still on the Throne

Located in Northern China, Chefoo School was launched by the China Inland Mission in 1881 to provide schooling for the children of CIM missionaries. It began with just three students, but the school grew considerably in size and importance until 1937, when the Japanese invaded China. During the invasion years, Chefoo tried to operate normally, but that became utterly impossible after the Japanese attacked Pearl Harbor at the end of 1941. On **November 5, 1942**, the frightened children and staff were rounded up by Japanese soldiers and marched away to internment camps where they remained, separated from anxious families, until the end of World War II. As they marched the last time out of the gates of their beloved Chefoo, the children sang this hymn, written by Kittie L. Suffield. Years later, survivors of this children's march still remembered how the rousing chorus bolstered the spirits of students and staff alike: "His promise is true, He will not forget you, / God is still on the throne"!

Have you started for glory and Heaven?
Have you left this old world far behind?
In your heart is the Comforter dwelling?
Can you say, "Praise the Lord, He is mine"?
Have the ones that once walked on the highway
Gone back, and you seem all alone?
Keep your eyes on the prize, for the home in the skies;
God is still on the throne.

God is still on the throne,
And He will remember His own;
Tho' trials may press us and burdens distress us,
He never will leave us alone;
God is still on the throne,
He never forsaketh His own;
His promise is true, He will not forget you,
God is still on the throne.

The LORD has established His throne in heaven,
and His kingdom rules over all.

—Psalm 103:19

Ask Ye What Great Thing I Know

How wonderful to be so excited about the gospel that we're begging people to ask us about it! This old hymn (often sung to the tune we use with "Take My Life and Let It Be") was penned by Johann C. Schwedler, a popular pastor in the early 1700s in the eastern German city of Niederwiese. Such crowds thronged his church each Sunday that he was busy from early morning to mid-afternoon in successive services. He wrote more than five hundred hymns, mainly on the themes of God's grace through Christ and the joy shared by those who trust Him. This hymn, which is based on 1 Corinthians 2:2 and Galatians 6:14, was published eleven years after Schwedler's death and was translated into English by the Anglican clergyman Benjamin Kennedy, who was born **November 6, 1804**, near Birmingham, England.

Ask ye what great thing I know,
That delights and stirs me so?
What the high reward I win?
Whose the name I glory in?
Jesus Christ, the Crucified.

Who is He that makes me wise
To discern where duty lies?
Who is He that makes me true
Duty, when discerned to do,
Jesus Christ, the Crucified.

This is that great thing I know;
This delights and stirs me so;
Faith in Him who died to save,
Him who triumphed o'er the grave:
Jesus Christ, the Crucified.

For I determined not to know anything among
you except Jesus Christ and Him crucified.

—1 Corinthians 2:2

Jesus Is All the World to Me

Will Lamartine Thompson, born **November 7, 1847**, in East Liverpool, Ohio, is the author of the famous invitational hymn "Softly and Tenderly," the exuberant hymn "There's a Great Day Coming" about the second coming of Christ, and this hymn of testimony, "Jesus Is All the World to Me." He began writing songs in 1870, and his hymns appeared in almost every songbook of the era. At age sixty-two, Thompson returned home from Europe aboard a steamer. He was suffering from pneumonia, and he was taken from the ship directly to the hospital. He died two weeks later, leaving behind a wife, a twelve-year-old son, and a legacy of praise.

> Jesus is all the world to me, my life, my joy, my all;
> He is my strength from day to day, without Him I would fall.
> When I am sad, to Him I go, no other one can cheer me so;
> When I am sad, He makes me glad, He's my Friend.
>
> Jesus is all the world to me, my Friend in trials sore;
> I go to Him for blessings, and He gives them o'er and o'er.
> He sends the sunshine and the rain, He sends the harvest's
>   golden grain;
> Sunshine and rain, harvest of grain, He's my Friend.
>
> Jesus is all the world to me, and true to Him I'll be;
> O how could I this Friend deny, when He's so true to me?
> Following Him I know I'm right, He watches o'er me day and
>   night;
> Following Him by day and night, He's my Friend.
>
> Jesus is all the world to me, I want no better Friend;
> I trust Him now, I'll trust Him when life's fleeting days shall end.
> Beautiful life with such a Friend, beautiful life that has no end;
> Eternal life, eternal joy, He's my Friend.

. . . that in all things He may have the preeminence.

—Colossians 1:18

All People That on Earth Do Dwell

Thousands of excited people jammed into the Moody Memorial Church in Chicago for its grand dedication service on **November 8, 1925**. Pastor P. W. Philpot chimed out a call to worship, and the organ began the majestic strains of "Old Hundredth"—which we use when we sing the Doxology. For over four hundred years, "All People That on Earth Do Dwell" has been sung to this tune at many great occasions in Christendom. It's a rendition of Psalm 100 ascribed to William Kethe that first appeared in the 1561 Genevan Psalter. It's even mentioned in one of the plays of William Shakespeare. As one of the oldest hymns in the English language, its power is ageless and its message is right from the heart of Scripture.

All people that on earth do dwell,
Sing to the Lord with cheerful voice.
Him serve with fear, His praise forth tell;
Come ye before Him and rejoice.

The Lord, ye know, is God indeed;
Without our aid He did us make;
We are His folk, He doth us feed,
And for His sheep He doth us take.

O enter then His gates with praise;
Approach with joy His courts unto;
Praise, laud, and bless His name always,
For it is seemly so to do.

For why? the Lord our God is good;
His mercy is for ever sure;
His truth at all times firmly stood,
And shall from age to age endure.

Enter into His gates with thanksgiving, and into His courts with praise. Be thankful to Him, and bless His name.

—Psalm 100:4

Praise, My Soul, the King of Heaven

On **November 9, 1947**, the *New York Times* announced that churches everywhere were preparing to celebrate the centenary of the death of hymnist Henry Lyte. According to the *Times*, the upcoming Sunday would find churches worldwide singing Lyte's hymns, such as "Abide with Me," which he wrote while dying. A memorial plaque to Lyte would be unveiled at Westminster Abbey, and a special memorial service would be broadcast on the BBC from the church Lyte had pastored a hundred years before in the small fishing village of Lower Brixton. During the service, "Praise, My Soul, the King of Heaven" would be sung, which, the *Times* reported, "was chosen by Princess Elizabeth as the opening hymn for her wedding to Lieut. Philip Mountbatten. It was also sung at the wedding of King George VI." It's one of our greatest hymns from one of our most beloved hymnists.

Praise, my soul, the King of Heaven;
To His feet thy tribute bring.
Ransomed, healed, restored, forgiven,
Evermore His praises sing:
Alleluia! Alleluia! Praise the everlasting King.

Praise Him for His grace and favor
To our fathers in distress.
Praise Him still the same as ever,
Slow to chide, and swift to bless.
Alleluia! Alleluia! Glorious in His faithfulness.

Angels, help us to adore Him;
Ye behold Him face to face;
Sun and moon, bow down before Him,
Dwellers all in time and space.
Alleluia! Alleluia! Praise with us the God of grace.

I . . . praise and extol and honor the King of heaven,
all of whose works are truth, and His ways justice.

—Daniel 4:37

Joyful, Joyful, We Adore Thee

Few people have enjoyed a more varied career than Henry Van Dyke, born in Germantown, Pennsylvania, on **November 10, 1852**—New York pastor, ambassador to the Netherlands, commander in the Navy, professor of English, president of the National Institute of the Arts, chairman of the committee that compiled the Presbyterian Book of Common Prayer, author, poet, novelist, essayist, and hymnist. He wrote this rousing hymn at Williams College in Massachusetts, handing the college president a piece of paper—this hymn—at breakfast. Van Dyke had written it that morning after gazing on the beauty of the surrounding Berkshire Mountains. "It must be sung to the music of Beethoven's 'Hymn of Joy,'" he said.

> Joyful, joyful, we adore Thee, God of glory, Lord of love;
> Hearts unfold like flowers before Thee, opening to the sun
>   above.
> Melt the clouds of sin and sadness; drive the dark of doubt
>   away;
> Giver of immortal gladness, fill us with the light of day!
>
> All Thy works with joy surround Thee, earth and heaven reflect
>   Thy rays,
> Stars and angels sing around Thee, center of unbroken praise.
> Field and forest, vale and mountain, flowery meadow, flashing
>   sea,
> Singing bird and flowing fountain call us to rejoice in Thee.
>
> Thou art giving and forgiving, ever blessing, ever blessed,
> Wellspring of the joy of living, ocean depth of happy rest!
> Thou our Father, Christ our Brother, all who live in love are
>   Thine;
> Teach us how to love each other, lift us to the joy divine.
>
> Mortals, join the happy chorus, which the morning stars began;
> Father love is reigning o'er us, brother love binds man to man.
> Ever singing, march we onward, victors in the midst of strife,
> Joyful music leads us sunward in the triumph song of life.

Do not sorrow, for the joy of the LORD is your strength.

—Nehemiah 8:10

Father, Whate'er of Earthly Bliss

Anne Steele has been called the most distinguished female writer of sacred song of the eighteenth century. Many of her hymns were personal prayers that flowed from the stresses she endured. Anne was born in an English village in 1716. Her Baptist father was a timber merchant and a lay pastor. A childhood accident left Anne partially disabled. At age fourteen, she was baptized and joined her father's church. At twenty-one, she became engaged to Robert Elscourt, but hours before the wedding he drowned while bathing in the river. As she recovered, Anne wrote out her hymns and prayers, but she was forty-five before she allowed any of them to be published. When she was in her early fifties, Anne's father died, and she never fully recovered from the shock. From that time, she was largely confined to her bedroom, until **November 11, 1778**, when she passed away at age sixty-one. Her last words were a triumphant, "I know that my Redeemer liveth!" She left us 144 hymns and 37 poetical versions of the Psalms.

Father, whate'er of earthly bliss
Thy sovereign will denies,
Accepted at Thy throne, let this
My humble prayer, arise:

Give me a calm and thankful heart,
From every murmur free;
The blessing of Thy grace impart,
And make me live to Thee.

Let the sweet hope that Thou art mine
My life and death attend,
Thy presence through my journey shine,
And crown my journey's end.

My brethren, count it all joy when you fall into various trials, knowing that the testing of your faith produces patience.

—James 1:2–3

Stealing from the World Away

Attending church is a *countercultural* experience: we need to counteract the influence of the popular culture in our lives. When we go to church, we're participating in a global weekly network of a billion people who are doing the same thing at the same time. We're participating in an ancient practice that goes back to the origins of the church and to the beginning of the creation. And we're involved in a habit the Bible says is increasingly vital as time draws to a close. Regular church attendance honors the rhythm of life that God established, the worship that Scripture ordains, the spiritual family that Christ has formed, and the mission for which we're placed on this planet. Here's a hymn by Ray Palmer (born **November 12, 1808**) about retreating once a week to worship with the saints of God.

> Stealing from the world away,
> We are come to seek Thy face;
> Kindly meet us, Lord, we pray,
> Grant us Thy reviving grace.
>
> Yonder stars that gild the sky
> Shine but with a borrowed light:
> We, unless Thy light be nigh,
> Wander, wrapped in gloomy night.
>
> Sun of righteousness! dispel
> All our darkness, doubts and fears:
> May Thy light within us dwell,
> Till eternal day appears.
>
> Warm our hearts in prayer and praise,
> Lift our every thought above;
> Hear the grateful songs we raise,
> Fill us with Thy perfect love.

. . . not forsaking the assembling of ourselves together.

—Hebrews 10:25

Open Our Eyes to See

Among the many hymnals that found their way into Victorian British homes was this one: *Hymns Written for Wigston Magna Church School By William Romanis, Vicar of Wigston Magna, Leicestershire.* It was published in London in 1878, and it contains this simple hymn. Romanis was a hymnist of the Victorian era whose works retained little of their popularity past his death on **November 13, 1899**. But this hymn with its lovely first verse reminds me of the two disciples on the Emmaus road to whom Jesus opened the Scriptures. It's a good prayer for today.

Open our eyes to see
Thy Presence, Lord, around;
How all the heaven is full of Thee,
And earth is holy ground.

Open our ears to hear
The still small voice from within
That gently whispers, Thou art near,
And warns away from sin.

Open our hearts to hold
Streams from the tideless flood
Of the deep Love Thy Christ has told
And witnessed with His blood.

Open my eye, ear, mind
Open my heart and will,
That Thou mayst all things ready find,
And with Thy fullness fill.

Did not our heart burn within us while He talked with us on the road, and while He opened the Scriptures to us?

—Luke 24:32

Turn Your Eyes upon Jesus

Helen Lemmel was born into a Methodist pastor's family in Wardle, England, on **November 14, 1864**. When she was twelve, she and her family emigrated to America where she eventually became a popular soloist, traveling widely and giving concerts. Later she taught voice at Moody Bible Institute in Chicago and Biola University in Los Angeles. During her ninety-eight years, she wrote more than five hundred hymns and a successful book for children. This is Helen's most popular hymn, and it was written in 1918 after she read a tract containing these words: "So then turn your eyes upon Him, look full into His face and you will find the things of earth will acquire a strange new dimness."

O soul, are you weary and troubled?
No light in the darkness you see?
There's a light for a look at the Savior,
And life more abundant and free!

Through death into life everlasting
He passed, and we follow Him there;
Over us sin no more hath dominion—
For more than conquerors we are!

His Word shall not fail you—He promised;
Believe Him, and all will be well:
Then go to a world that is dying,
His perfect salvation to tell!

Turn your eyes upon Jesus,
Look full in His wonderful face,
And the things of earth will grow strangely dim,
In the light of His glory and grace.

. . . looking unto Jesus, the author and finisher of our faith.

—Hebrews 12:2

There Is a Fountain Filled with Blood

Today is the birthday of one of hymnody's most troubled lyricists. William Cowper (pronounced Cooper), who was born **November 15, 1731**, suffered mental illness and bouts of severe depression all his life. He discovered Christ as his Savior at age thirty-three in an insane asylum while reading from the book of Romans. His happiest years were subsequently spent alongside his dear friend and pastor, John Newton, in the village of Olney, England. The two collaborated on one of the most famous hymnals in British church history—the *Olney Hymns*. Included was "There Is a Fountain Filled with Blood," published under the title "Praise for the Fountain Opened"—Zechariah 13:1.

There is a fountain filled with blood drawn from Emmanuel's veins;
And sinners plunged beneath that flood lose all their guilty stains.
Lose all their guilty stains, lose all their guilty stains;
And sinners plunged beneath that flood lose all their guilty stains.

The dying thief rejoiced to see that fountain in his day;
And there have I, though vile as he, washed all my sins away.
Washed all my sins away, washed all my sins away;
And there have I, though vile as he, washed all my sins away.

Dear dying Lamb, Thy precious blood shall never lose its power
Till all the ransomed church of God be saved, to sin no more.
Be saved, to sin no more, be saved, to sin no more;
Till all the ransomed church of God be saved, to sin no more.

E'er since, by faith, I saw the stream Thy flowing wounds supply,
Redeeming love has been my theme, and shall be till I die.
And shall be till I die, and shall be till I die;
Redeeming love has been my theme, and shall be till I die.

In that day a fountain shall be opened for the house of David and for the inhabitants of Jerusalem, for sin and for uncleanness.

—Zechariah 13:1

Go, Heralds of Salvation, Forth

On **November 16, 1895**, the distinguished Baptist leader Dr. Samuel Smith, age eighty-seven, stepped aboard a train at the New England Railroad Station in Boston, found his seat, and settled in. Just before the train pulled out of the station, Smith turned to speak to a friend. He half opened his mouth, gave a gasp, threw his hands up, and fell back dead. News of his passing flashed around the world, for Dr. Smith was famous for a patriotic hymn he'd written as a seminary student, "My Country, 'Tis of Thee." But Smith's passion for the gospel wasn't limited to America. He understood the global reach of the Great Commission and was a lifelong advocate of missions. Smith mastered several languages, wrote books tracing the missionary movement around the world, and penned several missionary hymns such as this one.

> Go, heralds of salvation, forth;
> Go in your heavenly Master's name;
> From east to west, from south to north,
> The glorious Gospel wide proclaim.
>
> Go forth to sow the living seed;
> Seek not earth's praise, nor dread its blame;
> Nor labors fear, nor trials heed;
> Go forth to conquer in His name.
>
> Lo, I am with you, saith the Lord,
> My grace your spirit shall sustain;
> Strong is My arm, and sure My Word;
> My servants shall not toil in vain.
>
> Go forth in hope; my burden take,
> Till God's great reaping day shall come;
> Then they who sowed in tears shall wake,
> And hail the joyful harvest home.

Go into all the world and preach the gospel to every creature.

—Mark 16:15

Who Is on the Lord's Side?

This call to arms comes from two women—the British lyricist Frances Havergal and the German composer Louise Reichardt. The latter was born into a musical home, but her childhood was disrupted by her mother's death and by Napoleon's invasion of Europe. Moving to Hamburg, Louise opened a voice studio and became engaged to a poet, Friedrich Eschen, who died suddenly before their wedding. She was then engaged to a painter, but he also died before their wedding. Louise later devoted herself to sacred music, composing two books of hymns before her death on **November 17, 1826**. This tune, called "Armageddon," fits Havergal's words perfectly as we sing, "We are on the Lord's side—Savior, we are Thine!"

Who is on the Lord's side? Who will serve the King?
Who will be His helpers, other lives to bring?
Who will leave the world's side? Who will face the foe?
Who is on the Lord's side? Who for Him will go?
By Thy call of mercy, by Thy grace divine,
We are on the Lord's side—Savior, we are Thine!

Not for weight of glory, nor for crown and palm,
Enter we the army, raise the warrior psalm;
But for love that claimeth lives for whom He died:
He whom Jesus nameth must be on His side.
By Thy love constraining, by Thy grace divine,
We are on the Lord's side—Savior, we are Thine!

Fierce may be the conflict, strong may be the foe,
But the King's own army none can overthrow;
'Round His standard ranging, victory is secure,
For His truth unchanging makes the triumph sure.
Joyfully enlisting, by Thy grace divine,
We are on the Lord's side—Savior, we are Thine!

Whoever is on the LORD's side—come to me!
—Exodus 32:26

Tell Me the Old, Old Story

When felled by serious illness, Kate Hankey used her recovery to compose an extended poem entitled "The Old, Old Story," which was finished and dated **November 18, 1866**. It began, "Tell me the old, old story, / of unseen things above." The second part of the poem tells the life of Christ in rich, rhyming verse. Though seldom read today, Kate's poem is immortalized by its adaptation into this beloved hymn with a score by composer Howard Doane. (Another adaptation of the same poem is found in the hymn "I Love to Tell the Story"—see August 13.)

Tell me the old, old story of unseen things above,
Of Jesus and His glory, of Jesus and His love.
Tell me the story simply, as to a little child,
For I am weak and weary, and helpless and defiled.

Tell me the story slowly, that I may take it in,
That wonderful redemption, God's remedy for sin.
Tell me the story often, for I forget so soon;
The early dew of morning has passed away at noon.

Tell me the story softly, with earnest tones and grave;
Remember I'm the sinner whom Jesus came to save.
Tell me the story always, if you would really be,
In any time of trouble, a comforter to me.

Tell me the same old story when you have cause to fear
That this world's empty glory is costing me too dear.
Yes, and when that world's glory is dawning on my soul,
Tell me the old, old story: "Christ Jesus makes thee whole."

Tell me the old, old story, tell me the old, old story,
Tell me the old, old story, of Jesus and His love.

We cannot but speak the things which we have seen and heard.

—Acts 4:20

O the Deep, Deep Love of Jesus

I find it fascinating and comforting that in Ephesians 3:18 the love of Jesus is described as being cube-shaped, perfect on all its sides, infinite in all its dimensions—long, high, wide, and deep. Drawing from this verse, Samuel Trevor Francis, who was born in England on **November 19, 1834**, makes the love of Christ real to us in this immortal hymn. His vivid image came from his own background. As a child, Samuel wrote poems and sang in the church choir; but as a young man he struggled with questions and considered drowning himself in the River Thames. Then he was wonderfully changed by a personal experience of the love of Christ. He eventually became a London merchant, but his real love was hymn writing and open-air preaching, which occupied him all his life, until his death at age ninety-two.

O the deep, deep love of Jesus, vast, unmeasured, boundless, free!
Rolling as a mighty ocean in its fullness over me!
Underneath me, all around me, is the current of Thy love
Leading onward, leading homeward to Thy glorious rest above!

O the deep, deep love of Jesus, spread His praise from shore to shore!
How He loveth, ever loveth, changeth never, nevermore!
How He watches o'er His loved ones, died to call them all His own;
How for them He intercedeth, watcheth o'er them from the throne!

O the deep, deep love of Jesus, love of every love the best!
'Tis an ocean full of blessing, 'tis a haven giving rest!
O the deep, deep love of Jesus, 'tis a heaven of heavens to me;
And it lifts me up to glory, for it lifts me up to Thee!

. . . that you, being rooted and grounded in love, may be able to comprehend with all the saints what is the width and length and depth and height—to know the love of Christ which passes knowledge; that you may be filled with all the fullness of God.

—Ephesians 3:17–19

I Need Thee Every Hour

Annie Hawks of Brooklyn faithfully attended Hanson Place Baptist Church, pastored by the celebrated hymnist Dr. Robert Lowry. With his encouragement, she began writing Sunday school songs for children. "One day as a young wife and mother of 37 years," she wrote, "I was busy with my regular household tasks. Suddenly I became so filled with the sense of the nearness of the Master that, wondering how one could live without Him, either in joy or pain, these words, 'I Need Thee Every Hour,' were ushered into my mind. Dr. Lowry wrote the tune and chorus, and this hymn was first sung at the National Baptist Sunday School Convention in Cincinnati on **November 20, 1872**."

I need Thee every hour, most gracious Lord;
No tender voice like Thine can peace afford.
I need Thee, O I need Thee; Every hour I need Thee;
O bless me now, my Savior, I come to Thee.

I need Thee every hour, stay Thou nearby;
Temptations lose their power when Thou art nigh.
I need Thee, O I need Thee; Every hour I need Thee;
O bless me now, my Savior, I come to Thee.

I need Thee every hour, in joy or pain;
Come quickly and abide, or life is vain.
I need Thee, O I need Thee; Every hour I need Thee;
O bless me now, my Savior, I come to Thee.

I need Thee every hour; teach me Thy will;
And Thy rich promises in me fulfill.
I need Thee, O I need Thee; Every hour I need Thee;
O bless me now, my Savior, I come to Thee.

Whom have I in heaven but You? And there is none upon earth that I desire besides You.

—Psalm 73:25

It Is Well with My Soul

The fog had finally lifted on Saturday evening, **November 21, 1873**, as Anna Spafford and her four daughters retired to their berths aboard the *Ville du Havre*. The ship glided through the mid-Atlantic at twelve knots. Suddenly, in the wee hours there was a violent shock. The *Ville du Havre* and a Scottish clipper had collided. Passengers were thrown from beds, screams filled the air, fires broke out, masts crashed to the deck; and within twelve minutes the *Ville du Havre* sank to the depths, bow first. Only sixty-one passengers were saved. The *New York Times* reported, "Mrs. Spafford, of Chicago, lost four children . . . [She] sank with the ship, but floated up again." Her husband, Horatio Spafford, caught the next available ship to join his wife; and as he passed the spot where his daughters had drowned, he was inspired with the words, "It is well." They became the basis of his famous hymn, "It Is Well with My Soul."

> When peace, like a river, attendeth my way,
> When sorrows like sea billows roll;
> Whatever my lot, Thou has taught me to say,
> It is well, it is well, with my soul.
>
> Though Satan should buffet, though trials should come,
> Let this blest assurance control,
> That Christ has regarded my helpless estate,
> And hath shed His own blood for my soul.
>
> And Lord, haste the day when my faith shall be sight,
> The clouds be rolled back as a scroll;
> The trump shall resound, and the Lord shall descend,
> Even so, it is well with my soul.
>
> *It is well, with my soul,*
> *It is well, it is well, with my soul.*

And she said, "It is well."

—2 Kings 4:23

There Shall Be Showers of Blessing

Major Daniel Whittle entered the world on **November 22, 1840**. He served in the 72nd Illinois Regiment during the Civil War, worked for a watch-making company in Chicago, and then devoted the rest of his life to Christian service and to writing timeless gospel songs like this one.

There shall be showers of blessing:
This is the promise of love;
There shall be seasons refreshing,
Sent from the Savior above.

There shall be showers of blessing,
Precious reviving again;
Over the hills and the valleys,
Sound of abundance of rain.

There shall be showers of blessing;
Send them upon us, O Lord;
Grant to us now a refreshing,
Come, and now honor Thy Word.

There shall be showers of blessing:
Oh, that today they might fall,
Now as to God we're confessing,
Now as on Jesus we call!

Showers of blessing,
Showers of blessing we need:
Mercy drops round us are falling,
But for the showers we plead.

I will cause showers to come down in their season; there shall be showers of blessing.

—Ezekiel 34:26

Jesus of Nazareth Passeth By

Ira Sankey was all nerves on **November 23, 1873**. He was in charge of a mass meeting of Scottish ministers in Edinburgh, and they only sang metrical psalms. He had planned to introduce some gospel songs before D. L. Moody's sermon, but Moody had fallen ill and stayed in bed. After the opening prayer, Sankey led in a safe choice, singing Psalm 100. Then, with a deep breath, he started singing a solo called "Jesus of Nazareth Passeth By." The crowd melted. He later wrote, "The singing of this song at once assured me that even 'human hymns,' sung in a prayerful spirit, were indeed likely to be used of God to arrest attention and convey gospel truth to the hearts of men in bonny Scotland, even as they had in other places."

What means this eager, anxious throng,
Which moves with busy haste along—
These wondrous gatherings day by day,
What means this strange commotion, pray?
In accents hushed the throng reply,
"Jesus of Nazareth passeth by."

Again He comes! From place to place
His holy footprints we can trace;
He pauseth at our threshold—nay,
He enters—condescends to stay:
Shall we not gladly raise the cry?
"Jesus of Nazareth passeth by."

But if you still His call refuse,
And all His wondrous love abuse,
Soon will He sadly from you turn,
Your bitter prayer for pardon spurn,
"Too late! too late!" will be the cry—
"Jesus of Nazareth has passed by."

And they told him, that Jesus of Nazareth passeth by.
—Luke 18:37 KJV

I Sing the Mighty Power of God

On **November 24, 1748**, anxious friends gathered by the bed of the "Father of English Hymnody," Rev. Isaac Watts, who was seventy-four years old. He was dying. His attendant begged him to take some liquid to moisten his mouth, and he received three teaspoons. The attendant remarked that Watts had taught his friends how to live, and now he was teaching them how to die. "If God should raise me up again," said Watts, "I may finish some more of my papers, or God can make use of me to save a soul, and that will be worth living for. If God has no more service for me to do, through grace I am ready; it is a great mercy to me that I have no manner of fear or dread of death. . . . I trust all my sins are pardoned through the blood of Christ. . . . I have no fear of dying." He passed away shortly afterward, leaving us a treasure trove of praise. Here's my favorite Watts hymn, a celebration of God's creative power that made heaven and earth. It first appeared in his *Divine Songs Attempted in Easy Language for the Use of Children*, published in 1715.

> I sing the mighty power of God, that made the mountains rise,
> That spread the flowing seas abroad, and built the lofty skies.
> I sing the wisdom that ordained the sun to rule the day;
> The moon shines full at His command, and all the stars obey.
>
> I sing the goodness of the Lord, who filled the earth with food,
> Who formed the creatures through the Word, and then pronounced them good.
> Lord, how Thy wonders are displayed, where'er I turn my eye,
> If I survey the ground I tread, or gaze upon the sky.
>
> There's not a plant or flower below, but makes Thy glories known,
> And clouds arise, and tempests blow, by order from Thy throne;
> While all that borrows life from Thee is ever in Thy care;
> And everywhere that we can be, Thou, God art present there.

Lift up your eyes on high, and behold who hath created these things . . . he is strong in power.

—Isaiah 40:26 KJV

Nothing but the Blood of Jesus

While pastoring in Brooklyn, New York, during the 1860s, Robert Lowry became involved in hymnology. By his death on **November 25, 1899**, he had written such favorites as "How Can I Keep From Singing?" "Up from the Grave He Arose," "Shall We Gather at the River?"—and this hymn about the cleansing power of the blood of Jesus Christ.

What can wash away my sin?
Nothing but the blood of Jesus;
What can make me whole again?
Nothing but the blood of Jesus.

For my pardon, this I see,
Nothing but the blood of Jesus;
For my cleansing this my plea,
Nothing but the blood of Jesus.

Now by this I'll overcome—
Nothing but the blood of Jesus,
Now by this I'll reach my home—
Nothing but the blood of Jesus.

Glory! Glory! This I sing—
Nothing but the blood of Jesus,
All my praise for this I bring—
Nothing but the blood of Jesus.

Oh! precious is the flow
That makes me white as snow;
No other fount I know,
Nothing but the blood of Jesus.

And when I see the blood, I will pass over you.

—Exodus 12:13

God Moves in a Mysterious Way

On November 15 we celebrated the birth of William Cowper, who wrote "There Is a Fountain Filled with Blood." Well, today is his birthday too. Many authorities list Cowper's birthday as **November 26, 1731**. The confusion comes from the British Calendar Act of 1751. In an attempt to align the calendar more accurately to the solar year, the government declared that the day after Wednesday, September 2, 1752, would be Thursday, September 14. People went to bed one night and woke up, so to speak, twelve days later. I'm glad we can celebrate twice with Cowper, because I wanted a chance to include this hymn. It's one of my favorites and was reportedly composed after the melancholy hymnist had been saved from a suicide attempt.

God moves in a mysterious way
His wonders to perform;
He plants His footsteps in the sea
And rides upon the storm.

Ye fearful saints, fresh courage take;
The clouds ye so much dread
Are big with mercy and shall break
In blessings on your head.

Judge not the Lord by feeble sense,
But trust Him for His grace;
Behind a frowning providence
He hides a smiling face.

Blind unbelief is sure to err
And scan His work in vain;
God is His own interpreter,
And He will make it plain.

I am going to do something in your days that you would not believe, even if you were told.

—Habakkuk 1:5 NIV

We Praise Thee, O God, Our Redeemer, Creator

This great Thanksgiving hymn was first sung on Thanksgiving Day, **November 27, 1902**. The author is Julia Bulkley Corey, who wrote it at the request of J. Archer Gibson, the organist at the Brick Presbyterian Church in New York City. Gibson wanted to use the tune to the Thanksgiving hymn "We Gather Together," but he wanted new words. Julia, an active member at Brick Presbyterian, penned these new words, and they were a hit. A month later, at the request of her father, a prominent New York architect, Julia added a verse to make it a suitable Christmas hymn: "Thy love Thou didst show us, Thine only Son sending, / Who came as a babe and whose bed was a stall, / His blest life He gave us and then died to save us; / We praise Thee, O Lord, for Thy gift to us all."

We praise Thee, O God, our Redeemer, Creator,
In grateful devotion our tribute we bring;
We lay it before Thee, we kneel and adore Thee,
We bless Thy holy Name, glad praises we sing.

We worship Thee, God of our fathers, we bless Thee;
Through life's storm and tempest our guide have Thou been;
When perils o'ertake us, escape Thou wilt make us,
And with Thy help, O Lord, our battles we win.

With voices united our praises we offer,
To Thee, great Jehovah, glad anthems we raise.
Thy strong arm will guide us, our God is beside us,
To Thee, our great Redeemer, forever be praise.

Oh, give thanks to the LORD, for He is good! For His mercy endures forever. Let Israel now say, "His mercy endures forever." Let the house of Aaron now say, "His mercy endures forever." Let those who fear the LORD now say, "His mercy endures forever."

—Psalm 118:1–4

No Night There

Born in an Irish village on **November 28, 1868**, John Clements emigrated to America with his family. At age seventeen, he heard D. L. Moody preach in Binghamton, New York. He was converted on the spot and devoted his remaining sixty years to spreading the gospel by soul winning and hymn writing. Over seventy composers set his words to music. The best known of his five thousand hymns are "Somebody Did a Golden Deed" and this cheering song about heaven.

In the land of fadeless day,
Lies "the city foursquare,"
It shall never pass away,
And there is "no night there."

All the gates of pearl are made,
In "the city foursquare,"
All the streets with gold are laid,
And there is "no night there."

All the gates shall never close,
To "the city foursquare,"
There life's crystal river flows,
And there is "no night there."

There they need no sunshine bright,
In "that city foursquare,"
For the Lamb is all the light,
And there is "no night there."

God shall "wipe away all tears"
There's no death, no pain, nor fears;
And they count not time by years,
For there is "no night there."

Its gates shall not be shut at all by day
(there shall be no night there).

—Revelation 21:25

Now I Resolve with All My Heart

Anne Steele, one of the most prolific of eighteenth-century Baptist hymnists, has been called the Poet of the Sanctuary. Her father was a British timber merchant and a man who prayed for his children. When Anne wrote her first book of poems and hymns, she sent them off in search of a publisher while her dad prayed. On **November 29, 1757**, he wrote in his diary: "This day Nanny [Anne] sent part of her composition to London to be printed. I entreat a gracious God, who enabled and stirred her up to such a work, to direct in it, and bless it for the good of many. . . . I pray to God to make it useful, and to keep her humble." Anne's book *Poems on Subjects Chiefly Devotional*, finally made it to print in 1760. Included was this poem of consecration.

> Now I resolve with all my heart,
> With all my powers, to serve the Lord:
> Nor from His precepts e'er depart,
> Whose service is a rich reward.
>
> O be His service all my joy;
> Around let my example shine
> Till others love the best employ
> And join in labors so divine.
>
> Be this the purpose of my soul,
> My solemn, my determined choice,
> To yield to His supreme control,
> And in His kind commands rejoice.
>
> O may I never faint nor tire,
> Nor wandering leave His sacred ways;
> Great God, accept my soul's desire,
> And give me strength to live Thy praise.

I am resolved to obey Your statutes to the very end.

—Psalm 119:112 HCSB

Hosanna, Loud Hosanna

It's not Palm Sunday, but never mind—we can always shout "Hosanna!" Jennette Threlfall did. The daughter of a British wine merchant, she was orphaned early in life and was raised by loving relatives. An accident left her disfigured and lame, and a subsequent accident left her disabled and bedridden until her death on **November 30, 1880**, at St. George's Hospital in London. Jennette was known for her cheerful disposition, and her poems and hymns all breathe the holy air of "Hosanna!" Perhaps her secret is found in a prayer she once wrote: "O loving Father, give Thy poor child strength! Thou knowest she has none: / O loving Father, give her strength to say, 'Thy will be done!'" Jennette's hymn "Hosanna, Loud Hosanna" is sung to the German tune "Ellacombe," which is often used with "I Sing the Mighty Power of God."

Hosanna, loud hosanna, the little children sang;
Through pillared court and temple the lovely anthem rang.
To Jesus, who had blessed them close folded to His breast,
The children sang their praises, the simplest and the best.

From Olivet they followed mid an exultant crowd,
The victor palm branch waving, and chanting clear and loud.
The Lord of men and angels rode on in lowly state,
Nor scorned that little children should on His bidding wait.

"Hosanna in the highest!" that ancient song we sing,
For Christ is our Redeemer, the Lord of heaven our King.
O may we ever praise Him with heart and life and voice,
And in His blissful presence eternally rejoice!

Hosanna! "Blessed is He who comes in the name of the Lord!" Blessed is the kingdom of our father David that comes in the name of the Lord! Hosanna in the highest!

—Mark 11:9–10

Ye Christian Heralds

As we sing out our faith in church every week, we should include a mixture of mission songs, for we have the greatest calling in history. We're to take the gospel to every creature under heaven. "Ye Christian Heralds," though seldom heard today, was once a favorite missionary hymn. It was written by Rev. Bourne Hall Draper, who was born near Oxford in 1775. His parents were Anglicans who wanted their son to prepare for Holy Orders, but they didn't have the money for his education, so he became a printer with Oxford Press. While there, he began attending a Baptist church and was eventually ordained into the Baptist ministry, pastoring in Isaac Watts's hometown of Southampton. Draper wrote this hymn as a young man for the farewell service of a group of missionaries leaving for India on **December 1, 1803**.

Ye Christian heralds, go proclaim
Salvation through Emmanuel's name;
To distant climes the tidings bear,
And plant the Rose of Sharon there.

Ruler of worlds, display Thy power,
Be this Thy Zion's favored hour;
Bid the bright morning star arise,
And point the nations to the skies.

Set up Thy throne where Satan reigns,
On Afric shores, on India's plains;
On wilds and continents unknown,
And be the universe Thine own!

And when our labors are all o'er,
Then we shall meet to part no more;
Meet with the blood-bought throng to fall,
And crown our Jesus, Lord of all!

Then, having fasted and prayed, and laid hands on them, they sent them away.

—Acts 13:3

I Am Trusting Thee, Lord Jesus

This simple hymn summarizes the testimony of its radiant author, Frances Ridley Havergal. Born into the home of a musical pastor, Frances was a beloved poet and soloist who gave herself wholly to Jesus Christ after reading a little book titled *All for Jesus*. When her sister later asked about her experience, Frances replied: "Yes, it was on Advent Sunday, **December 2, 1873**, I first saw clearly the blessedness of true consecration. I saw it as a flash of electric light, and what you see you can never un-see. There must be full surrender before there can be full blessedness. God admits you by the one into the other. He Himself showed me all this most clearly." She wrote this hymn the next year, and it was said to have been her favorite.

I am trusting Thee, Lord Jesus,
Trusting only Thee;
Trusting Thee for full salvation,
Great and free.

I am trusting Thee for pardon;
At Thy feet I bow;
For Thy grace and tender mercy,
Trusting now.

I am trusting Thee to guide me;
Thou alone shalt lead;
Every day and hour supplying
All my need.

I am trusting Thee, Lord Jesus;
Never let me fall;
I am trusting Thee forever,
And for all.

Blessed is the man who trusts in the LORD, and whose hope is in the LORD. For he shall be like a tree planted by the waters, which spreads out its roots by the river.

—Jeremiah 17:7–8

O Lord, I Will Delight in Thee

Rev. John Ryland was proud of the son who bore his name. In 1764, he wrote, "John is now eleven years and seven months old. He has read Genesis in Hebrew five times through; he read through the Greek New Testament before nine years old." Three years later, Ryland had the joy of baptizing his son; and in 1771, at the age of eighteen, John Ryland Jr. preached his first sermon. Father and son worked side by side in the ministry until November 11, 1785, when John Ryland Jr. became his father's successor. The junior Ryland also became a prime supporter of missionary William Carey and one of the founders of the British Missionary Society. He was also a hymnist, and this song, written **December 3, 1777**, reveals the secret of his ministry. "I recollect deeper feelings of mind in composing this hymn," he said, "than perhaps I ever felt in making any other."

O Lord, I will delight in Thee
And on Thy care depend,
To Thee in every trouble flee,
My best, my only Friend.

When all created streams are dried,
Thy fullness is the same;
May I with this be satisfied
And glory in Thy name.

No good in creatures can be found
But may be found in Thee;
I must have all things and abound
While God is God to me.

O Lord, I cast my care on Thee,
I triumph and adore;
Henceforth my great concern shall be
To love and please Thee more.

*Delight yourself also in the LORD, and He
shall give you the desires of your heart.*

—Psalm 37:4

Gentle Mary Laid Her Child

As we prepare for another Christmas, let's remember that Jesus was born amid the songs of heavenly choirs singing glory to God in the highest. In fact, the nativity story is packed with original hymns: Mary's hymn of praise, Zechariah's hymn of praise, the songs of the angels over shepherds' fields, and the song of Simeon in Luke 2. Christmas is a golden season for hymns celebrating the incarnation of Jesus, who is Immanuel, "God with Us." This Canadian carol was written by Rev. Joseph S. Cook. He was born in Durham County, England, on **December 4, 1859**, but emigrated to Canada early in life and became an ordained Methodist preacher. He wrote the hymn in 1919 for a Christmas carol competition sponsored by a Canadian Methodist magazine. It is sung to the tune "Tempus Adest Floridum" ("Good King Wenceslas").

Gentle Mary laid her Child lowly in a manger;
There He lay, the undefiled, to the world a Stranger:
Such a Babe in such a place, can He be the Savior?
Ask the saved of all the race who have found His favor.

Angels sang about His birth; wise men sought and found Him;
Heaven's star shone brightly forth, glory all around Him:
Shepherds saw the wondrous sight, heard the angels singing;
All the plains were lit that night, all the hills were ringing.

Gentle Mary laid her Child lowly in a manger;
He is still the undefiled, but no more a stranger:
Son of God, of humble birth, beautiful the story;
Praise His name in all the earth, hail the King of glory!

The angel answered and said to her, "The Holy Spirit will come upon you, and the power of the Highest will overshadow you; therefore, also, that Holy One who is to be born will be called the Son of God. . . . For with God nothing will be impossible." Then Mary said, "Behold, the maidservant of the Lord!"

—Luke 1:35–38

The Birthday of a King

Here's another Christmas favorite. Both the words and the music were written by a Brooklyn-born composer with a big heart for disabled children. William Harold Neidlinger was widely respected in the upper echelons of the music world as a church organist and conductor, but he also specialized in child psychology. He became well-known for his music books for kindergarteners; better known for the New Jersey school he founded for mentally handicapped children; and best known for his children's Christmas Carol "The Birthday of a King." Neidlinger passed away during the Christmas season, on **December 5, 1924**.

> In the little village of Bethlehem,
> There lay a Child one day;
> And the sky was bright with a holy light
> O'er the place where Jesus lay.
>
> 'Twas a humble birthplace, but O how much
> God gave to us that day,
> From the manger bed what a path has led,
> What a perfect, holy way.
>
> *Alleluia! O how the angels sang.*
> *Alleluia! How it rang!*
> *And the sky was bright with a holy light*
> *'Twas the birthday of a King.*

Where is He who has been born King of the Jews? For we have seen His star in the East and have come to worship Him.

—Matthew 2:2

I Am Not Skilled to Understand

When we can't lean on our own understanding, we can trust Him who does all things well. The author of "I Am Not Skilled to Understand" was Dorothy (Dora) Greenwell, born **December 6, 1821**, in Durham, England; she wrote from her own experience. She was born into a comfortable family, but her father's death caused economic problems resulting in the family estate being sold. After moving to London, Dora struggled with health problems, but that didn't stop her from engaging in a ministry to handicapped and mentally challenged children or from writing a series of spiritually powerful books. This hymn was published as a poem titled "Redemption" in her 1873 book *Songs of Salvation*.

I am not skilled to understand
What God hath willed, what God hath planned;
I only know that at His right hand
Is One who is my Savior!

I take Him at His word indeed;
"Christ died for sinners"—this I read;
For in my heart I find a need
Of Him to be my Savior!

That He should leave His place on high
And come for sinful man to die,
You count it strange? So once did I,
Before I knew my Savior!

Yea, living, dying, let me bring
My strength, my solace from this Spring;
That He who lives to be my King
Once died to be my Savior!

They were astonished beyond measure, saying,
"He has done all things well."

—Mark 7:37

At the Name of Jesus

As a teenager, Caroline Maria Noel wrote a few poems; but she abandoned the attempt when she was about twenty years old. Only after becoming bedridden by a serious illness in her forties did she again take up her pen in the hope of encouraging others who were suffering. For twenty-five years she ministered with pen and ink from her sickbed, before passing away at age sixty on **December 7, 1877**. Her best-known hymn is this paraphrase of Philippians 2:4–11, and it first appeared in her book *The Name of Jesus, and Other Verses for the Sick and Lonely*. Notice the sturdy theology of this hymn. Sentimental rhyme does little to encourage us when sick and suffering; we need the strong name of Jesus before whom every knee will bow. (Try singing this hymn to the tune of "Like a River Glorious.")

At the name of Jesus, every knee shall bow,
Every tongue confess Him King of glory now;
'Tis the Father's pleasure we should call Him Lord,
Who from the beginning was the mighty Word.

Mighty and mysterious in the highest height,
God from everlasting, very light of light:
In the Father's bosom with the spirit blest,
Love, in love eternal, rest, in perfect rest.

At His voice creation sprang at once to sight,
All the angel faces, all the hosts of light,
Thrones and dominations, stars upon their way,
All the heavenly orders, in their great array.

Humbled for a season, to receive a name
From the lips of sinners unto whom He came,
Faithfully He bore it, spotless to the last,
Brought it back victorious when from death He passed.

That at the name of Jesus every knee should bow.

—Philippians 2:10

What Time I Am Afraid

I was driving through Ohio recently when my wife called. "Rob," she said in grave tones, "I have bad news." My heart sped up like firecrackers exploding. Then she said meekly, "I broke the vase we bought the other day." I have to admit I raised my voice. "Don't ever do that to me again," I said. "A broken vase is not *bad news*. Someone dying is *bad news*! You nearly made me wreck." This hymn tells us that we can trust the Lord whatever the news. "What Time I Am Afraid" is the Scottish version of Psalm 56. It was set to music by Uzziah Burnap, who died on **December 8, 1900**. Though he graduated with a music degree from the University of Paris and was a prominent New York organist for decades, Uzziah Burnap paid the bills by running a dry goods store in Brooklyn. His tune for "What Time I Am Afraid" is titled "Holy Guide."

What time I am afraid
I put my trust in Thee;
In God I rest, and praise
His Word, so rich and free.

In God I put my trust,
I neither doubt nor fear,
For man can never harm
With God my Helper near.

In God, the Lord, I rest,
His word of grace I praise,
His promise stands secure,
Nor fear nor foe dismays.

For Thou hast saved from death,
From falling kept me free,
That in the light of life
My walk may be with Thee.

Whenever I am afraid, I will trust in You.

—Psalm 56:3

O for a Closer Walk with God

William Cowper, the melancholy hymnist, was distressed by a friend's illness when he wrote the words of this hymn. "I began to compose them yesterday morning [**December 9, 1769**] before daybreak, but fell asleep at the end of the first two lines; when I was awaked again, the third and fourth verses were whispered to my heart in a way which I have often experienced." It later appeared in *Olney Hymns* under the title "Walking with God," based on Genesis 5:24.

> O for a closer walk with God,
> A calm and heavenly frame,
> A light to shine upon the road
> That leads me to the Lamb!
>
> Where is the blessedness I knew,
> When first I saw the Lord?
> Where is the soul refreshing view
> Of Jesus and His Word?
>
> What peaceful hours I once enjoyed!
> How sweet their memory still!
> But they have left an aching void
> The world can never fill.
>
> Return, O holy Dove, return,
> Sweet messenger of rest!
> I hate the sins that made Thee mourn
> And drove Thee from my breast.
>
> The dearest idol I have known,
> Whate'er that idol be
> Help me to tear it from Thy throne,
> And worship only Thee.

And Enoch walked with God; and he was not, for God took him.

—Genesis 5:24

God Our Father, We Adore Thee

There are two fathomless doctrines at the heart of Christianity: the Trinity (God as three Persons, yet one God) and the Duality (Jesus as both God and Man, yet one Person). "God Our Father" is one of Christianity's premier Trinitarian hymns. The words are by the British evangelist George W. Frazer; the tune, "Beecher," was written by the German composer John Zundel, whose birthday is today. He was born **December 10, 1815**, near Stuttgart.

> God, our Father, we adore Thee! We, Thy children, bless Thy
>   name!
> Chosen in the Christ before Thee, we are "holy without blame."
> We adore Thee! We adore Thee! Abba's praises we proclaim!
> We adore Thee! We adore Thee! Abba's praises we proclaim!
>
> Son Eternal, we adore Thee! Lamb upon the throne on high!
> Lamb of God, we bow before Thee, Thou hast brought Thy
>   people nigh!
> We adore Thee! We adore Thee! Son of God, who came to die!
> We adore Thee! We adore Thee! Son of God, who came to die!
>
> Holy Spirit, we adore Thee! Paraclete and heavenly Guest!
> Sent from God and from the Savior, Thou hast led us into rest.
> We adore Thee! We adore Thee! By Thy grace forever blessed:
> We adore Thee! We adore Thee! By Thy grace forever blessed!
>
> Father, Son, and Holy Spirit, Three in One! We give Thee praise!
> For the riches we inherit, heart and voice to Thee we raise!
> We adore Thee! We adore Thee! Thee we bless, through end-
>   less days!
> We adore Thee! We adore Thee! Thee we bless, through end-
>   less days!

. . . elect according to the foreknowledge of God the Father, in sanctification of the Spirit, for obedience and sprinkling of the blood of Jesus Christ.

—1 Peter 1:2

Silent Night

On **December 11, 1792**, a baby was born into the family Mohr in snow-clad Salzburg, Austria. He was named Josef, and as a boy he sang as a chorister in the cathedral choir of his native city. In 1815, Josef was ordained by the Roman Catholic bishop of Salzburg and two years later became assistant priest at St. Nicholas Church of Oberndorf, in Austria's alpine region. One Christmas Eve, he discovered the organ in the church wasn't working. According to the traditional story, Josef quickly wrote the words to this carol and asked the acting organist, Franz Gruber, to compose the tune. It was sung with guitar accompaniment that evening, December 24, 1818.

Silent night, holy night,
All is calm, all is bright
Round yon virgin mother and Child.
Holy Infant, so tender and mild,
Sleep in heavenly peace,
Sleep in heavenly peace.

Silent night, holy night,
Shepherds quake at the sight;
Glories stream from heaven afar,
Heavenly hosts sing Alleluia!
Christ the Savior is born,
Christ the Savior is born!

Silent night, holy night
Wondrous star, lend thy light;
With the angels let us sing,
Alleluia to our King;
Christ the Savior is born,
Christ the Savior is born!

And she brought forth her firstborn Son, and wrapped
Him in swaddling cloths, and laid Him in a manger,
because there was no room for them in the inn.

—Luke 2:7

Look, Ye Saints! The Sight Is Glorious

For two hundred years, this hymn has been a favorite of church-goers on Ascension Sunday (approximately forty days after Easter). It was written by the Irish poet Thomas Kelly, author of one of my favorite hymns, "Praise the Savior, Ye Who Know Him." There are several melodies attached to this hymn, but a very common one is "Bryn Calfaria." It was composed by William Owen, born **December 12, 1813**. Owen was a native of Wales who worked in the Penrhyn slate quarries. He was a gifted singer who published a book of hymn tunes in 1886.

> Look, ye saints! the sight is glorious:
> See the Man of Sorrows now;
> From the fight returned victorious,
> Every knee to Him shall bow;
> Crown Him, crown Him,
> Crown Him, crown Him,
> Crowns become the Victor's brow,
> Crowns become the Victor's brow.
>
> Crown the Savior! angels, crown Him;
> Rich the trophies Jesus brings;
> In the seat of power enthrone Him,
> While the vault of heaven rings;
> Crown Him, crown Him,
> Crown Him, crown Him,
> Crown the Savior King of kings,
> Crown the Savior King of kings.

And while they looked steadfastly toward heaven as He went up, behold, two men stood by them in white apparel, who also said, "Men of Galilee, why do you stand gazing up into heaven? This same Jesus, who was taken up from you into heaven, will so come in like manner as you saw Him go into heaven."

—Acts 1:10–11

Since I Have Been Redeemed

If you could summarize your testimony, your attitude, and your condition in just one line, what would it be? How about, "I have a song I love to sing, since I have been redeemed"? That was the testimony of Edwin O. Excell. He was born into the home of a German Reformed pastor on **December 13, 1851**, in Stark County, Ohio. As a young man, he worked as a plasterer and bricklayer, but he loved singing and song leading. One day he was invited to lead the music during a Methodist revival, and there he was saved. He became a renowned song leader, music publisher, composer, and hymn writer. This is his hymn of testimony, published in 1884.

I have a song I love to sing,
Since I have been redeemed,
Of my Redeemer, Savior King,
Since I have been redeemed.

I have a Christ who satisfies
Since I have been redeemed,
To do His will my highest prize,
Since I have been redeemed.

I have a home prepared for me,
Since I have been redeemed,
Where I shall dwell eternally,
Since I have been redeemed.

Since I have been redeemed,
Since I have been redeemed,
I will glory in His name,
Since I have been redeemed,
I will glory in the Savior's name.

And they sang a new song, saying . . . "You were slain
and have redeemed us to God by Your blood out of
every tribe and tongue and people and nation."

—Revelation 5:9

God from on High Hath Heard

J. R. Woodford was consecrated Bishop of Ely on **December 14, 1873**, in London's Westminster Abbey. He was a popular preacher, an honorary chaplain to Queen Victoria, and an educator who founded Ely Theological College. Woodford wrote hymns of his own and translated those of others. This delightful carol was written in Latin by the French poet Charles Coffin. Woodford rendered it into English for his 1852 book, *Hymns Arranged for Sundays.*

God from on high hath heard;
Let sighs and sorrows cease;
Lo! from the opening Heav'n descends
To man the promised Peace.

Hark! through the silent night
Angelic voices swell;
Their joyful songs proclaim that "God
Is born on earth to dwell."

See how the shepherd band
Speed on with eager feet;
Come to the hallowed cave with them
The Holy Babe to greet.

Art Thou the Christ? the Son?
The Father's image bright?
And see we Him whose arm upholds
Earth and the starry height?

Our sinful pride to cure
With that pure love of Thine,
O be Thou born within our hearts,
Most Holy Child divine.

And the Word became flesh and dwelt among us, and we beheld His glory.

—John 1:14

O Little Town of Bethlehem

When you sing this carol from a hymnal, notice that the title of the tune is "St. Louis." It's not named for a city or a saint, but for the composer of the music, Lewis H. Redner (born **December 15, 1830**). Here's what happened: In 1865, Phillips Brooks, the famed Boston pastor, visited the Holy Land and stopped in Bethlehem, the birthplace of Jesus. He was so moved that, returning home, he wrote this hymn for the children in his Sunday school. He handed the words to his organist, Lewis Redner, asking him to compose the melody. "If it's a good tune," added Brooks, "I'll name it 'St. Lewis' after you." Lewis couldn't come up with a suitable tune until the evening before the song was to be performed; but it was an instant hit, and Brooks did name it for the organist, changing the spelling to avoid embarrassing him.

O little town of Bethlehem, how still we see thee lie!
Above thy deep and dreamless sleep the silent stars go by.
Yet in thy dark streets shineth the everlasting Light;
The hopes and fears of all the years are met in thee tonight.

For Christ is born of Mary, and gathered all above,
While mortals sleep, the angels keep their watch of wondering love.
O morning stars together, proclaim the holy birth,
And praises sing to God the King, and peace to men on earth!

How silently, how silently, the wondrous Gift is giv'n;
So God imparts to human hearts the blessings of His Heav'n.
No ear may hear His coming, but in this world of sin,
Where meek souls will receive Him still, the dear Christ enters in.

O holy Child of Bethlehem, descend to us, we pray;
Cast out our sin, and enter in, be born in us today.
We hear the Christmas angels the great glad tidings tell;
O come to us, abide with us, our Lord Emmanuel!

*Jesus was born in Bethlehem of Judea
in the days of Herod the king.*

—Matthew 2:1

God Will Take Care of You

In 1904, the evangelistic team of Walter and Civilla Martin moved temporarily into a Bible institute in Lestershire, New York, when Walter agreed to compile a hymnbook for the school. One Sunday while Walter was out preaching, Civilla stayed in bed, feeling sick. Alone in her room, she wrote the words of this hymn. When Walter returned, she handed him the lyrics. He went immediately to his little organ and composed the tune. It was sung that night and included in the hymnbook he was assembling. Walter passed away on **December 16, 1935**, in Atlanta. He was seventy-three. Civilla remained alive and active into her eighties, and is the author of several other beloved hymns, including the ever-popular "His Eye Is on the Sparrow."

> Be not dismayed whate'er betide,
> God will take care of you;
> Beneath His wings of love abide,
> God will take care of you.
>
> All you may need He will provide,
> God will take care of you;
> Nothing you ask will be denied,
> God will take care of you.
>
> No matter what may be the test,
> God will take care of you;
> Lean, weary one, upon His breast,
> God will take care of you.
>
> *God will take care of you,*
> *Through every day, o'er all the way;*
> *He will take care of you,*
> *God will take care of you.*

The LORD will take care of me.

—Psalm 27:10

Let Us, with a Gladsome Mind

Though not a Christmas carol, the joyful lyrics of this hymn and its festive melody fit any holiday program. The words were written by the poet John Milton in 1623, when he was only fifteen years old. Much of the hymn's popularity comes from its merry tune, "Monkland," written by John Antes, a Moravian watchmaker from Pennsylvania. Antes led a global life for Christ, serving in Germany and Egypt before his death in England on **December 17, 1811**.

Let us, with a gladsome mind,
Praise the Lord, for He is kind.
For His mercies [shall] endure,
Ever faithful, ever sure.

Let us blaze his Name abroad,
For of gods He is the God.
For His mercies [shall] endure,
Ever faithful, ever sure.

He with all commanding might
Filled the new made world with light.
For His mercies [shall] endure,
Ever faithful, ever sure.

All things living He doth feed,
His full hand supplies their need.
For His mercies [shall] endure,
Ever faithful, ever sure.

Let us, with a gladsome mind,
Praise the Lord, for He is kind.
For His mercies [shall] endure,
Ever faithful, ever sure.

Praise the LORD of hosts, for the LORD is
good, for His mercy endures forever.

—Jeremiah 33:11

Rejoice, the Lord Is King

I was tempted to use "Hark! The Herald Angels Sing" for today's hymn. After all, it's the Christmas season, and today is the birthday of its author, the immortal Charles Wesley, who was born in the Epworth parsonage on **December 18, 1707**. But I can't leave out one of my most deeply loved hymns, "Rejoice, the Lord Is King." It also was written by Wesley. In a curious coincidence of hymnological history, the composer of the hymn's majestic melody, John Darwall, died on **December 18, 1789**. So today marks both the birth of the lyricist and the death of the composer. But the hymn itself is timeless. It's one of the greatest ever written and a perfect anthem for celebrating the birth of our Lord, the newborn King.

> Rejoice, the Lord is King! Your Lord and King adore;
> Rejoice, give thanks and sing, and triumph evermore;
> Lift up your heart, lift up your voice;
> Rejoice, again I say, rejoice!
>
> Jesus, the Savior, reigns, the God of truth and love;
> When He had purged our stains, He took His seat above;
> Lift up your heart, lift up your voice;
> Rejoice, again I say, rejoice!
>
> His kingdom cannot fail, He rules o'er earth and heav'n,
> The keys of death and hell are to our Jesus giv'n;
> Lift up your heart, lift up your voice;
> Rejoice, again I say, rejoice!
>
> Rejoice in glorious hope! Our Lord the Judge shall come,
> And take His servants up to their eternal home.
> We soon shall hear th'archangel's voice;
> The trump of God shall sound, rejoice!

The LORD is King forever and ever.

—Psalm 10:16

Blessèd Night

The hymns of Horatius Bonar, the "Prince of Scottish Hymn Writers," are a source of endless comfort. He was a Bible scholar and pastor who wrote more than six hundred hymns. Today is his birthday, **December 19, 1808**, and it's also the anniversary of his book of hymns, the preface to which he composed on his forty-eighth birthday, **December 19, 1856**. Bonar included several carols in his *Hymns of Faith and Hope*, such as this picturesque song, originally titled "The Shepherd's Plain."

> Blessèd night, when first that plain
> Echoed with the joyful strain,
> "Peace has come to earth again."
> Alleluia!
>
> Blessèd hills, that heard the song,
> Of the glorious angel throng
> Swelling all your slopes along.
> Alleluia!
>
> Happy shepherds, on whose ear
> Fell the tidings glad and clear,
> "God to man is drawing near."
> Alleluia!
>
> We adore Thee as our King,
> And to Thee our song we sing,
> Our best offering to Thee bring,
> Alleluia!

The shepherds said to one another, "Let us now go to Bethlehem and see this thing that has come to pass, which the Lord has made known to us."

—Luke 2:15

O Come, O Come, Emmanuel

In medieval Europe, there were cathedral services each evening leading up to Christmas Eve. Each service would begin with an *antiphon*, a choral call to worship. There were seven "Great O Antiphons," beginning with the Latin word *vini* ("come"), followed by the Latin words for "O Wisdom," "O Lord," "O Branch of Jesse," "O Key of David," "O Dayspring," "O King of Nations," and "O Emmanuel." These choral prayers were rooted in messianic titles used by the prophets in the Old Testament, pleas for God to come. During the 1800s, various English translations of the "Great O Antiphons" were made. This well-loved British version is the work of Thomas Alexander Lacey, who was born **December 20, 1853.**

O come, O come, Emmanuel!
Redeem thy captive Israel
That into exile drear is gone,
Far from the face of God's dear Son.

O come, thou Branch of Jesse! Draw
The quarry from the lion's claw;
From the dread caverns of the grave,
From nether hell, thy people save.

O come, O come, thou Dayspring bright!
Pour on our souls thy healing light;
Dispel the long night's ling'ring gloom,
And pierce the shadows of the tomb.

Rejoice! Rejoice! Emmanuel
Shall come to thee, O Israel.

"They shall call His name Immanuel,"
which is translated, "God with us."

—Matthew 1:23

Sweeter Sounds Than Music Knows

John Newton kept preaching even after old age had robbed him of eyesight and a clear mind. Not long before his death, he met his friend William Jay of Bath and they chatted about their infirmities. "My memory is nearly gone," said Newton, "but I remember two things—that I am a great sinner, and that Christ is a great Savior." Newton died in his eighty-third year on **December 21, 1807**. He left behind a remarkable legacy and a rich collection of hymns—but not many nativity hymns. Here is a rare Newton Christmas carol, found in the Olney collection under the title "Praise for the Incarnation." It can be sung to any 7777 meter. Try the tune "Gloria" ("Angels We Have Heard on High"), adding the *Gloria in excelsis Deo*.

Sweeter sounds than music knows
Charm me, in Emmanuel's name;
All her hopes my spirit owes
To His birth, and cross, and shame.

When He came the angels sang
"Glory be to God on high,"
Lord, unloose my stammering tongue,
Who should louder sing than I?

Did the Lord a man become
That He might the law fulfill,
Bleed and suffer in my room,
And canst thou, my tongue, be still?

O my Savior, Shield, and Sun,
Shepherd, Brother, Husband, Friend,
Every precious name in one;
I will love Thee without end.

*But when the fullness of the time had come, God
sent forth His Son, born of woman, born under the
law, to redeem those who were under the law.*

—Galatians 4:4–5

Away in a Manger

For years, everyone assumed Martin Luther had written this carol; in songbooks it was usually subtitled "Luther's Cradle Hymn." According to tradition, the Reformer had written this hymn, which consisted of only two stanzas at the time, for his little son, Hans. We now believe the first two stanzas of "Away in a Manger" came from an anonymous German Lutheran in Pennsylvania, not from Luther himself. We also know who added the tender third verse that begins, "Be near me, Lord Jesus." It was John T. McFarland, who was born January 2, 1851, in Mount Vernon, Indiana, and passed away on the morning of **December 22, 1913**, at his home in Maplewood, New Jersey. McFarland was a Sunday school leader and children's worker whose life's mission was to nurture children in the instruction of the Lord. It was McFarland who introduced graded instruction to American Sunday schools. How fitting that he would complete the most famous children's Christmas carol of all time.

> Away in a manger, no crib for a bed,
> The little Lord Jesus laid down His sweet head.
> The stars in the sky looked down where He lay,
> The little Lord Jesus, asleep on the hay.
>
> The cattle are lowing, the Baby awakes,
> But little Lord Jesus, no crying He makes;
> I love Thee, Lord Jesus, look down from the sky
> And stay by my cradle till morning is nigh.
>
> Be near me, Lord Jesus, I ask Thee to stay
> Close by me forever, and love me, I pray;
> Bless all the dear children in Thy tender care,
> And fit us for Heaven to live with Thee there.

This will be a sign to you: You will find a baby wrapped in cloths and lying in a manger.

—Luke 2:12 NIV

Come, Thou Long Expected Jesus

On **December 23, 1855**, London's new preaching sensation, twenty-one-year-old Charles Spurgeon, wove this carol by Charles Wesley into his Christmas sermon as skillfully as a weaver braids a golden thread into a tapestry: "A very singular thing is this, that Jesus Christ was said to have been 'born the king of the Jews.' Very few have ever been 'born king.' Men are born princes, but they are seldom born kings. I do not think you can find an instance in history where any infant was born king. He was the Prince of Wales, perhaps, and he had to wait a number of years, till his father died, and then they manufactured him into a king, by putting a crown on his head; and a sacred chrism, and other silly things; but he was not born a king. I remember no one who was born a king except Jesus; and there is emphatic meaning in that verse that we sing 'Born thy people to deliver; Born a child, and yet a king.' The moment that He came on earth He was a king."

Come, Thou long expected Jesus
Born to set Thy people free;
From our fears and sins release us,
Let us find our rest in Thee.
Israel's Strength and Consolation,
Hope of all the earth Thou art;
Dear Desire of every nation,
Joy of every longing heart.

Born Thy people to deliver,
Born a child and yet a King,
Born to reign in us forever,
Now Thy gracious kingdom bring.
By Thine own eternal Spirit
Rule in all our hearts alone;
By Thine all sufficient merit,
Raise us to Thy glorious throne.

Jesus said to them . . . "I came from God and now am here."

—John 8:42 NIV

Angels from the Realms of Glory

British publisher James Montgomery, the orphaned son of Moravian missionaries, wrote this carol for the **December 24, 1816**, edition of his newspaper, the *Sheffield Iris*.

Angels from the realms of glory,
Wing your flight o'er all the earth;
Ye who sang creation's story
Now proclaim Messiah's birth.

Shepherds, in the fields abiding,
Watching o'er your flocks by night,
God with us is now residing;
Yonder shines the infant light:

Sages, leave your contemplations,
Brighter visions beam afar;
Seek the great Desire of nations;
Ye have seen His natal star.

Saints, before the altar bending,
Watching long in hope and fear;
Suddenly the Lord, descending,
In His temple shall appear.

All creation, join in praising
God, the Father, Spirit, Son,
Evermore your voices raising
To th'eternal Three in One.

Come and worship, come and worship,
Worship Christ, the newborn King.

Then the angel said to them, "Do not be afraid, for behold, I bring you good tidings of great joy which will be to all people."

—Luke 2:10

O Come, All Ye Faithful

The Christmas truce on Flanders Field in Belgium is a timeless testimony to the power of the birth of Christ. On the western front of World War I, a brief, unofficial cessation of hostilities occurred between British and German forces. It began on Christmas Eve 1914, when German soldiers in their trenches began singing "Silent Night." The British stopped firing and began singing English carols. Soon the troops were greeting each other across no-man's-land and exchanging small gifts. According to the written account of an unknown British soldier, the next morning, **December 25, 1914**, was foggy and very cold. Neither side began firing; the truce held. Some British troops went over to the German side to help bury a slain soldier and then returned for a Christmas worship service. "How we did sing, 'O Come, All Ye Faithful,'" he wrote his family. "I never expected to shake hands with Germans between the firing lines on Christmas Day, and I don't suppose you thought of us doing so. So after a fashion we've enjoyed our Christmas." The next day the war resumed.

O come, all ye faithful, joyful and triumphant,
O come ye, O come ye, to Bethlehem.
Come and behold Him, born the King of angels;

Sing, choirs of angels, sing in exultation;
O sing, all ye citizens of heaven above!
Glory to God, all glory in the highest;

Yea, Lord, we greet Thee, born this happy morning;
Jesus, to Thee be all glory given;
Word of the Father, now in flesh appearing.

O come, let us adore Him,
O come, let us adore Him,
O come, let us adore Him,
Christ the Lord.

For there is born to you this day in the city of
David a Savior, who is Christ the Lord.

—Luke 2:11

The Hope of the Coming of the Lord

Christmas is a red-letter reminder of our Lord's return, for as surely as He came the first time He will come again. This "blessed hope" was on evangelist D. L. Moody's mind in the fall of 1899 as he planned the details of his own funeral. He didn't expect it to occur as soon as it did. Moody passed away just before Christmas that year, and his funeral occurred **December 26, 1899**. The service was just as Moody wanted, and it concluded with this hymn by Daniel Whittle. The melody is by May Moody (Whittle's daughter and Moody's daughter-in-law). She's the composer who also wrote the music for "Moment by Moment."

A lamp in the night, a song in time of sorrow;
A great glad hope which faith can ever borrow
To gild the passing day, with the glory of the morrow,
Is the hope of the coming of the Lord.

A star in the sky, a beacon bright to guide us;
An anchor sure to hold when storms betide us;
A refuge for the soul, where in quiet we may hide us,
Is the hope of the coming of the Lord.

A call of command, like trumpet clearly sounding,
To make us bold when evil is surrounding;
To stir the sluggish heart and to keep in good abounding,
Is the hope of the coming of the Lord.

Blessèd hope, blessèd hope,
Blessèd hope of the coming of the Lord;
How the aching heart it cheers,
How it glistens through our tears,
Blessèd hope of the coming of the Lord.

. . . looking for the blessed hope and glorious appearing
of our great God and Savior Jesus Christ.

—Titus 2:13

The Lord Bless You and Keep You

As we conclude the old year, it's a good time to study the bene-dictions of the Bible. The word *benediction* is a Latin-based term meaning a concluding prayer of blessing. My wife's favorite verse in the Bible is the benediction of Romans 15:13: "May the God of hope fill you with all joy and peace as you trust in him, so that you may overflow with hope by the power of the Holy Spirit" (NIV). And I'm very fond of the benediction in Hebrews 13:20–21, which says, "May the God of peace, who through the blood of the eternal covenant bought back from the dead our Lord Jesus . . . equip you with everything good for doing his will" (NIV). The two foun-dational benedictions of the Bible are the apostolic benediction of 2 Corinthians 13:14 ("The grace of the Lord Jesus Christ, and the love of God, and the communion of the Holy Spirit be with you all. Amen.") and the Aaronic blessing in Numbers 6:24–26. The latter is the basis of this magnificent choral prayer by Peter C. Lutkin, a gifted composer and organist who spent most of his life and ministry in Chicago. Lutkin wrote the tunes to several of our hymns, including this rendition of the Aaronic blessing, with its fabulous sevenfold "Amen." Today is the anniversary of Lutkin's homegoing. He passed away **December 27, 1931**.

The Lord bless you and keep you
The Lord lift His countenance upon you,
And give you peace, and give you peace;
The Lord make His face to shine upon you,
And be gracious, and be gracious;
The Lord be gracious, gracious unto you.
Amen, Amen,
Amen, Amen,
Amen, Amen,
Amen!

And the LORD spoke to Moses, saying: "Speak to Aaron and his sons, saying, 'This is the way you shall bless the children of Israel. Say to them: "The LORD bless you and keep you; the LORD make His face shine upon you, and be gracious to you; the LORD lift up His countenance upon you, and give you peace."'"

—Numbers 6:22–26

Hark, the Glad Sound

John Bauman was a Lutheran clergyman who fled Prague under persecution and settled in England. His daughter Monica married a London merchant named Daniel Doddridge, and they named their twentieth child Philip. Eighteen of their previous children had died in infancy; and, indeed, Philip appeared to be stillborn. But he survived and went on to become a celebrated pastor, educator, author, and hymnist. His bestselling book is *The Rise and Progress of Religion in the Soul,* and his best-known hymn is the rousing "O Happy Day!" The hymn "Hark, the Glad Sound" is considered one of his best. It was written for a Christmas sermon from Luke 4:18–19, which Doddridge preached on **December 28, 1755**. The first verse is especially worth memorizing.

> Hark, the glad sound! The Savior comes,
> The Savior promised long;
> Let every heart prepare a throne,
> And every voice a song.
>
> On Him the Spirit, largely poured,
> Exerts His sacred fire;
> Wisdom and might, and zeal and love,
> His holy heart inspire.
>
> He comes the broken heart to bind,
> The bleeding soul to cure;
> And with the treasures of His grace
> To enrich the humble poor.
>
> Our glad hosannas, Prince of Peace,
> Thy welcome shall proclaim;
> And Heav'n's eternal arches ring
> With Thy belovèd name.

The Spirit of the Lord is upon Me, because He has anointed Me to preach the gospel to the poor.

—Luke 4:18

Hallelujah! What a Savior!

On **December 29, 1876**, as the Pacific Express train chugged onto a bridge over the Ashtabula River at 7:28 p.m., passengers were alarmed by loud groans and cracks from beneath them. Suddenly the bridge gave way, and eleven cars plunged seventy feet into the icy water below. On board, kerosene heaters and lamps burst into flames and became instant infernos. Among the ninety-two fatalities was the young but already-famous gospel songwriter Philip Bliss, who died while vainly trying to save his wife. Bliss had composed the melody for "It Is Well with My Soul" and the words and music for other classics, such as "Almost Persuaded," "Jesus Loves Even Me," "My Redeemer," "Wonderful Words of Life," and this pensive hymn based on Isaiah 53:3.

"Man of Sorrows!" what a name
For the Son of God, who came
Ruined sinners to reclaim.
Hallelujah! What a Savior!

Guilty, vile, and helpless we;
Spotless Lamb of God was He;
"Full atonement!" can it be?
Hallelujah! What a Savior!

Lifted up was He to die;
"It is finished!" was His cry;
Now in Heav'n exalted high.
Hallelujah! What a Savior!

When He comes, our glorious King,
All His ransomed home to bring,
Then anew this song we'll sing:
Hallelujah! What a Savior!

He is despised and rejected by men, a Man of sorrows and acquainted with grief.

—Isaiah 53:3

A Year of Precious Blessings

Fanny Crosby, the blind hymnist, was dearest friends with song leader Ira D. Sankey, but she also had a special place in her heart for Sankey's son, Ira Allen Sankey. The two wrote many songs together, Aunt Fanny providing the words and young Sankey the music. Fanny died in February of 1915 at age ninety-four. On December 20 of that year, Ira Allen married Anna Underhill Meighan, and the two left for the Caribbean on their honeymoon. He was suffering from tonsillitis when they boarded the steamship *Korona*, and his condition quickly worsened. He died on **December 30, 1915**, and was buried at sea. We can be sure he and Aunt Fanny immediately resumed their partnership writing hymns for heaven. Here is their song for ending the year with praise.

A year of precious blessings
And glorious victories won,
Of earnest work progressing,
Its onward course has run;
To Thee, O God, our Refuge,
Whose goodness crowns our days,
Within Thy earthly temple,
We lift our souls in praise;

Thou Master of assemblies
In mighty power descend,
Behold our glad reunion,
Conduct it to the end;
Inspire our hearts with courage
And deeper love for Thee,
That all, Thy Name may honor,
Where'er our field may be,

Blessed be the God and Father of our Lord Jesus Christ, who has blessed us with every spiritual blessing in the heavenly places in Christ.

—Ephesians 1:3

Another Year Is Dawning

This is one of my favorite hymns by one of my favorite hymnists, the British nightingale, Frances Ridley Havergal. I try to sing this hymn three times a year—on New Year's Day, on the first Sunday of the New Year at church, and on my birthday. It was written for **December 31, 1874**, and it's one of several New Year's hymns from the pen of Frances Havergal. Often called the Hymnist of Consecration, another of her hymns begins, "Standing at the portal of the opening year, / Words of comfort meet us, hushing every fear." And yet another Havergal New Year's hymn, written on December 31, 1859, says, "As thy days thy strength shall be! / This should be enough for thee." If you aren't familiar with "Another Year Is Dawing," you'll appreciate knowing that it's usually sung to the tune "Aurelia" by Samuel Wesley, which is also used for "The Church's One Foundation."

Another year is dawning, dear Father, let it be
In working or in waiting, another year with Thee.
Another year of progress, another year of praise,
Another year of proving Thy presence all the days.

Another year of mercies, of faithfulness and grace,
Another year of gladness in the shining of Thy face;
Another year of leaning upon Thy loving breast;
Another year of trusting, of quiet, happy rest.

Another year of service, of witness for Thy love,
Another year of training for holier work above.
Another year is dawning, dear Father, let it be
On earth, or else in Heaven, another year for Thee.

Therefore, my beloved brethren, be steadfast, immovable, always abounding in the work of the Lord, knowing that your labor is not in vain in the Lord.

—1 Corinthians 15:58

Permissions

January 17

© Van Ness Press, Inc. (ASCAP) (admin. by LifeWay Worship c/o Music Services, www.musicservices.org). All rights reserved. Used by permission.

March 28

Copyright © 1965 Hanna Street Music (BMI) (adm. at CapitolCMGPublishing.com). All rights reserved. Used by permission.

April 16

Words: Stuart K. Hine; Music: Swedish folk melody/adapt. and arr. Stuart K. Hine; © 1949, 1953 The Stuart Hine Trust CIO. All rights in the USA its territories and possessions, except print rights, administered by Capitol CMG Publishing. USA, North and Central American print rights and all Canadian and South American rights administered by Hope Publishing Company. All other North and Central American rights administered by The Stuart Hine Trust CIO. Rest of the world rights administered by Integrity Music Europe. All rights reserved. Used by permission.

June 9

Words: Thomas O. Chisholm Music: William M. Runyan © 1923, Ren. 1951 Hope Publishing Company, Carol Stream, IL 60188. All rights reserved.

September 7

© 1934. Renewed 1962 Broadman Press (SESAC) (admin. by LifeWay Worship c/o Music Services, www.musicservices.org). All rights reserved. Used by permission.

Index of First Lines and Titles

Titles are in italics
First lines are in lightface

Robert J. Morgan is a Gold Medallion Award–winning author and has served as pastor of The Donelson Fellowship in Nashville, Tennessee, for over thirty years. He is the author of thirty books, including *Then Sings My Soul* and *The Red Sea Rules*; his books on the stories behind great hymns of faith have sold over a million copies. He holds degrees from Columbia International University (BS), Wheaton Graduate School (MA), and Luther Rice Seminary (MDiv). He and his wife have three daughters and ten grandchildren.

Visit Rob's website: www.robertjmorgan.com.